Where there's Muck,
there's Bras

# LOST STORIES OF THE
# AMAZING WOMEN OF THE NORTH

## KATE FOX

Harper
North

HarperNorth
Windmill Green
24 Mount Street
Manchester M2 3NX

A division of
HarperCollins*Publishers*
1 London Bridge Street
London SE1 9GF

www.harpercollins.co.uk

HarperCollins*Publishers*
Macken House
39/40 Mayor Street Upper
Dublin 1
D01 C9W8

First published by HarperNorth in 2022
This edition published 2023

1 3 5 7 9 10 8 6 4 2

A catalogue record for this book
is available from the British Library

ISBN: 978-0-00-847292-4

Printed and bound in Great Britain by
CPI Group (UK) Ltd, Croydon

This book is produced from independently certified FSC™ paper
to ensure responsible forest management.

For more information visit: www.harpercollins.co.uk/green

*To Rosemary, my Stepmum, and all those other extraordinary, ordinary Northern women whose superpower is love.*

# Contents

# 1

# The Forgotten Queens of the North

*Cartimandua was a Northern Queen,*
*more powerful and cannier than Boadicea*
*what made one stay in the memory*
*and the other disappear?*

*An unsculpted statue cannot crumble*
*an unpainted portrait cannot fade*
*a memory cannot be forgotten*
*if it was never made.*

I wondered if it was just the chip on my shoulder. The fat, greasy, chip-shop chip that seagulls love chip on my shoulder that meant I noticed that notable women in all sorts of fields were always being described as 'not as well known as you'd think', 'underrated' or 'forgotten'. The chip on my shoulder that meant when I trained as a radio newsreader, hoping to work for Northern radio stations, I was told I sounded 'too Northern'. Or, the one that weighed me down when I noticed a lot of people who worked in writing and broadcasting couldn't get their head round the fact I lived in the North and worked in writing and broadcasting: 'Have you travelled down today?' they'd ask in shock when they realised I really didn't live in London, as if suddenly realising there actually were roads and railway lines, possibly even aeroplanes, that went beyond the Watford Gap.

Once I realised you really were less likely to be remembered by history, or noticed in the present, if you were Northern or a woman (and the likelihood of not being remembered or noticed increases with every additional marginality you have – such as being from an ethnic minority, disabled or LGBTQI+), I felt distinctly miffed about this exclusion. I wanted to make a fuss. But there's a Catch-22. It's not very Northern to make a fuss. In fact, if a certain Russian punk feminist band were from the North, they'd have to be renamed Pussy Kerfuffle. But basically, I didn't know if I should go on about it too much, or who would care. Did it matter that if you asked people to name a Northerner, they would almost certainly name a man first? And second. And third. Probably a man in the great tradition of Northern Curmudgeons – that is, men who must not ever betray that they are happy about anything or anybody and who would say, even of an experience transporting them to their greatest height of transcendent beauty and euphoria, 'It were alreet.' Men like Geoffrey Boycott or Noel Gallagher or Michael Parkinson – who is so Northern he is even named after a Northern type of ginger cake. (As I toured round the North, I realised that some places call it parkin and some call it ginger cake. At least that's not as divisive as the bread roll. Which might be a bap or a barm cake or a stottie or an oven-bottomed muffin or a bun or a teacake ... Audiences can get very passionate about this. More passionate than about class and gender regional inequalities, to be honest. Sometimes I lost all hope of us ever overcoming our intra-Northern differences and developing a united identity. 'Pan Northern' is not just a kind of Northern casserole, I wanted to say.)

Then first a ripple, then a wave of activity began around the centenary of women getting the vote, which meant that money was made available to councils around Britain to celebrate women who had contributed to the cause (a fifth of that was awarded to a statue project in London, but no, I'm not making a fuss, not me . . . ). Along with the Me Too movement and the campaigns of feminist activists such as Caroline Criado Perez (who successfully campaigned for Jane Austen to be the first woman, apart from the Queen, celebrated on a banknote) and Laura Bates, who pointed out that only 15 per cent of statues in the UK were women, this wave coincided with women in history being taken more seriously and recognized as more likely to have been erased from the records than men.

Then came The Festival of the North, an idea of George Osborne, then chancellor of the exchequer, to showcase the culture of the 'Northern Powerhouse', a catchy title which is not actually the nightclub in Barnsley it sounds like. It's an initiative to help the North's economy catch up to that of London and the South East, since the North has massively less government investment in infrastructure like transport, training, and the arts; has big ongoing social problems caused by the death of manufacturing industries like mining and shipbuilding; and has higher ill-health and death rates than London and the South East. (George tended not to talk much about these structural issues, instead placing the emphasis on the need for the North and its businesses to attract national and international investment.)

Before applying to be part of the festival, I amused myself by googling 'Northern Powerhouse', which uniformly brought up images of either men in suits at long council tables brandishing documents in red folders, or men in hard hats and high-vis jackets pointing at things on building sites, in order to let us know that they personally were building the Northern Powerhouse. I suppose there was at least some diversity of colour because some of the hard hats were blue instead of yellow. But on the whole, it was local and national politicians showing us a North in their image. White, male and middle-aged. So I was chuffed when my proposal for a stand-up show about Northern women who had been forgotten in the past or should be remembered in the future was accepted. Who could have resisted it with a title like *Where There's Muck, There's Bras* which, as you will know, is a pun on the Northern saying about the value of farming land to industry: 'Where there's muck, there's brass'. One of my favourite things has become hearing posh and/ or Southern people being unable to pronounce the pun correctly because they say 'bras' and 'brass' in exactly the same way.

I soon discovered that there were a LOT more notable Northern women than I knew about. A lot. Women who have been lost from the collective memory in the way that many women are lost – because their names don't go down on the marriage certificates and we lose track of them through time – but many more who were just downplayed. One illustration of how quickly this can happen is in the story of the politician Mo Mowlam: she played a crucial role in the Good Friday peace agreement of 1998 when she was Northern Ireland secretary but was missed off magazine covers commemorating the twentieth anniversary of the process she had been so important to. One of her predecessors, also a much-loved North East MP, Ellen Wilkinson, tipped as a future leader of the Labour Party in the 1940s, still doesn't have a statue commemorating her (though one is finally on its way). And what about Helen Sharman from Sheffield, who went into space in 1991, yet Tim Peake was routinely described as 'the first British astronaut' when he went up a whole twenty-four earth years later.

I remembered how, growing up in the eighties in Bradford, we did learn about Margaret McMillan, who successfully campaigned for big improvements to nursery schools at the turn of the twentieth century, but, ironically, we didn't learn about the brilliant Bradford writer Andrea Dunbar, whose work, including the film *Rita, Sue and Bob Too*, was shining a light on poor kids in Bradford at that moment, rather than eighty years earlier. Meanwhile, my Asian classmates were not getting any light at all shone on role models from their parents' culture. Even the most well-meaning histories and narratives are often skewed and partial or downright oppressively biased.

---

There's a lot of history in this book but I also wanted to make sure I wrote about women who are shaping the stories of the North now – women like the screenwriter Sally Wainwright, whose dramas *Last Tango in Halifax* and *Happy Valley* are redefining the type of roles available to Northern female actors. I am also strongly aware that ethnic minority women are massively underrepresented in history generally, in the history of the North and, consequently, in this book. So it is exciting to see women who are shaping future narratives of the North, like Syima Aslam, who runs the hugely influential and expanding Bradford Literature Festival; poet Suhaiymah Manzoor-Khan, originally from Leeds, whose work challenges what it is to be British, Muslim, and of immigrant origin; and Umme Imam from Newcastle, whose leadership of the Angelou Centre for black and ethnic minority women has seen them provide a strong voice for women in the city who face violence and oppression. There is definitely a danger when talking about Northern women that you end up suggesting there is something inherent about being born in the North that makes you a certain way. I don't think that for a minute. For me, gender, ethnicity and regional identity are all much more culturally constructed rather than innate. I hope and know that future narratives of the North's lasses will have a far more diverse range of identities – including ethnic minorities, trans women, disabled women and women from Cleckheaton (sorry, women from Cleckheaton, I haven't left you out on purpose). I don't know if outsiders understand that 'out-Northern-ing' each other is a camp sort of game we sometimes play up to, to amuse ourselves. I'll always treasure the exchange with a shop assistant at Northallerton station that started with me saying, 'I'll have a bag of the Yorkshire crisps, please,' and them replying, 'Our finest Yorkshire crisps from God's Own County,' and ended up with me saying, 'Lovely Yorkshire tea,' and them agreeing, 'Gathered on the slopes of India' as we laughed at our own ridiculous pride.

I have felt a pressure to include every Northern woman who's ever lived to make up for our relative exclusion from official narratives, and resigned myself to the dispiriting knowledge that I will be missing out many women who people think should be included, either through accident, ignorance, inverted snobbery or lack of space. I know I have to own this though, and just say that this is a subjective list. It's a start. Get in touch with me about those I've missed out. But I also hope it will act as an incentive for you to notice the women around you now. Shout about them, amplify their voices, make it even harder for history to forget them. There is also something traditional and perhaps reactionary about lists of notables. I mean, most of the crucial people – your mum, your gran, your cousin's best friend – will still not be recorded, and who am I to say that those who were able to access a public life in the narrow range of categories I've looked at (culture, politics, protesting, sport and exploration, mainly) have had a life worth remembering? We've all spoken to someone at the fish shop or the bus stop or the pub whose story makes our jaws drop. I've realised that's not a reason not to make such lists, though. Even flawed acts of remembering prompt us to remember why remembering is important. Plus, though I say it myself, these are a heck of a lot of interesting women whose stories have inspired, excited and cheered me.

As well as asking which women should be included, I had to decide what constitutes 'The North'. People often ask 'But where does the North end?' as if this was an impossible conundrum. Attempting to define it is a great illustration of the point that the North is both a geographical and a cultural construct. I love definitions like 'You're in the North when the washing is on lines, rather than spinners', though obviously this could lead to some households in Plymouth being rather surprised to find they're suddenly Northern. I'm aware there are some parts of what I would probably class as the Midlands – Mansfield, say – that 'feel' Northern because people there identify with aspects of what's perceived to be a Northern identity. I mainly use Dave Russell's boundary of the traditional seven counties of the North: Cheshire, Lancashire, Cumberland, Westmorland, Northumberland, Durham and Yorkshire.

Enjoying our Northern grit is part of that culture (we *have* had to be pretty resilient in the face of persistent socio-economic inequalities) and there's always been a receptivity to tales of this. It's why people might name a Northern woman like Grace Darling from Bamburgh in Northumberland, who helped her lighthouse-keeper dad save nine people from a boat shipwrecked off Longstone Island in 1838. Her bravery and goodness sent Victorian Britain a bit doolally and she became a heroine. Twelve portrait painters sailed to the island to ask her to sit for them, and people sent her the equivalent of thousands of pounds in crowdfunding for no apparent reason. (Sadly, she died of tuberculosis four years after her rise to national heroism, aged just twenty-six.) People might also think of Hannah Hauxwell, the Yorkshire farmer whose life at a farm on the High Pennines without water or electricity was chronicled in the documentary *Too Long a Winter* in 1972 and then in a follow-up nearly two decades later. Or of Amanda Owens, the Yorkshire Shepherdess, whose hilarious and heart-warming tales of life on her remote South Cumbrian farm bringing up her nine children sell thousands of books and net millions of TV viewers.

I am aware, however, that I'm applying the term 'Northern' to women who might not apply it to themselves. Certain parts of the region have identities which are so strong they will trump Northernness in terms of self-definition. Someone from Liverpool is more likely to refer to themselves as a Scouser first, someone from Newcastle will call themselves a Geordie, someone from Yorkshire will call themselves a Goddess (sorry, us Tykes do love ourselves). I do think there's a value in asserting that unified Northern identity, though – if you're in some ways a subordinate culture to the dominant culture of the South then you need all the solidarity you can get (at the same time, you don't want to lose your pride in your own particular local area. My ideal description of where I'm from makes me think of how schoolchildren sometimes write their addresses – I'm a proud Whitley Bay-er, Yorkshirewoman, Northerner, British, European, citizen of Earth and the Universe).

Most of the women in this book were born in the North of England, but my criteria was whether they were strongly enough associated with the North in some way. So, Baroness Tanni Grey-Thompson, who is very definitely Welsh, is in because she has laid down such roots on Teesside that she chose to become Baroness of Eaglescliffe, the Teesside town where she and her family have made their home. Her Paralympic achievements were mostly not won in the North, but her work as an influential disability rights advocate is conducted from here and she is chancellor of Northumbria University. Radio pioneer Olive Shapley was born in Peckham but spent over forty years of her career in Manchester, making work in and about the North of England.

Many of the women do not have what is taken to be the most defining characteristic of Northern identity: a Northern accent. When I was performing a show that asked the question of whether I was middle class, which concluded that I wouldn't be read as such because of my strong Northern accent, women would often come up to me and apologetically say that they didn't sound Northern anymore because they had lived elsewhere, or experienced pressure to lose their accent in order to be taken more seriously in education or work, but they still felt Northern even though other people didn't recognize them as such. They experienced an identity which seemed to be very much between two worlds. Sometimes I felt like a priest taking confession and then absolving them of the sin of not being Northern enough.

Accent is, of course, the primary way that Northernness is detected and discriminated against. Research in universities has shown how a regional accent marks people out as working class and, according to shocking prejudices that still exist, as stupid and uneducated. One striking study found that no female university professors had kept a regional accent, even if they'd grown up with one, whereas senior men were more likely to not only keep theirs but even to exaggerate them. Katie Edwards, an academic from Doncaster, said people would openly mock her Northern accent at academic events. My doctorate involved researching how researching how stand-up performance can be used by Northern English women to portray their regional identity. (Doing a PhD in stand-up comedy was a bit confusing to people. 'What, are you going to need a PhD to go on *Live at the Apollo* now?' they'd ask incredulously. 'No,' I'd reply. 'A penis would help, but not a PhD.') After interviewing lots of performers and analysing over 260 newspaper reviews, I found that national newspapers were several times more likely to comment on the voice, regional identity and body shape of Northern performers than of comedians from the South. Being Southern, even if you identified as working class like Sara Pascoe or Russell Howard, meant you were seen as sort of 'neutral' in your identity, whereas Northernness was not neutral and was often disparaged and not taken seriously. It was also harder for performers based in Manchester, and even more so for those based further from London, such as in the North East, to be noticed by national scouts and people in the media industry. They were also less likely to have had access to cultural and educational opportunities, partly because there were fewer in the North and it cost more to access national opportunities, which were invariably based in London. I called this mixture of social, economic and cultural factors impacting on what Northern creatives could earn and do the 'Northernness Effect' (which I know sounds like a sixties film starring Richard Burton). Other post-industrial areas of the UK are subject to a very similar mixture of factors (the West Midlands, say), but the point I'm making is that if you ever ask why it's harder to get on in certain professions if you're from the North of England, you need to take factors such as accent prejudice into account alongside other measures of class and economic disadvantage.

The very successful actor Maxine Peake (Bolton, Lancashire, the North, England, Europe, the World) has talked about this mixture of prejudices openly and hilariously. She says we need to tell new stories about the North that go beyond the stereotypes of poverty and struggle and women as 'brassy, bold, outspoken but loose', and that casting directors should note that 'being Northern isn't a character trait!'

One woman who would be a great candidate for the Maxine Peake treatment would be Cartimandua, who became a kind of guiding spirit for this project. When I was touring the *Where There's Muck, There's Bras* show, I would ask audiences to put their hands up if they had heard of Boadicea, the warrior queen who led a rebellion against the invading Romans. Every audience member would put their hands up. Then I would ask if they'd heard of Cartimandua, queen of the Brigantes – the tribe that held territory from the equivalent of today's Scottish Border, across to the Wash and down to Chester. No hands would go up, or maybe the occasional one. Seeing the confirmation of her relative obscurity would turn me a bit indignant all over again, forgetting that I'd only heard of Cartimandua when I started researching the show.

I developed a hunch that there would be warrior queens from the North of England that I just didn't know about, and googled 'warrior queens' and 'North of England'. Two really interesting facts came up: first of all, that Iron Age female skeletons had been found buried with their chariots, horses and weaponry in East Yorkshire, mostly notably in the splendidly named Wetwang. The only other evidence of women being buried with their chariots is in Northern France. It was amazing to imagine these women, hair flying in the wind, blue and red necklaces round their necks as they carried news and goods and power between tribal settlements. And secondly, there was a queen called Cartimandua who lived at the same time as Boadicea, but instead of rising up against the Romans (which, sadly, in Boadicea's case led to the slaughter of many thousands of her people in battle, and her own death), she made a deal with them to supply goods and cooperate with them in return for being mostly left alone. She ruled for a long time, possibly at least thirty years; was the hereditary ruler in her own right (because Celtic tribes were matriarchal); and experienced a split with her consort husband Venutius that makes Angie and Den's divorce in *EastEnders* look tame. There, a pub was at stake; for Cartimandua, it was her kingdom, possibly her life. It is thought that her headquarters were at Stanwick, eight miles north of Richmond in North Yorkshire, where the settlement of what was clearly an important Celtic ruler has been uncovered, along with glassware and pottery, imported jewellery, and wine and oil containers.

According to our main source of knowledge about Cartimandua, the Roman historian Tacitus (who should theoretically have loved her given that he was Roman and she was their ally, but who seemed a bit perturbed by the whole idea of a strong woman queen, as women were generally more subordinate in Rome), she lost popularity with her people when she handed over King Caratacus in chains to the Romans after he sought refuge with her following his failed rebellion against them in AD 51. Arguably, although this meant she was off his Christmas card list, it would have meant that, strategically, her people were left alone by the occupying invaders. After she married again, to the armour bearer Vellocatus in AD 57 (while he was not of low status, he was definitely of lower status than queen), Venutius led an uprising of the Brigantes against her, which the Romans sent troops to help quash. But when he gave it another go in AD 69, the Romans were not there in sufficient numbers to help, and Cartimandua fled, possibly to the new Roman headquarters at Deva (Chester), possibly eventually to Rome, or possibly she was killed.

But what we do know is that she disappears at that point from history. Or at least, from the tiny amount of official history she appears in. Boadicea lives on in fiction, song, myth and national identity (who doesn't love a plucky underdog, fighting for freedom, especially a glamorous warrior queen avenging the violation of her daughters and her people?), whereas Cartimandua, Northern woman, strategist, leader, apparently no pushover and protector of her people, disappears. No Cartimandua Arms pubs, no Cartimandua history lessons, no Cartimandua statues (though there is a star-map artwork set into Wincobank Hill in Sheffield which refers to her as the 'star-crossed queen').

Perhaps it is possible to tap into how her people felt about her if you connect with Celtic myth. By which I mean that the Brigantes tribe which she ruled had an association with the goddess Brighid. As with Boadicea, it is possible that the people of her tribe identified her, as leader, with the goddesses they worshipped. Brighid is an amazingly capable mythic figure. She's an ironsmith, she's a prophetess, a story-teller, a healer. She looks after animals, crops and her people. Were she real and alive today, she'd be interviewed in *Cosmo*, telling them how she manages to 'do it all'. It appears that the Romans, ever-practical in their co-option of the local deities in places they invaded, worshipped her too, as there are Roman altars bearing inscriptions to Brigantia near Leeds, Halifax, and South Shields. I want to suggest that myths, as a form of meme, live on in fragments and traces in places associated with them. Despite the stereotypes attached to a Northern woman now, at some level there is a deep-held memory of the powerful multiplicity of what we could be. (I'm going to just let that sentence hang there, glad that this isn't a PhD where I have to justify big statements like that and cite references. Instead, it's a knowledge I feel I hold in my body, like the hills hold it in their depths.)

As soon as you start looking at the women of the North, an interesting thing happens: you move beyond the domi-nant narratives of the North as the home of gritty, working-class, industrial realism in a line running somewhere from

Elizabeth Gaskell's *North and South* to *Billy Elliot* and *The Full Monty* via *Saturday Night and Sunday Morning* and *Kes*. You'll get plenty of that, don't get me wrong – I talk about Gaskell, *Coronation Street* and Shelagh Delaney. But you also hear of Northern women who are (gasp) middle class, Northerners who travel (out of the North, and not just to London), Northerners whose dominant modes are surrealism and who are more concerned with the future than the present or past (Margaret Cavendish, say, or Leonora Carrington or Ngozi Onwurah). You also move beyond the dominant cities of Manchester and Liverpool and the counties of Lancashire and Yorkshire to discover stories of the North East and Cumbria as well. The working-class politician Ellen Wilkinson, who was instrumental in the Jarrow March; aristocrat Gertrude Bell, who was the architect of modern Iraq; the Van Gogh of Cumbria – Sheila Fell; the outspoken Sunderland singer Nadine Shah. All of them hammering out their words, their ideas and their creations after forging them in the smithy of the Northern landscapes and cities, far from the centres of power – except that they could travel there in their chariots, bring back new treasures, become prophets, seers, storytellers and er . . . fishwives. There are so many of them to discover. In the words of Ellen Wilkinson and many another Northern woman, let's crack on . . .

# 2

# The Hildas

In this chapter we're going to meet four Northern women who share a name. The archetypal Northern female name. They are a religious leader, an Olympic swimmer, a comedian and a soap character. They all had to fight through obstacles, employing more than their share of the famed Northern resilience and grit – and this struggle is embodied in their name. Hilda comes from the German word for 'battle'. Conjure up a Hilda in your mind and you might see her wielding a sweeping brush and dustpan, with wrinkled stockings and curlers. But think of a screaming Valkyrie like Brunhilde and we come closer to its original meaning.

I wrote this and then realised I couldn't imagine what a screaming Valkyrie looked like. But apparently they're very beautiful, strong, mythical Norsewomen who get to choose who lives and who dies in battle and is taken to Valhalla, where cheering crowds line the walls. Sort of like *X Factor* judges.

In the eighth century, the North of England was invaded by Vikings who then liked it here ('the people are just so friendly, everyone chats to you at the longboat stop'), stayed, and ruled into the tenth century. These Norse people had different myths to the existing Anglo-Saxon inhabitants of the North, different lifestyles, even different hair. Apparently,

Norsemen wore theirs shaved at the back and shaggy at the front, while the Anglo-Saxons generally had long locks. I am now imagining strong Hilda-women holding on to these reverse mullets during vigorous sex, before downing a flagon of mead.

Obviously, if there were women among these Viking raiders who found monastic communities in places like Holy Island and Iona to be easy targets to nick things from (monks being more likely to show hospitality to strangers and to share their worldly possessions – possibly running after the thieves, saying, 'Would you like my sandals as well, they'd go lovely with your helmet?') then history has barely recorded it. I'm going to go out on a limb, though, and say that there would of course have been real-life shield maidens among the Norse raiders. Remember – where there is history, there are women who've been written out of it . . .

In 2019, a documentary for the National Geographic channel did a facial reconstruction of a woman found buried in a Viking graveyard in Norway. Although she had been buried among other Viking warriors, with arrows, a sword, an axe and a spear, had a sword wound in the middle of her skull so deep it had dented the bone, and was buried with her head resting on a shield, she wasn't thought to be a warrior because she was a woman. Presumably, earlier archaeologists and historians just thought she had especially stabby make-up applicators.

Conversely, a warrior skeleton dug up in Birka in Sweden over a hundred years ago, with the full kit of a professional warrior, including weapons, a mare and a stallion, and gaming pieces that showed they were engaged in high-level military tactics and strategy, wasn't initially thought to be female because they were a warrior. But scientists recently tested the skeleton and discovered she was definitely a lass. What's more, her DNA showed that she had a genetic link with Swedes, but also with people from Iceland and the Orkneys – and England and Scotland. I was really hoping they would be more specific and add 'and people from Wakefield' or something. But I think we can safely say that Viking women warriors would have been among the Norse people who went on to shape some of the distinctive culture and DNA of the North of England.

Some of that distinctive culture is about a directness and straightforwardness in speech and manner, different to the later Normans, who phrased things in fancy language and courtly manners and didn't really say what they meant. We can see this operating in the myths (and possibly realities) of shield maidens like Brunhilde. Like their male counterparts, shield maidens were more honest and more concerned with honour than the cunning and seductive maidens who usually turn up in medieval myths, deceiving their suitors. They would have called a shield a shield, and a spade a bloody shovel.

Anyway, our Hildas' stories mostly consist of things they did very much in their own right as women who had to battle through to achieve the things they wanted to achieve. First, we're going to travel back to the earliest days of Britain as a nation, when the idea of the North was only just beginning to exist, to start with a woman who was one of the greatest educators and leaders who ever lived, and who played a part in shaping not only the entire future of the Church of England, and what eventually became Great Britain, but also perceptions of the North.

## Hilda of Whitby

Whitby is known for Dracula, Whitby Abbey and goths. I think it should also make more of a fuss about one of the most influential Northern women who ever lived – Saint Hilda of Whitby. In researching her I developed a bit of a girl crush on Hilda. If someone printed a 'What Would Hilda Do?' T-shirt, I would definitely buy it.

I picture her, a slight, grey-haired woman in her fifties wearing a simple woven blue shawl, standing out as an elderly woman for her time, with kind eyes, crinkled at the corners, walking through the wooden buildings of the abbey she ran in Whitby. Taking a moment to look up at the big grey North Yorkshire sky and the waves crashing onto the cliffs below. She knew how to sink into a moment and be in it, after all those hours of silent prayer. But she also knew to smile and listen to the people who approached her to ask advice. They might ask her about practical matters: 'How much honey shall we add to the mead?' 'Bernard is still sweating a fever, shall I apply another poultice?' They might ask her about spiritual matters: 'Mother (everyone called her mother), sometimes in the dark I hear a voice, how do I know it is God?' 'At matins sometimes my mind drifts to the villagers I left behind when I came to be a nun here, how do I stay with my prayers?'

She was a woman of the world who, as a former princess, could talk to kings and bishops and visiting church officials from Rome in their own language, but could also speak to a shy cowherd in a way that drew him out of himself like nobody had before. Her eyes seemed to have a light in them. Sometimes playful, sometimes wise. When her mother was an infant, she had dreamt of a bright necklace that would light the whole world. The eighth-century historian Bede would say that was symbolic of Hilda herself. But she had become adept at sidestepping the expectations others had of her, meeting them in the moment, person to person, and putting them at ease.

Pretty much all that we know about her (sadly not that much, given her importance) comes from Bede. Now, he was generally not sufficiently interested in women to indicate he would be up for wearing a 'Male Feminist' T-shirt, but he did approve of Hilda. He was a fellow Northerner, a monk who had given his life to the church just as she had, and he had a geeky interest in when Easter should fall. One of Hilda's biggest gigs was presiding over the Synod of Whitby — a gathering that decided, among other things, how Easter should be calculated. It also spent an inordinate amount of time deciding how monks should wear their hair, but we'll get to that.

Hosting an event at which the future of Christianity was decided wasn't the most obvious path for Hilda when she started off in life. She was actually born a pagan princess. Which sounds much cooler, and more *Game of Thrones*, than being a Christian saint. When she was born in AD 614, Britain was a chaotic place (lucky that things are so different now . . . ). After Roman rule collapsed in the fifth century, Britain split into multiple warring kingdoms of Angles and Saxons. Hilda's dad was in the running for the crown of one of the biggest kingdoms — Northumbria — which nowadays is Northumberland and most of Yorkshire. He was poisoned while in exile when she was still a baby and she was brought up in her uncle's court in Northumbria.

Amid all this chaos, Christianity was spreading like a virus across the country. Well, not a virus. Like a meme. Sort of. Christianity promised certainty and an afterlife and structure. There were two distinct strains at that time. Sorry, not strains – let's call them types. One came from Rome and was a bit more focused on nice churches and shiny gowns and incense and stuff. The other, Celtic Christianity, came from Ireland and was less hierarchical. It was more about leading a simple lifestyle and emphasising a direct connection to your spirituality rather than having it mediated by priests in bling.

This type was much more Hilda's thing and, despite having been baptised into Roman Christianity along with the rest of her uncle's court when she was 13 (in a wooden church erected on the site of York Minster), she became close to some of the leading figures in Celtic Christianity, such as Aidan, Bishop of Lindisfarne. As an example of how he practiced this more rugged Christianity, Aidan waded out into the sea every morning and recited the Psalter. That's a hundred and fifty psalms. Nowadays he'd probably have a wild swimming blog.

His apprentice Cuthbert also stood in the sea praying, and two otters were once seen coming to dry his feet with their fur. This was before towels, obviously. Cuthbert then went a step further and became a hermit on one of the Farne Islands for ten years, though people did keep sailing up to him on little boats and asking for advice and spiritual healing. He probably thought he'd get some peace when he was dead, but because his body was still intact in 698, eleven years after he died – which confirmed his ability to do miracles and consequently his sainthood – religious people kept digging him up to see if he had decomposed yet. He still hadn't by the eleventh century, nor even during the Reformation, though by the time he was at last interred at Durham Cathedral and curious monks had another peep in

1827, he'd finally become a skeleton after all that oxygen exposure.

For many years, Cuthbert was seen as a protective figure for the North East. This was symbolised by Cuddy ducks being named after him – eider ducks which he tamed and looked after on the Farne Islands. So it wasn't just the otters he liked hanging out with.

I note this partly because it's endlessly amusing to me to go on about a saint rubbing himself on cute furry animals, but partly because Hilda's possible role as a protector of Northern identity seems to have been lost to history, along with many other parts of her life.

She only comes into historical view in 647 when Aidan asked her to run the monastery at Hartlepool. Before that, she'd become a nun and had been going to join her sister in a convent in France. It may be fair to say that not many people turn down a sunny retreat in France in order to take a job in Hartlepool, but Hilda was no ordinary woman. We don't know what her secular life consisted of up until the age of 33, but in the time of warring kingdoms and chaos she may well have had a husband who died in battle and chil- dren who died in childbirth.

The community at Hartlepool was all women, and she set it up and ran it. There were supplies to get in, meals to plan, buildings to run, as well as the prayer and devotional routines of the community's day. Plus, visitors to greet, books to study and transcribe and, I would like to guess, as a lover of the North East's changeable sea and skies, walks to have along the long beaches. It would be another fifteen hundred years before these beaches acquired the Ridley Scott backdrop of chemical works shooting flames into the sky. (The Teesside chemical plants inspired the look of his film, *Blade Runner*.

This is one of my top Teesside fascinating facts. Alongside how Stockton on Tees is the home of the safety match, and long proudly announced this fact with a large, phallic-looking match in the middle of a roundabout as you entered the town.)

By 657 she was running the new monastery on the headland at Whitby. It was a mixed community of monks and nuns, who slept separately but had communal meals, worship and tasks. Bede says that Hilda ran a regime of 'justice, piety, chastity' (presumably code for 'keep to your own beds folks, even though those Yorkshire winters can be cold') and 'particularly of peace and charity . . . no one there was rich and none poor for they had all things in common'. This must have been a tonic after growing up with murder, threat, and battles over territory as the backdrop to her life. It was certainly not a life of retreat and withdrawal, though. Several monks from Whitby went on to become prominent bishops, and Hilda received lots of visits from clerics and royals seeking advice.

She is also responsible for the first English poet we know the name of: Caedmon. In the evenings at the abbey, there would be sing-songs and gatherings round fires. Caedmon, a cowherd, was too shy to join in, but apparently Hilda once heard him singing to his cows and coaxed him to share his songs with the abbey residents. After she had gone all Simon Cowell and spotted his talent, his conversion of biblical stories into the plain Anglo-Saxon of ordinary people proved an excellent way to convert more of them.

All of her achievements culminated in the Synod of Whitby in 664, which set the direction of the church in Britain for hundreds of years to come. You know those party political conferences in seaside resorts where everybody stays in B&Bs and gets drunk at late-night discos? Well, this wasn't like that. But maybe a bit. And it was sparked because a king and his wife disagreed about when Easter should be. Not content to have two Easter eggs instead of one, this major meeting was called to resolve it.

Hilda's heart was with the Celtic monks but she presided over the Synod with characteristic humility and efficiency. Although this might seem like it foreshadows the battle for control of England's church that took place during the Reformation in the sixteenth century, the Celts and Romans generally got on and saw they had more in common than divided them. Perhaps Hilda would have helped smooth things over too. Just a few monks stropped off to Iona to do things their way. And perhaps, with the greater authority of the Roman strand of Christianity, local hairdressers were kept busy because Celtic Christians had free flowing locks, perhaps reflecting their freer ways, whereas the Roman monks had the distinctive tonsure bald in the middle, with hair round the sides. A look which hasn't proved to be a classic down the ages, funnily enough, though Bill Bailey made a good go at bringing it back into fashion during *Strictly Come Dancing* in 2020.

Hilda was seriously ill for the last six years of her life, and on the day she eventually died, aged 66, the nuns at the neighbouring abbey of Hackness said they'd had visions of her and were already saying psalms in her honour when the messenger arrived to tell them she was gone. Myths and legends grew up around her even before she was sainted and before Bede wrote about her, more than a hundred years after her death. In the Middle Ages, people told stories of how in Hilda's time there had been a plague of snakes in Whitby and how she prayed to God to first remove their heads and then turn their bodies to stone. This is not the most efficient method recommended by Rentokil if you're afflicted by a snake plague. In fact, the headless snakes are the beautiful ammonite fossils plentiful on the shorelines round Whitby. These spiral stones date from the Jurassic period of 145 million to 200 million years ago, and Victorians did a roaring trade in them, especially when they added snake heads.

At least Hilda was being remembered, and still is when people visit the abbey in Whitby, although maybe a bit below Dracula in the minds of goths and other tourists. She most often crops up in connection with education now – in the schools and colleges which bear her name, not least St Hilda's College, Oxford, founded in 1893. For me she stands out as an example of wise leadership, of her abbey, her chosen religion and, less obviously, of her region and country, at a time when it was riven with tribal conflicts and factional fighting. Through opening up the abbey, becoming involved in reading, writing, and translating texts, and recognizing the simple power of words like Caedmon's to share ideas, Hilda helped promote a way of life that was about simple routine and ritual, looking out for your neighbour, living harmoniously and communally, and of equality between the genders and between different strands of thought. She doesn't strike me as a leader who was about power for power's sake, or as one who wanted to consolidate the structures and buildings and riches of the church. She just wanted people to live good lives.

Nowadays she'd have spent quite a lot of her time on panels titled 'Female Leadership in the Church: The Way Forward' but in this particular window of history, she wasn't unusual as a female leader. We were yet to have the Norman invasion, which brought the concept of marriage in which women were the property of men. She was recognized in her own right. How bizarre she might have found it to know that future synods of the church would be obsessed with the question of whether women could even be vicars. Or that it would take until 2014 for a synod to give women bishops the go-ahead. There are still only 25 of them, out of 115 in total. Progress isn't always linear. Though as Hilda herself might remind us, her name means to battle, to struggle on . . .

### Hilda James

Now for a Northern woman who embodies all the qualities associated with Hildas – the resilience, the rebellion, the directness and the bravery. Her story fascinates me in itself – and it also fascinates me because I so nearly never knew it. Hilda James makes me think of all the other women whose stories will be forgotten, or never told in the first place. It also fascinates me because it includes a mother who was a bit of a cowbag. I'm familiar with that particular type, but the cowbaggery of Hilda's mum seemed to be on a different scale. There can be mums who stop you going to the youth club dressed 'like that', or to the disco because you haven't done your homework, or out with that boy who makes Shia LaBeouf look like Francis of Assisi. But Hilda's mum cost her daughter a sporting dream that would have resonated around the world.

She had started swimming when she was eleven, and only because her parents didn't want her to go to religious studies classes and sent her to swimming lessons instead. Her bathing costume was knitted from wool and sagged down to her knees. However, Bill Howcroft, the inspirational coach of the Garston swimming club in Liverpool, saw something in her. And despite the conflicts it caused with her mum, who seemed to be jealous of the medals she started bringing home and the freedom and sense of family she found with her Garston teammates, she kept on going. In fact, only five years later, aged just 16, she, along with two other speedy female swimmers from Garston (Grace McKenzie and Charlotte Radcliffe) and her greatest rival Connie Jeans from Nottingham, celebrated winning the silver medal at the 1920 Olympics in Antwerp. They had come second in the 4 x 100 metre freestyle relay. That was a triumph, but the Americans had sped past them in every other race, with their newly developed freestyle stroke, gracefully scything through the water while the British still did the more laborious stroke known as 'the Trudgen' (named after a man called John Trudge. And not because it's a trudge. Though as it uses freestyle arms but side scissoring legs and you keep your head out of the water, it's a lot less aerodynamic than the stroke we know today as freestyle).

It was Hilda who cheekily asked the American coach Lou Handley to teach her the new stroke, and Hilda who took it back to the UK and set records with it in pools, at every distance, from Aberdeen to Penzance.

Hilda had a sense of humour. She'd talk to anyone in her Scouse lilt and keep them entertained at swimming competitions with her trick dives, doing the crab and the periscope and the dolphin. No wonder Cunard Line spotted her and wanted her to be the celebrity swimming coach on their first purpose-built cruise liner, the *Carinthia*. No wonder she was such a star during the swimming exhibition races in America in 1922. She even acquired a nickname, becoming known as 'the English Comet'.

But the biggest thing that lay on the horizon was the 1924 Paris Olympics, where she was tipped to win multiple medals. As the best swimmer in Britain and one of the best swimmers in the world, this was practically guaranteed. But her mum put her foot down. She decided her daughter had already had too much freedom and so she insisted she had to come as chaperone. If she couldn't, which the British Olympic Committee wouldn't allow, then Hilda was not going to Paris – gold medal chance or no gold medal. Hilda was under 21, not yet an adult, so she couldn't go against her parents' wishes. Bill, the team coach, came to the house and there was an almighty row. Afterwards, her dad hit her so badly with his belt that she couldn't sit down. It led to a sort of intervention. The Cunard bosses stepped in to make sure she had a home and a job of her own as soon as she was over twenty-one. But it was too late for Hilda to go to those Olympics.

She married William McAllister, an engineer on the Cunard liner where she became a celebrity swimming coach. There was talk of her swimming the Channel but the attempts never got underway. Then she had children and settled into life as a mum and a grandma, and hardly even swam. But her body remembered. And one day, Hilda had one final flare as the English Comet, at the age of 76, when her swimming days seemed to be long forgotten. She was a little, hunched woman, with a pacemaker then. Walking along the edge of Garston Pool draped with bunting for the annual gala, crowds lining the sides, she dipped her toe into the water gingerly, then stepped back. Earlier in the day she had ignored her daughter-in-law, who had an inkling something was up and said, 'You're not going to swim are you?', not knowing Hilda already had her swimming costume on under her sensible Marks and Sparks cardie and slacks. She had asked her old teammate, who was running the gala, if she could swim in the break between heats. He knew it wasn't every day that a septuagenarian Olympian makes a comeback at a local swimming gala and was thrilled to agree. The crowd had no idea who she was. As she stepped onto the poolside, there was a tannoy announcement. Something about the Garston team from the Antwerp Olympics. Hilda something.

Hilda had come to the gala because her daughter-in-law had been concerned her formerly chirpy mother-in-law was losing her zest for life. She had encouraged Hilda to give a talk at the local old people's home about her swimming career. She didn't know much about it because Hilda didn't talk about it much, but she knew there was a dusty medal box in the attic. Hilda mentioned once that her mum had thrown most of her medals away. But she still had one or two. She spoke to a room full of old people sitting in the lounge, who looked up in surprise when Hilda brought out her silver Olympic medal. Their eyes brightened when she said she'd danced with Tarzan once: Johnny Weissmuller, a swimmer nearly as successful as she was. She'd loved America and the Americans. The glamorous American swimmers Gertrude Ederle and Helen Wainwright, who took her under their wing during the 1922 racing season, had kitted her out in a beautiful ballgown and watched as she waltzed off with Tarzan himself, who stole a kiss. It sounded like a film. It should have been a film if she'd swept the board at those Paris Olympics, but she was too modest to say that.

Back in Garston pool, where she had set some of her records decades earlier, she painfully creaked into the water.

Nice of them to let an old lady into the pool while the real swimmers are resting, they must have thought, failing to realise she was teasing them.

Then suddenly, after she'd carefully climbed out to polite, baffled applause for this grey-haired pensioner who had apparently won some things once, she shot back into the water with a perfect dive, slashing down the pool at a rate of knots. This can't be that same little old lady? Faster than most of the swimmers they'd seen in the competition today? Now she's doing these trick dives in the water, as if she's a crab, a porpoise, a periscope. She's funny, playing with the crowd, winking. Then back up and down the pool with that perfect front crawl. The crowd are on their feet – they can't believe what they've seen. They have no idea this woman once held the British and European freestyle record at every distance from 100 metres to a mile, and nine world records as well.

Hilda had forgotten all this too. She'd settled into life as a wife and mother and grandmother, not dwelling on those far-off days in swimming pools, in American ballrooms, on the Cunard liners. The days there were, and the days there could have been. But in the water at that gala in Garston she remembered. She remembered with every muscle who she used to be, as her arms sliced the air and her eyes tracked the line on the bottom of the pool, and she breathed again in that old rhythm and propelled herself forward as if she was flying, and the applause of the crowd reached her ears muffled by the water.

It pleases me that one of her grandchildren, Ian, later stepped in to make sure the rest of the world remembered too. He wrote a book about her swimming career called *Lost Olympics*, and successfully applied to have her inaugurated into the International Swimming Hall of Fame in 2016, thirty-four years after her death.

She was the English Comet and she is mostly forgotten. Now, when I swim front crawl, which I only learnt in the summer of my forty-second year, basically because I was scared to put my face in the water and didn't like messing my hair up, I swoosh up and down the pool feeling like Superman and I think of Hilda, as you might now, the first British woman to swim this stroke. I think of her blazing American summer in the spotlight and the freedom she found in the water, and of how she shone so brightly despite her mother's attempts to dim her light.

### Hylda Baker

At the start of the Second World War, the tiny, sharp, fiery Lancastrian comedian Hylda Baker had been treading the boards for twenty-four years, ever since starting out in her dad's music-hall show aged ten. She was making a living and had worked with some top names but hadn't achieved her dream of being a star. She did, however, spot an opportunity to start producing her own shows. She would be the first woman to do so. That, and the performances she did after finally attaining the stardom she craved at the age of fifty, is why her biographer, the actor Jean Ferguson (famous for playing Marina in *Last of the Summer Wine*) calls her a 'pioneer and a genius who was ahead of her time'.

She was a music-hall and variety turn for many years, then became most known for acting as pickle-factory boss Nellie Pledge in the Seventies sitcoms *Nearest and Dearest* and *Not on Your Nellie*, as well as taking film roles. But Hylda was a comedian to her core, and, unlike many famous Northern comedians such as Bernard Manning or Roy

Chubby Brown, she wrote her own material and devised her own act in a way that is more similar to the stand-up comics of today. And as so many Northern comedians do, she took inspiration from the people she saw and heard around her. In an interview she said:

> I am a student of life. I take ordinary conversation and use it in a way that makes it appear outlandish, ludicrous and extremely funny, but the truth is that every housewife speaks one of my comedy lines every time she goes out to do the family shopping. There is nothing pretentious or phoney about it, because I watch the people around me and draw the material from everyday life.

After landing a role in a show called *Meet the Girls (the Boys Have Left Behind)*, billed as 'the first all-woman show featuring the original and only crazy gangstress Hylda Baker . . . a feminine attack on the blackout blues', she recognized the potential of producing all-women shows herself. She took the big step of leaving the North and moving to London, as she realised that's where she needed to be based to get noticed. She then produced her own show called *The Girls They Left Behind*. Producing meant she basically did everything. She wrote, directed, and starred in the show; booked the acts and venues; designed and transported the sets and posters; liaised with the theatres and even, on one occasion, stepped in to conduct the orchestra when the conductor was ill! It was a variety show featuring singers, dancers and bands, a whistler (that is, a woman called Gladys who sang and whistled, not a painting by Whistler), a ukulele-playing contortionist, and knockabout comedy sketches about the war, including one in which the women were in army uniform.

She remembered playing Clapham during the Blitz and there was such a massive air-raid outside that they couldn't leave the theatre when the show finished at 10.30 that night. They performed the show twice more and still made the audience laugh, even with the bombs whistling overhead. They finally finished at 4 a.m., after the audience joined a singalong of songs like 'I'll Be Seeing You' and 'The White Cliffs of Dover'. (I can't imagine doing a gig with bombs overhead. I have performed in cafés where the cappuccino machine is too loud, but that's not quite the same . . . )

Hylda pushed her innovation further with her next show and said, 'God'll strike me down,' because *Meet the Men and Me* was an all-male revue featuring female impersonators and Hylda dressed as a man in elegant suit and trilby hat. Her biggest success, though, came after the war was over, with a show called *Bearskins and Blushes* which ran for over three years and featured nudity among the singing and sketches with 'Six Parisian Models and Eight Blushing Beauties'. In revues in those days, women would stand nude in a series of poses announced with titles like 'Now, here are some artistic poses depicting the beauty of womanhood'. Under strict rules that applied until 1968, they were not allowed to move – and adherence to those rules was another thing Hylda had to manage as producer. Who knew the line between art and porn was staying still? ('Yes, I'm watching Porn Hub, but it's on FREEZE FRAME. I might as well be at the National Gallery.') She was still doing everything herself, partly out of necessity and partly out of perfectionism. Sometimes theatre managers would try to cheat her by fiddling box office receipts. Once, in Lincoln, the stage crew refused to put the scenery up because they didn't want to take orders from a woman. There would have been dozens of incidents like this. She became adept at getting things done anyway, this four-foot-eleven Northern woman who was funny in everyday life as well as being able to speed-read an audience, who was known as warm and caring by the young performers she mentored, but who could also be assertive and strong enough to literally make the show go on night after night. So of course she was known as 'a difficult woman'.

After eleven years producing her own shows and being booked to do her own act in variety shows and pantomimes in between, she was burnt out and became ill. She'd spent nearly forty years living out of a suitcase, in dingy digs – and finally she'd had enough. Stardom didn't seem to be on the horizon. With 'Tex' Martin, one of a series of men not nearly as capable as her that she fell in love with, she decided to give ordinary life a go and went back to run the family fish and chip shop in Plodder Lane, Farnworth (she had already had a short-lived marriage aged 24 to a man who ran off with some of her money, and never wanted to try that again). But after six months, an adrenaline-craving Hylda was back to health and desperate to be back on the stage where she felt she belonged. A theatrical agent said he wanted her act, but not her variety show, and she started to move up from the grottier 'Number Three' theatres to headline the plusher 'Number Two' venues and to support big singing acts like Frankie Vaughan and Al Martino.

By this point she had developed an act in which she played a drill sergeant suggestively threading a hosepipe through the squad's legs. One of the squad, who was played by a very tall man, kept getting it wrong, leading to Hylda's classic line 'She's able, I'm bodied'. From the huge reaction to the sketch and the dynamic between them, Hylda knew there was something there. Though little did she realise it would be the act that finally made her name.

When I performed the show *Where There's Muck, There's Bras* that led to this book, I would ask audiences if they remembered the comedian and music hall star Hylda Baker. If the audience was older – rows of spectacles glinting back at me and anoraks on laps, in places like Barnsley and Halifax and Sheffield – more than half the hands would go up. If they were younger, hardly any would. Then I'd ask who remembered Matthew Kelly. As in 'Tonight, Matthew, I'm going to be . . .' Remembering the singing show *Stars in Their Eyes*, which Kelly had hosted until 2004, most hands would go up, across people of all ages.

Then I'd surprise the audience by saying that these two people, who seem to belong to utterly different eras, actually worked together. Matthew was the last in a succession of tall, silent men dressed as women who played Hylda Baker's friend Cynthia. The Cynthias' job was to stand while Hylda, dressed in a badly-fitting checked jacket and an ostrich feather boa, gossiped about her friend who was 'tall and blonde with aquamarine features'. She would utter her catchphrase 'She knows, you know' and lament the passing of time, saying, 'I must get another hand put on this watch.' She was trying to be 'posh' but said her words wrong. People loved Hylda's act for her malapropisms: 'I've had lessons in electrocution you know,' and 'I can say this without fear of contraception,' or 'I'm not menthol and I am not suffering with illuminations.' The start of this act where she is looking for her friend Cynthia, urging her to 'be soon won't you, I'm stood standing here', can't help but make you think of Victoria Wood, in yellow raincoat and beret, beseeching the audience 'I'm looking for my friend, Kimberley. Have you seen her? She's really, really tall and really, really wide. If she had a suitcase on her head she'd look like a fitted wardrobe.'

Undoubtedly, Hylda was part of Victoria Wood's lineage. Though given that Victoria was still almost on her own as a woman selling out her own comedy shows in the 1980s, Hylda's achievement in doing this as a woman on her own from the early part of the twentieth century, and for several decades, stands out as even more pioneering, though this is barely recognized in entertainment history. That's even more astonishing once you realise how very, very famous she became. An overnight success at the age of 50, as she joked. The thing that gave Hylda her big break was the thing that was killing the variety industry she had worked in for forty years. But in 1955, her call to appear on TV on *The Good Old Days*, where audiences dressed up like old-school music hall crowds in evening dress – suits for the men, long dresses and plumed hats for the women – for a live performance broadcast from the City Varieties Music Hall in Leeds, was what changed everything for her. She had always thought it might. But when it finally happened, she didn't feel ready:

> In the theatre and the music hall it's before thousands, but in front of the camera and TV's millions, I wanted to do something special. But the ideas wouldn't come. I did 'Cynthia' and the same act that thousands of variety goers in the North knew but now I was standing in front of about five million people. Really it didn't seem much different to me from all the preceding years in stage – not until we were off air, and people began phoning up. There were so many calls for me I had to run away and hide!

After that point, she adopted the eccentric star persona she had always been moving towards. She drove a car with 'She knows, you know' inscribed across the front, bought a big house at Cleveleys in Blackpool and put a flagpole outside, that catchphrase emblazoned across the flag. She bought two unruly monkeys, Mickey and Coco, as substitutes for the children she had desperately wanted but wasn't able to have, and sometimes surprised co-stars by asking them to hold them if they were crying. She took her mother to Paris and Monte Carlo as she'd always said she would when she 'came into my own!'.

She devised various radio and TV shows and worked constantly for the next decade, including starring in the sitcom *Nearest and Dearest*. She and comedian Jimmy Jewell played Nellie and Eli Pledge, where their on-screen sparring mirrored their real-life relationship, which deteriorated so drastically that filming of the sixth series resembled all-out war. Realising she was getting less screen time than her co-star, she said, 'Hang on, I'm in and out of this scene like a fart in a colander' and began adding bits of comic business to make sure the camera stayed on her.

It was ironic that Hylda fought to get out from under the shadow of the various double acts she was tied into throughout her life, be it her marriage or love affairs with disappointing men, her characters or her co-stars. Maybe she was most herself when she was a solo turn but part of an ensemble show of players who relied on her. They became her collaborators and perhaps a recreation of the music hall family in which she had started off, all those years ago in Farnworth in Lancashire.

In the last few years of her career, Hylda, always forgetful, struggled to learn her lines, and cue cards had to be written out for her and left all over the set, even on the side of bushes and billboards when they filmed outside. It became clear she had dementia and eventually she couldn't work any more and went into a retirement home for performers, then into a nursing home. It feels even more poignant that, as well as forgetting her lines and who she was, such a pioneer was herself forgotten, with only ten people at her funeral and sparse obituaries not recognizing her contribution as an innovative producer and comedian. Ironically, comedy is not taken seriously as an art form, and until recently much of its history has been written by amateur enthusiasts. Had she been one of the first and only female producers in theatre, or opera, I'd guess we'd have much more documentation putting her importance as an early figure into context.

However, perhaps Hylda herself would call someone having the need for affirmation in that way, 'a big girl's blouse' (a phrase that she coined). Hers was a life lived on stage, in front of audiences who recognized her as one of their own and who loved her and enjoyed the gift and skill she had honed over so many years with a rare determination, focus and down-to-earth resilience. As she said:

> A woman who makes her name must fight more than a man to keep at the top. People have tried to push me back a few times but I haven't let them. I've had to be a bit of a battle-axe or I'd have been trodden on. I don't want people's sympathy, just their laughter and, if possible, their affection. Then I'm a contented woman.

### Hilda Ogden

When I mentioned I was writing about *Coronation Street*'s Hilda Ogden to one friend she said, 'I felt like I grew up with her . . . like she was my auntie or my grandma.' Thanks to the intimacy of the soap, which reflected the real lives of millions of people, it really did feel like we knew the characters as they came into our living rooms.

Hilda was played by Jean Alexander for twenty-three years, from 1964 to 1987. Hilda and her onscreen husband Stan formed a legendary double act, with the scene in which she wept over his glasses case after his death being described as one of the most moving in television history.

We'll meet some of *Coronation Street*'s other women in another chapter, but I've included Hilda Ogden here because it feels like, with her perpetual pinny and headscarf and rollers, she is visual shorthand for the archetype of a particular Northern woman. A good-hearted battler, a working-class wife and mother trying to keep house and family together but getting no particular help to do it. Latterly, she was a surrogate mum or grandma to lodgers Eddie Yeats, and Sally and Kevin Webster; she was a busybody who knew everything that was going on in her street and was looked down on by residents who had pretensions, but she had plenty of her own, most legendarily summed up with her 'murial' (mural) of a mountain scene and the three pottery flying ducks in the middle of it (the middle one being positioned downwards to look like it was in a permanent nose-dive was Jean Alexander's idea). When Hilda moved out of the street in 1987, she revealed the deep emotional importance of these features when she said to Percy Sugden: 'I've come in here more times than I care to remember, cold, wet, bone-tired, not a penny in me purse. And seeing them ducks and that muriel . . . well they've kept me hand away from gas tap and that's a fact.'

Hilda knew she and Stan were seen as a joke by their neighbours and it bothered her. But as a character she was a constant source of comedy which overlaid the daily tragedies of her life in the way that the Street has always done so masterfully and which underlines the resilience of the Northern archetype.

She was so appreciated as the spirit of *Coronation Street*, and as a symbol of something the nation liked to see in itself, that in 1979 the British League for Hilda Ogden was formed by legendary actor Laurence Olivier, broadcasters Michael Parkinson and Russell Harty, writer Willis Hall, and former poet laureate John Betjeman. Three of them were knights of the realm – recognition that would never come Jean Alexander's way as a dame. They had their first meeting at the Garrick Club in London and made 5,000 pin badges. As we shall see later, Hilda's iconic style still persists as a defining image of Northern womanhood, and has been deployed by drag queens and environmental activists, among others.

On hearing that I was writing a chapter about Hildas of the North, my partner's daughters exclaimed, 'Oh, Hilda, with blue hair, on Netflix!' After googling and explaining and getting distracted by a piano that plays notes with a 'meow' noise, and the twelve mobile phones and laptops that accompany any pack of young people, I discovered that the name and spirit of Hilda lives on for a new generation. The 2019 series *Hilda* follows the adventures of fearless Sparrow Scout Hilda and her pet deerfox, Twig, who move from her native forest to the Norwegian city of Trolberg and outwit various monsters and spirits. It's based on an original graphic novel series by a young creative called Luke Pearson, who, given that the series was originally picked up for screen by a producer who saw it in an indie bookstore in New York, I had originally assumed was a cool New Yorker. I let out a bit of a scream when I saw that he was actually born in Stockton on Tees, not twelve miles from where Hilda of Whitby ran her first monastery in Hartlepool (and, lest we forget, home of the friction match . . . )

Pearson was particularly inspired by William A. Craigie's book on Scandinavian folklore from 1896 and so, here, we come full circle back to our Hilda Valkyries. He said he wanted to write a character who does things because of her curiosity, empathy and sense of adventure. Who is interested in everything and constantly questions the things that happen to her. And who never resolves her problems with a fight. How wonderful that the spirit of the Hilda, which had become an old-fashioned name that was dying out (just five babies were named Hilda in the UK in 2018), has been revived for a new, global generation. A generation which so badly needs it.

# 3

# Sibyls, Suffragettes and (re)Sisters

Fighting and resisting is often something that's better done together. Whether you're witches in a village, fighting for the vote, or telling developers to frack off, collective action is more likely to protect you and get you what you want. Northerners have a long history of acting together, perhaps because a collective spirit was forged in the factories and mills of the Industrial Revolution, and in socialising in clubs, pubs and on terraced doorsteps. And before that, in places far from the centre of power where people had to make their own . . .

### The Pendle Witches

Here's a rule: in order for somebody to be designated as clean, somebody else has to be designated as dirty. In order for somebody to be designated as normal, then somebody else has to be set up as weird. In order for a singer like Leona Lewis to shine out as a star on *The X Factor*, you needed Bob from the fish shop to audition, with a voice like a hamster being strangled in a wind tunnel. In order for monarchs to set themselves up as godly, pure and rightful rulers, they needed some lawless, wild-haired women from forests and rural villages as a contrast. Enter the witches. They were mainly working-class women who scraped a living by selling herbs and possibly spells in their villages. At their best they were perhaps the Denise Robertsons (the late, much-loved *This Morning* agony aunt) of their communities, dispensing herbs and wise counsel, or low-rent Gwyneth Paltrows selling ineffective but harmless potions. Peak witch-hunting time was from 1450 to 1750, with an estimated 40,000—50,000 people burned at the stake in Europe and the Americas, 80 per cent of them women over 40 (one of the few times in history when middle-aged and old women have had big audiences for anything).

One of the biggest trials took place in the North of England when the Pendle witches were tried and executed in 1612. One very hot summer, I went on a bit of a pilgrimage to witch country – visiting Lancaster Castle and the cold stone jail where the witches were held and tried. I walked up the solitary green wedge of Pendle Hill, and to the village of Roughlee, where there is a beautiful life-sized statue of one of the accused witches, Alice Nutter, shackled on her way to the trial. It was erected in 2012 to mark the trial's 400th anniversary. The sculptor David Palmer wanted to get away from the pointy nose and warts caricature and has created a dignified representation of an ordinary woman in chains due partly to the prejudices of the time and partly to petty rivalries and feuds. Locals have taken her to their hearts and often place posies of flowers in her clasped hands.

The execution of twelve people started with a tiny event one cold March day on the road to Colne. A young woman, Alizon Device, asked to buy a pin from a travelling pedlar and cursed him when he refused. He may or may not have suspected she wanted it for witchcraft. She may or may not have been trying a newfound ability to do spells. He may or may not have collapsed with a stroke at exactly the wrong (or right) moment. Either way, his son reported Alizon to the local magistrate for witchcraft and she implicated her grandma Demdike (known as 'Old Demdike') and a rival wise old woman in the village (known as 'Old Chattox'). At that point, years of buried annoyances and rivalries came to the fore, like some sort of hyped-up *Jeremy Kyle Show* episode climax, and two more women ended up being accused alongside Demdike and Chattox of everything from summoning the devil, to killing people with their spells. They were sent for trial at Lancaster Castle. The Demdike and Device families then held a meeting (a crisis meeting, a conspiracy to blow up the castle, a Catholic mass, a witchy ritual – who knows?) at a local tower on Good Friday, and were shopped to the magistrates too. Nine-year-old Jennet Device was at the meeting and became the chief prosecution witness, possibly having been coached by the prosecutors.

This little girl later stood in the wood-vaulted court room at Lancaster Castle, among many of her relatives, and told the magistrates her brother had killed a sheep because the devil hadn't been able to find them food for their feast, and gave other incriminating details of the meeting, pointing out others who had been there, even as her mother, Elizabeth, shouted at her (Jennet calmly asked for her to be removed from the room). We know all this because the clerk of the court, Thomas Potts, wrote an account of the trial with the excellent title *The Wonderfull Discoverie of Witches in the Countie of Lancaster*. Again, this was all deeply *Jeremy Kyle* but with the consequence that ten people, including Jennet's mother, were hanged at the gallows (one was found not guilty and one – 80-year-old Demdike – died in the harsh prison conditions). Jennet herself last appears in the historical records in 1636 in jail on witchcraft charges herself. Those were certainly scary times to be a Northern woman with a liking for herbs and giving advice. Female Waitrose shoppers would definitely have found themselves in danger.

## Mother Shipton

Along with Alice Nutter, there is another statue in Yorkshire that intends to rescue a witchy figure from the prejudices of history. Ursula Sontheil was born in a field during a thunderstorm in 1488. Her mother, Agatha, gave birth to her when she was only fifteen and was cast out by the villagers of Knaresborough for the crime of being a teenage single mum. One story says Agatha was tried as a prostitute, and she pointed out that having a bastard baby didn't make her a prostitute, and that the judge had himself got one of his serving girls pregnant. She raised Ursula in a cave for two years until a local bishop arranged for Ursula to be taken in by a local family and for Agatha to go to a nunnery. Agatha never saw her daughter again.

Ursula was apparently a strange-looking, hunched child who spent a lot of time on her own learning how to make potions and poultices. She married a carpenter from York, called Tobias Shipton, when she was twenty-four. He died a few years later and they didn't have children. Although still on the fringes of village life, it feels like Ursula found a way to make herself valuable and noticed. Perhaps she had always had to be alert and spot patterns, being a woman on her own and probably under constant threat of teasing and mockery (also, maybe there's such a thing as having visions of the future – but the jury is still out on that). Either way, she began to make predictions. Some of them were very specific, such as when she said that Cardinal Wolsey would never visit York. Henry VIII had made him Archbishop of York in 1514, but he didn't get round to visiting the city until a trip was planned in 1529, which puts the reluctance of some cabinet ministers to travel beyond the Watford Gap into perspective. Apparently, Cardinal Wolsey was so annoyed by her prophecy that he sent three noblemen to remonstrate with her. Satisfyingly, though, she was right – he got to within thirty miles of the city, then had to turn back because of a fire and died on the return journey. The 1641 pamphlet which recounts this is convincing in its specificity, and suggests that, a century after her death, Ursula was a well-known figure who needed no introduction. As the years went on, though, she and her prophecies began to be inflated, mythologised and caricatured.

It's exciting to think the future can be foretold – even if you're pinning the predictions on a quirky Yorkshirewoman who died in 1561 at the ripe old age of seventy-three. Samuel Pepys said when London burned during the Great Fire of 1666: 'Mother Shipton's word is out', which further confirms that her name and words were still common knowledge over a century after she died. However, a couple of centuries later, mass-market books sensationalised her predictions. A Victorian editor called Charles Hindley, who produced some of these books, confessed that he wrote what is still commonly thought to be one of her most famous prophecies, about how 'The world then to an end will come in eighteen hundred and eighty one.' He probably also wrote 'A carriage without a horse shall go/Disaster fill the world with woe . . . In water iron then shall float/As easy as a wooden boat.' I remember my mum intoning this in a witchy voice around the house. We wanted to believe Mother Shipton could foretell the future, a future we were living in, just like we want to believe that fellow Lancastrian Mystic Meg could four centuries later.

There is something special, however, about the cave where Ursula was raised, and today Mother Shipton's 'petrifying well' in Knaresborough, where objects like shoes and teddy bears can be turned to stone in a matter of weeks, still gets a steady stream of visitors. But the transformations wrought there are due not so much to magic as to minerals.

It's a beautiful spot down there by the river. I remember vividly a lovely day out with a friend's family when we were about eight. We hired a rowing boat and then drank Coke at a café on the riverside. I definitely wouldn't have thought then to question the idea that Mother Shipton was a scary old crone. The books we read were full of them. I'm glad that depictions of history are moving on, though, and since 2017 there has been a statue of her, sitting on a bench in the town centre, looking like a real woman, not a cartoon witch. The sculptor Chris Kelly (hooray for more statues of Northern women by sympathetic and skilled sculptors. I can't help hoping for one to be sculpted by a woman at some point, though) said in a BBC interview that in the first literary print of her she actually looked like a well-to-do Tudor noblewoman and he wanted to try and reflect the real woman. No stick-on warts required.

Mother Shipton could be called a folk hero- a figure representing resistance against the forces of the establishment. Dolly Peel of South Shields in the North East is another, and her statue stands overlooking the Tyne. With her headscarf and basket and homely face, she looks like any other fishwife of the early nineteenth century, and indeed the memorial is intended to celebrate the strength of ordinary working women. But like Mother Shipton, Dolly was anything but ordinary. Her life highlights included smuggling and hawking contraband goods, hanging out in the town square writing topical poems, including one to her pal, the town's Liberal M.P and - most spectacularly- stowing away on the ship where her husband and son had been press-ganged into being sailors during the Napoleonic Wars in an attempt to rescue them, being discovered and becoming a much valued nurse on the ship. Once back on dry land, she was pardoned because of her usefulness and her family were exempted from ever being press-ganged again - but she still saved other men of the town from the same fate, sometimes by hiding them under her voluminous skirts. A 1923 play about her was revived at the town's theatre in 2005 and the statue stands as a monument not just to her rebellious spirit but that of the town's people who can also drink in a pub bearing her name.

### Chartist Women

While some marginalised women gained what power they could from spells and prophecy, there were other groups of women who wanted to redress imbalances of power. Namely, that they didn't have any and small groups of rich men had loads of it. We will sadly never know the names and details of many of the individual women who were involved in these fights, but these movements drew in many thousands of Northern women down the years. They gained solidarity in numbers and discovered the power of the collective – something that was made easier by men and women gathering in large numbers to work in the mills and factories of the Industrial Revolution. Suddenly, people lived more densely than ever before and injustices could be seen as shared troubles. They found solidarity in recognizing the contrast between their hard lives and the profits they generated for their rich employers. Women worked for lower pay than men, and in difficult conditions in the cotton and textile mills of Lancashire, Cheshire and Yorkshire. Some of them were among the approximately eighteen people who died, and thousands injured, in the infamous Peterloo Massacre of 1819, when military men on horseback, armed with sabres, charged a peaceful Manchester crowd who had gathered to hear radical reformer Henry Hunt argue for better working and living conditions and fairer representation in parliament. There were women's reform groups – some of them had attended that day wearing white gowns to signify purity, including Mary Fildes, president of the Manchester Female Reformist Society, who stood alongside Hunt on the platform. There were also women in the crowd whose stories will never be fully known, but who were caught up in the violence when the soldiers started attacking the crowd. Margaret Downes died after being 'dreadfully cut in the breast', and Elizabeth Gaunt was 'cut and trampled on the field' and suffered a miscarriage after her arrest and imprisonment. Her unborn child is listed as one of the massacre's victims. No one was prosecuted and there was never any retribution for the victims of that day – instead, the chief constable was commended for his brutal actions, and it became harder for groups to gather.

The desire for reform continued to ferment, however. The Chartists were begun by a group of six people in London in 1836. There were more people called John in this group (two) than women (none). They were not the Chartists until 1838 when they drew up a charter of six demands aimed at opening up parliament to ordinary men; the demands included votes for all men over 21, payment for MPs, equal sizes of constituencies, and annual elections. Many Chartists did want votes for women too, but it was believed that asking for this would be too controversial and put back the cause as a whole. However, from Lancaster Jail – the same place where the Pendle witches had been imprisoned – Salford Chartist R. J. Richardson earned his 'Male Feminist' badge by arguing in his pamphlet of 1840, *The Rights of Women*, that if women could rule as queens, then they should also be allowed to vote.

Women were supposed to be confined to the domestic sphere at this time, according to the prevailing norms of the day. However, many Northern cities did have very active women's Chartist groups. In Hyde, Manchester, for example, the society had 300 men and 200 women and, as the *Northern Star* newspaper put it, 'The women were more militant than the men'. Women were not generally to the fore as leaders in the movement but there were over a hundred women's groups and a third of the signatories of the charter were women.

Across the north, town after town and city after city found women giving voice to the movement. Elizabeth Hanson of Halifax formed the Elland Female Radical Association in 1838. She managed to not upset the applecart by framing their activism as supporting their men, saying, 'It is our duty both as wives and mothers . . . to give and receive instruction in political knowledge and cooperate with our husbands and sons in their great work of regeneration.' The local newspaper described her as one of the movement's best speakers and said she 'melted the hearts and drew forth floods of tears'. Women Chartists who addressed crowds were described by the press as 'she-orators' (which I think I'll insist on being described as from now on). The Female Political Union of Newcastle issued a statement saying that although they had been told their province should be the home, the interests of their fathers, husbands and brothers were their interests too.

In Sheffield, Anne Knight founded the Female Political Association in 1851, along with Anne Kent and several other Sheffield women, and the following year they published the first petition in England that demanded universal suffrage. She called taxation without representation 'a tyranny'. The group also formed links with imprisoned revolutionary women in France and America. (Of course, I can't name all the women Chartists but I want to name some who ran this group so we get a sense of how many are missing from history – so thank you, Eliza Rooke, Abiah Higginbotham with her great name, Eliza Cavill, Kate Ash and so many more of you.) I bet if you asked most people to name the Northern city that first made the demand for women to get the vote they would say Manchester, so it's a bit sad to learn that when the government offered funding to key cities involved in the fight for women's suffrage to celebrate its centenary, Sheffield was not on the list because it didn't apply. Other Sheffield radical women at the time included Mary Anne Rawson, born in 1801 to wealthy parents who encouraged her involvement in good causes. The anti-slavery society she set up was the first one to call for an immediate end to slavery, rather than a gradual one. It was disbanded when slavery was abolished in 1833.

One way that women in particular were able to push the aims of the charter was through 'exclusive dealing' – that is, shopping only in places that supported it. In 1839, 600 women from the Bradford Female Radical Association walked down the city centre streets headed by a woman carrying a banner saying 'Exclusive Dealing' ('Ethical shopping' I suppose we would call it today).

In 1842 parliament rejected the Chartists' petition for the second time, and strikes and riots spread from Lancashire to Yorkshire. One procession of several thousand into Halifax was led by women singing Chartist hymns. They were later joined by women from Bradford, who were 'poorly clad and barefoot', and stepped in front of the military, daring them to kill them if they wanted to. Arrest records show that many women were beaten and imprisoned for taking part in these protests. Although it seemed like a lot of male Chartists still preferred that women helped behind the scenes or did nice gentle things like make banners and teas and organise temperance societies, there were plenty of women who were just as radical, or more radical, than the men.

Many people's knowledge of the fight for the vote for women starts and ends with the Pankhursts, but it is clear that the industrial (and rural) areas of the North were sowing the seeds of radical change and action among women well before that eminent family. (The Chartists, by the way, petered out after the third petition was rejected in 1848. Suffrage for men did come with the Reform Act of 1867, and another demand of the men, for secret ballots, was fulfilled in 1872. But most women were going to have to wait more than sixty years for their turn in this country.)

## *The Suffragists and Suffragettes*

Adela Pankhurst has just dodged another egg. A young lad this time, running off laughing with his mates. Having them thrown at her is just what happens at the start of meetings. They see the 'Votes for Women' banners, and her slight seven-stone figure on the platform in her white dress. Easy target. She's learnt how to get the crowd on her side. Make her voice louder without shouting. She likes Bradford and its elaborate gothic City Hall and its smoky streets – and the people. The women in their clogs and shawls. She can laugh with them. She must have seen every town and city in the North now. Her mother and sister have taken the headquarters of the Women's Social and Political Union down to London so they can be nearer the government. But she likes it here in the North. The people are real and they're kind to her. Anyway, there's still her school job in Manchester most of the time. Christabel has gone off to study law, so there was only enough money for Adela to be an apprentice teacher. She knows about long days, Though not like the ones the women have here in the mills and the factories, then coming back to make the dinner and do the housework. She wants to help them strike, to encourage them to speak up to the bosses and try to achieve better conditions, to see that giving women the vote will mean better working conditions for everybody. Lots of the men know that. Not this one, though. He looks up at her, then round at the other men stood with him in their flat caps and worsted suits. 'If you were my wife,' he throws out, 'I'd poison you.' Quick as a flash Adela replies, looking round at the crowd as she does, catching some women's eyes, 'No need for that, my friend,' she ripostes. 'If I were your wife, I'd take it!' The tension bursts and the whole crowd roars into laughter, a wave of it reaching the man's friends, one of whom cuffs him on the ear as he laughs ruefully at himself.

---

The cold tube makes Kathleen Brown gag. They had opened her jaws wider than they'd ever been opened before to put it in. She can feel the slop, warm down her windpipe, choking her, hands hard on her shoulders through the rough material of her prison dress. She was weak after four days without eating, but now her body is fighting again. That rush of something. She'd felt it when they arrested her. Two of the one hundred and twenty policemen in Newcastle that day reaching out and grabbing her by the arms. For a minute it felt like they were going to hug her. It had felt like all the rules were gone, upended that day. What a sight the procession had been. She'd never seen so many women and men in the centre of Newcastle. The band and the carriages. So many banners. 'Support the Bill', 'Who are the People?', 'No Taxation Without Representation'. Suffrage groups from all of the North East. It was like being part of something much bigger than she was. She'd got a glimpse of the chancellor in his car. That's why they'd come. She didn't see that posh woman throwing the stone. Lady Constance it was. The newspaper one of the other girls had managed to get said that it had a message wrapped round it: 'To Lloyd George. Rebellion Against Tyranny is Obedience to God. Deeds Not Words.' They've called what happened that day 'the Battle of Newcastle'. But it didn't feel like a battle, it felt like a party. She saw some of the other women in their purple and green sashes and white dresses smashing windows, even some at the Palace Theatre. She'd never heard the sound of glass breaking before. It was louder than she thought. It's cold here in Holloway, a draft blowing through the stone cell walls, the cement floor, the wooden plank bed. But she doesn't feel on her own. Her mother is in the movement too, and her sisters. Her father works on the railways and he thinks women should get the vote. Of course he does. Most people do, but the government just aren't listening to the peaceful petitions and the meeting interrupters. That's why they've had to become more militant. Now their own bodies are weapons and the police are scared. You can tell. Even this prison officer with the tube looks away when she looks him hard in the eyes.

———————

Mary Murdoch feels strong and ready even though it had been such a busy day. Downing three raw eggs before she dashed from her home on Beverley Terrace into the city centre helped. Today's patients flash across her mind, like snapshots. That girl with the ear infection, the boy with the sprained ankle, the baby with colic, though really it was the mother who just needed someone to talk to. It's like she's always said, 'From the day you put up your brass plate, never refuse a piece of work'. It feels good to be relied on, to know she was the first woman GP in Hull, but she wants more women to follow her. Women she can train, like Louisa, who has shared her house and so much of her life. She knows she can rouse people, get them to believe that women will have the vote. It was thanks to Lulu, dear Lulu (how she misses her, an ache sometimes in the pit of her stomach even though the days are so busy with surgery and dashing from meeting to meeting by train), that she had set up the Hull branch of the National Union of Women's Suffrage Societies. That was the issue. The one issue. Nobody could keep women's progress back now; it was an inevitable high tide. Now a by-election was coming and she must do her part to make sure the three candidates are on their side. She has her brake ready, and the ribbons in the new suffragist colours of red, white and green for the pair of chestnut horses, and her beloved dogs who will ride with her through the streets, the details of next week's meeting on the side of the carriage. The suffragettes thought they were doing so well they weren't even fielding a candidate. It wasn't that she didn't want them in Hull, but rational persuasion was turning the tide. They didn't need letterbox bombs or window breaking or hunger strikes in Hull. Their words and arguments were ready to unpack like the contents of her doctor's bag.

---

Mary Gawthorpe, who had traveled up to the meeting from Leeds, was used to making her voice reach right to the corners of the meeting rooms she found herself in so often now. She had said similar words before, too: 'We want a question answering at a woman's meeting representing unenfranchised women. Will you, if elected, move an amendment to the King's Speech in case woman's suffrage is not included in it?' Guy Wilson's face changed. He hadn't been expecting this, although, of course, anything could be asked of a candidate at a by-election meeting. Confusion clouded his brow as other voices started up. She was a suffragette, he surmised – there were others in. He mustn't inflame the situation. 'I ought to have notice of the question,' he said. Then, 'I am in favour of women's suffrage.' The hubbub continued. He picked up his hat. Mary Murdoch addressed the questioner and the rest of the meeting in a clear, calm voice from her chair's position behind the table, saying that the NUWSS was non-political but was supporting him as the Liberal candidate, and also the Labour candidate, though not the Tory 'who gave as a reason that woman was too good and too gentle to mix up in the mire of politics. But it was a remarkable fact that Sir George Bartleby had the assistance of a large number of ladies to do the nasty, dirty work of canvassing'. The audience laughed, including Mary Gawthorpe, who had asked the question. Mary Murdoch knew her of course, as one of Emmeline Pankhurst's bodyguards. A good and witty speaker, an experienced campaigner. She admired her, all of them, and certainly would not condemn them or their tactics in public, unlike some other NUWSS chairs. The local paper had quoted Mary Gawthorpe when they interviewed her at the station as she arrived from Leeds saying she would start a branch of the WSPU in Hull. She would send circulars to 3,000 local women reminding them that they couldn't vote for their own MP simply because they were women. They had photographed her teaching a children's choir a 'Votes for Women' song and included pictures of the suffragette card game featuring well known suffragettes, the ones who had been there when everything started in Manchester. Emmeline and Christabel Pankhurst, of course. The formidable duo who worked and lived together – Esther Roper and Eva Gore Booth – who had done so much to start things off. The mill workers Hannah Mitchell and Annie Kenney. Mary Gawthorpe was still there in Hull on the balcony of the City Hall at the count when Wilson got back in with a majority of three thousand. An involuntary chorus of the song they had sung outside parliament came into her head: 'Rise up, women! For the fight is hard and long; Rise in thousands, singing loud a battle song.' The passionate Leeds activist had come a long way since hearing about Christabel Pankhurst and Annie Kenney being imprisoned for demanding votes for women at a Liberal rally at the Free Trade Hall in Manchester in 1905. She had heard it as a call from her place as an Edwardian new woman, attending meetings on philosophy and ideas and art at Leeds Art Club, training as a teacher and dating her first love. She answered it, writing to Christabel in Strangeways that if it was necessary to go to prison in order to win the vote, she was ready. Like Mary Murdoch, she too had felt the coming change as a series of waves. She was a human cork, ready for some unknown harbour. It did take her to prison for a month when she was arrested at the opening of parliament, receiving several beatings from policemen; it took her away from her teaching career and all across the North as a full-time organiser for the Women's Social and Political Union. It took her, as an activist, speaker and writer, beyond where she might never have reached without becoming part of the movement for change.

---

It is a December day in Manchester in 2018. A crowd are stood with their right arms outstretched in front of them, imitating the statue of Emmeline Pankhurst that is being unveiled. She stands on a chair, as was common in meetings, in a white stone circle inscribed with 'Deeds Not Words'. The circle opens out onto the Free Trade Hall where she and some of the other suffragettes were arrested after inter-rupting that election rally in 1905 and, as Hannah Mitchell said at the time, 'The North was roused and neither Earnest Grey nor his party were ever able to tamp down the fire they lit that evening.'

The statue had been erected following five years of planning, after councillor Andrew Simcock looked round the city's Sculpture Hall and asked, 'Where are all the women?' Twenty notable Manchester women were shortlisted as subjects, six sculptors were shortlisted (three men and three women), and Emmeline Pankhurst won the vote by a landslide. Hazel Reeves's simple design, 'Rise Up Women' won. The next job was fundraising, and it's fascinating that the North—South divide once again raised its head as a factor. When it was announced that the government was making five million pounds available in 2018 for celebrations to commemorate the 100th anniversary of women getting the vote, the statue team got straight onto them. When the Manchester team pointed out that a million of the five million pounds was going to the Millicent Fawcett statue in London (Millicent Fawcett led the more moderate National Union of Women's Suffrage Society), an official said, 'Ah well, you see, that's a national project. Yours is in Manchester.'

Not that Emmeline herself wasn't perfectly savvy about the crucial role of London in influencing governmental opinion. A reason that I've included vignettes from suffragettes based across the North is that the crucial role played by some of them is sometimes underplayed in histories which focus on Emmeline and Christabel Pankhurst, and on the protests which centred on London. Emmeline was Northern, though, born in Manchester to a mother from the Isle of Man and a father who ran a calico and bleach works in Salford. Her grandfather was in the crowd at Peterloo and her parents were radicals too. Her mother,

Sophia Goulden, took her to abolitionist meetings and Emmeline said that when she heard the suffragist Lydia Becker speak at a meeting in Manchester when she was fourteen, she 'left the meeting a conscious and confirmed suffragist'. She spent some time at school in Paris, whose revolutionary fervour and high fashion left its mark, and on returning to Manchester she met lawyer Richard Pankhurst and they became a sort of socialist Posh and Becks of late nineteenth-century Manchester. She campaigned for the Married Women's Property Act, which he had written. Therefore, he was the kind of impressively woke husband who encouraged Emmeline's campaigning activities rather than wanting her to be chained to the kitchen sink (though I think maids would have done their washing up, to be fair). He tried unsuccessfully to get elected as an MP on a radical platform in Manchester, so Emmeline decided they might have more luck if they moved to London. She opened a high-end furnishings shop to keep them afloat financially, but although they enjoyed mixing with the free-thinking radicals of London, they decided to move back to Manchester after Richard still didn't manage to get elected. A son tragically died, but Emmeline was very close to her oldest daughter, Christabel, and, as her mother had done before her, initiated her in her causes and ideas. It felt like Christabel was her great hope and she invested in her law studies and in travelling with her to the continent, whereas, as we know, her youngest daughter, Adela, was only able to train as an apprentice teacher. After Richard died, Emmeline was forced to take on work as a registrar of births and deaths, and the poverty she saw among the women coming to her convinced her to step up her efforts to get women the vote.

She started the Women's Social and Political Union in her front room in 1903 and it soon became the biggest campaigning organisation for women, with its slogan 'Deeds Not Words'. Cotton and textile workers' unions in Lancashire were mobilised thanks to factory women who came on board, like Annie Kenney, and the incident at the Free Trade Hall in 1905 took their campaign to a different level. Once again, Emmeline saw London as the place where it was necessary to be in order to penetrate government, and the organisation's headquarters moved there in 1906. As Jill Liddington's brilliant book about the suffragette movement in Yorkshire – *Rebel Girls* – relates, Adela Pankhurst was left to spread the suffragette word around Northern towns, which suited her fine: 'My heart was with my own people in Yorkshire & Lancashire. With the poor & downtrodden, the fallen women and neglected children.' Adela was very much on track to become my favourite Pankhurst, given that she was the disadvantaged black sheep of the family, despite all the hard graft she put in for the cause, and was down to earth and funny and passionate. Plus, her mum, fearing she was deviating from her and Christabel's hard-line approach as they became more militant once the government refused to budge ('Broken windows are better than broken promises'), basically packed her off to Australia with twenty quid, some warm clothes and a few introductions. Adela never saw the rest of her family again (I suppose there's always bound to be tensions in political families – we see it with the Bushes, the Milibands, the Chuckle Brothers . . . ). Unfortunately, after marrying a union leader and a communist in Australia, Adela lurched dramatically to the right and became a staunch advocate for traditional families and Empire, and wrote favourably about Nazi Germany.

All the Pankhursts had a tendency to very, very strong views. Excellent for persisting and helping get women over 30 the vote by 1918, not so great for promoting harmony. Christabel and Emmeline promised the government they would suspend their increasingly violent campaign when the war started, and they became deeply pro-war, handing out white feathers to men who refused to sign up. Christabel eventually went off to America and preached the end of the world as a Seventh Day Adventist. Both she and Emmeline had failed campaigns to become Conservative MPs. Adela's older sister Sylvia, however, did keep espousing her father's socialist values, setting up anti-fascist newspapers through the thirties and writing against authoritarianism. After she went against the social norm and had a baby in 1927 with her partner, the Italian anarchist Silvio Corio, her mum didn't speak to her again. Nowadays ITV2 would probably have sponsored a reunion tour, twenty years on, Louis Walsh suggesting they sing 'Sisters Are Doing It for Themselves' and hug as white feathers rain down from the ceiling and they conclude that they'll all have to just agree to disagree, the important thing was that women had got the vote and everybody agreed Adela looked great with hair extensions.

---

As it is, some of the suffragettes and suffragists are remembered more than others, but the impact of their amazing efforts over many years is one of the most profound legacies of any campaign, anywhere, ever. All women over 21 got the vote in 1928. They could begin the work of legislating more in their own interests. They had worked collectively and strategically, disagreeing on tactics of course, as any group or movement does, but over time the gentle nudges and the violent outbursts took effect and the revolution felt like it had been inevitable all along. For those who lived it, of course, it wasn't. Women's futures as full citizens was at stake. For some women, including Emily Wilding Davison from Northumberland, who threw herself in front of the king's horse (possibly to pin a suffragette scarf to the horse's bridle) at the height of the suffragettes' militancy, and died (and is now commemorated with a statue in her home town of Morpeth), they literally gave their lives to make change happen. The women of the North's mills and factories were absolutely crucial to this, working alongside middle-class women like Leeds trade unionist Leonora Cohen, who, after saying she refused to recognize the legitimacy of the law in courts where she was answering criminal damage charges (such as for throwing an iron bar and breaking the glass case displaying the Crown Jewels in the Tower of London) because women had not helped make the law, went on to become one of the country's first female magistrates. There are so many of them, and most of their names will never be known, but they stand behind that statue of Emmeline Pankhurst and give her outstretched arm its power and reach, as it propelled all of them, all of us, into the future.

### Hull's Headscarf Revolutionaries

It is 1968. A big woman wearing a headscarf, her jaw set in a determined line, almost a grimace, clings on to a harbour guardrail and is held back by four police officers, one of them with a black-gloved hand over her chest. Earlier, a reporter had asked her, in his RP voice, 'Do you regard yourself as some sort of suffragette?' She had fixed him with a withering look and said in flat Yorkshire, 'Don't be daft.'

Lillian Bilocca had challenged the taboo of women going down onto Hull's dockside, pledging that she would stop any trawler sailing that didn't have a radio operator on board. 'All the best, flowers,' she had wished the deckhands lining the decks of the trawlers setting off for three weeks' fishing in the treacherous, icy waters, a thousand miles away in the middle of the Arctic. But then, when one trawler confirmed they didn't have a radio operator on board, just like the *St Romanus*, which had been lost at sea with all twenty of its crew three weeks earlier, she attempted to board the ship to stop it sailing. As Brian Lavery, author of *The Headscarf Revolutionaries*, said, if she had tried to leap onto that boat, she would have killed herself. But she was headstrong and absolutely determined to be listened to.

The close-knit fishing community of Hessle Road in Hull was now reeling from two trawler tragedies, as the loss of the *Kingston Peridot* was also confirmed on 30 January 1968, just as hopes were fading for the *St Romanus*. Lillian Bilocca's daughter Virginia remembers her banging her hand down and saying, 'Enough is enough!' The fish-factory worker, whose son worked on the boats (against her wishes because she knew how unsafe they were), started a petition for better safety measures on board the notoriously dangerous vessels, where 6,000 lives had been lost over a century of deep-sea fishing that was so vital to Hull. Within three days she had 10,000 signatures – from an area where 14,000 people lived. There was a feeling that at long last something was being done, and there was an upswell of support. Five hundred women packed a meeting at a church hall and Lillian Bilocca spoke, as did Yvonne Blenkinsop, whose dad had been lost at sea years earlier, leaving her mum a widow with six children to raise. Lillian said she was determined that the prime minister himself should hear what they had to say and force the trawler owners to implement basic safety measures, like having support ships sail out with medical expertise on board. It was decided that she, Yvonne, Mary Denness, and Chrissie Jensen would form a committee and go down to London. Big Lil said she would picket Harold Wilson's house if she had to, and nobody doubted she meant it. Not everybody was a supporter, though — some of the trawler men thought the women should stay in the kitchen and out of trouble, having long been conditioned not to complain for fear of losing their jobs. One of the company owners, a man in a suit and tie, caused outrage when he went on telly and said the women were 'getting carried away on a wave of mass hysteria'.

But something was shifting, despite how the press treated Lillian — commenting on her size and the fact that she was, literally, a fishwife. During a press conference, news came in that another vessel — the *Ross Cleveland* — had gone down, with the loss of all but one of her nineteen crew. Three trawlers and sixty-eight lives lost in less than a month. The women went to Downing Street and met Harold Wilson and presented their 'Fisherman's Charter'. Yvonne Blenkinsop later described how she said to one of the civil servants, 'Petal, are we going to have these changes then?' and he said, 'You are, my dear.' Sure enough, the women saw all eighty-eight of their safety recommendations implemented. As Mary Denness said when they got back to Hull, they achieved in six weeks what trade unionists and politicians hadn't managed in a century. Appropriately, the first change put in place was that the next trawler to sail out of Hull went with a 'mother ship' carrying equipment and medical backup. Lillian herself was an indomitable mother ship, galvanised by her fears for her son and for all the families in Hull's close-knit fishing community. The campaign was one of the biggest worker victories ever seen in UK industry. However, it has taken many years for Lillian Bilocca to be recognized as the folk hero she was. She lost her job and was blacklisted in the fishing industry. Her achievements were already forgotten by the time Hull's fishing industry collapsed when Iceland won the Cod Wars (which sounds like a reality show just waiting to happen) in 1976. When she died of cancer aged 59 in 1988, there were very few people at her funeral. However, in recent years Hull has begun to remember its history again. There have been two plays (including one by Maxine Peake, of course), a mural, songs, books, a plaque and a BBC documentary – *Hull's Headscarf Heroes*. It is impossible to watch it and not be moved by these women coming out of the domestic sphere – as Lil's daughter Virginia said, her mother was actually a private person, propelled by their need to make the fishing industry safe. They knew the men were only at home for three days at a time and therefore couldn't effectively organise in order to demand their rights. Out of necessity and outrage, they stepped up and found their voices. But it wasn't the last time women would rise with one voice against the giants of industry. Sixteen years later, the miners' strike would change the meaning of solidarity.

## Women Against Pit Closures

Somebody found Aggie Currie an orange box to stand on, because she was only little. Her legs were shaking but she told the packed meeting about the collecting they'd done for the miners at Markham Main pit. How people were cheering them on. Giving clothes and tins of food, and money so they could keep the soup kitchens going, and toys for the kiddies. She'd thought she'd have to say something clever, but one of the union leaders had told her before her speech (not that he thought women should be getting involved in this sort of thing) to speak from her heart, to talk about what she knew. Well, she did. The crowd stood up and clapped and clapped. People were coming up to her afterwards telling her how brilliant it was to hear from a miner's wife and to know that women had formed groups to support the miners. They wanted to know how they could help. Aggie let herself feel how well she'd done. 'You've cracked it, girl,' she said to herself. She went on to do lots of speeches and revelled in her new nickname – 'Gobshite'. Years later, when the university women came to talk about that year of strikes, from March 1984 to March 1985, and the role of the women married to the pit workers who went on strike for a year in an (ultimately doomed) attempt to halt pit closures, Aggie reflected on how she had become a different person:

> Miners' strike learned me to swear. I used to say before
> the strike, I must have been a bloody clockwork doll. Put
> the batteries in me. Right you can make breakfast. Then
> you're going to your mates. Go do shopping, go do
> cleaning. Get kids from school. Doing them duties.
> Everything were built round Pete and the kids. I'm a
> stronger person than what I ever was before.

It had been expected that the women would help out, as they had in previous strikes, with the women's stuff. The soup kitchens and the car boot sales, delivering food parcels and supporting their men after they came home from a hard day on the picket line – but many of them went further.

They joined the picket. They became political, started watching the news. Some of them went to university. It changed lives, gave them voices.

I love hearing the voices of women like Aggie. Funny, down to earth, unmistakably Northern. These voices were also captured by Maxine Peake (I swear now she's stalking me. I think she should have written this book, actually. Maxine? Maxine? Can you do a thousand words on Cartimandua for me?) for her play *Queens of the Coal Age*, commissioned by the Royal Exchange Theatre in 2018. She interviewed four of the women, miners' strike veterans, who occupied Parkside Pit in Newton-le-Willows in 1983. The pit employed more than 800 people and was seen as one of the most modern, efficient and clean pits possible, with twenty-five working years left in its coal reserves. Inspired by the anti-nuclear camps at Greenham Common, the Lancashire Women Against Pit Closures group set up a pit camp, which provided a community focus for their campaign.

At Easter weekend they occupied the pit itself after passing themselves off as visitors, complete with safety jackets and helmets, and travelling down the lift in the miners' cage and refusing to come up again. The miners would greet them as they came down to work in the cage, and play cards with them, bring pots of tea and 'mucky books'. As Lesley Lomas said, 'Normally I'd have been quite offended but, in the circumstances . . .' When they decided to go back up after four days (without any more supplies than they'd taken underground with them), Anne made them clean up before they travelled back above ground. Elaine said she heard the comedian Jo Brand saying on television, 'And I bet they left it tidy,' and she wrote to her and said, 'I'm Elaine, one of the Women Against Pit Closures, and I'm ashamed to say, yes we did!' She described how, as they came back up in their disguise of miner's hat, belt and battery that they'd used to get down the pit, a policeman said to her, 'You lost,' and she said, 'Yeah, but we went down fighting. And that matters. That matters.'

### The Fracking Nanas

A grey-haired woman in a bright yellow T-shirt that says 'Don't frack with me', one with a bright yellow tabard that says 'Nana Dancing Queen' on the front, a pink-haired girl with a yellow tabard and yellow headscarf tied in a knot in the middle of her hair. Brightly coloured bunting, placards saying 'Frack Free Preston'. It's only in writing about the Fracking Nanas, whose thousand-day camp eventually saw off the fracking giants Cuadrilla, that I realise they are a mash-up of so many powerful Northern tropes. We have Hilda Ogden, and grans generally, in the comforting Northern word 'Nana'. We have the suffragettes in the headscarves and their militancy. We have, like the witches, another group of Lancashire women using rituals and chanting to keep their territory safe (they dress up in white on Wednesdays to hold a 'call for calm') and who are, like the Women Against Pit Closures and the Headscarf Revolutionaries, absolutely focused on how their goals must benefit future generations of their families, of all our families.

Some of them came to one of my *Where There's Muck, There's Bras* shows in Preston. They had performed a short theatrical piece, 'Nanas With Banners', about their campaign before my show and there was some kerfuffle in the audience when an angry man in a very knitted jumper started shouting and was led away through the foyer. Wherever there are female protestors, there's always some angry men.

The group was formed in summer 2014 in response to Cuadrilla's application to frack land in Blackpool. They say it's a clean, green-energy way to bring shale gas out of the ground. As it can cause earthquakes and soil contamination, there are understandably some concerns about this claim. Indeed, there have now been several earthquakes near the fracking site in Blackpool – previously, the seaside town only experienced them on Saturday nights when all the couples turned in to their B&B beds at once. (Oops. The Seventies have called and would like their joke back.) A key moment for the Nanas was when they claimed squatters' rights in a field for three weeks at the Preston New Road site where Cuadrilla was trying to get a licence for exploratory drilling. Fourteen thousand residents supported their petition and Lancashire County Council turned the application down, though that decision was later overturned by the government.

Fifty-six-year-old Nana Tina Rothery (Nana name: Nana Queenie) explains some of the benefits of their Nana personas: 'If you want to slow a truck down, have someone with a Zimmer frame walk in front . . . The police don't want to manhandle an old lady who looks like she has brittle bones or a colostomy bag. They don't want the mess on their hands, literally.' Forty-nine-year-old Anjie Mosher (Nana name: Nana Inappropriate) told a *Guardian* profiler:

> A few of us wanted to engage the public without being
> threatening or aggressive. There's nothing more gentle
> and unthreatening than your nana, and if your nana tells
> you something you listen because nana knows best.
> We took the old matriarchal image of Hilda Ogden, put
> on our yellow tabards and headscarves, armed ourselves

with feather dusters and little teapots and went to capture
that field at daft o'clock in the morning.

After nearly a thousand days of action by the Fracking
Nanas, Cuadrilla withdrew from the site. Multiple earthquakes and the playful but angry nanas had seen them off.
Meanwhile, as with all these protest movements, many of
the women involved are left with a greater sense of their
own ability to speak up and out for what they believe in,
with a sense of solidarity, camaraderie and creativity. And
they have reminded us that Northern matriarchs are still the
true Queens of the North.

# 4

# Politicians

## *The Real Northern Powerhouse*

On a cold February morning I stood with a group of other women in men's suits and ties, yellow hard hats and hi-vis jackets. We were holding banners saying 'Lass War' and 'We Are the Northern Powerhouse' and handing out leaflets to smartly dressed delegates on their way into Manchester's Central Exhibition Centre. We bantered with them and many of them told us 'well done'. At one point we burst into a shy and slightly out of tune rendition of 'Where Have All the Flowers Gone?' with the lyrics changed to 'Where have all the lasses gone? When will the fellas learn?', hastily taught to us by singer-songwriter Sharon Jagger of the feminist duo Union Jill. This earned us a headline in the *Manchester Evening News* of 'Choir Protest At Northern Powerhouse Conference'. So I now hold the distinction of being part of the world's worst choir. I also may hold the distinction of having said the most mildly Northern thing ever at a demonstration when I told *The Guardian* newspaper, who had come along to photograph us, that I had spent the last two years looking at male-heavy images of the Northern Powerhouse and 'tutting'.

We were there because the Northern Powerhouse conference of 2017 was being held in that space, in order to discuss the economic and social future of the North of England – and out of ninety-eight speakers, only thirteen were women. I had suggested we dress up in the uniform of the ultimate Northern Powerhouse man . . .

Women were not in these pictures. Women were not in these pictures for two reasons: firstly, the photo opportunity of women in hard hats and bright jackets just didn't seem to appeal to newspaper photographers and PR agencies; and secondly, there are still relatively few powerful female politicians in the North of England. There are more metro mayors (mayors of major city regions who now hold budgets for training and transport) called Andy and Dan (two of each) than there are women (one in total). The first female Metro Mayor Tracy Brabin (former actor, including in *Coronation Street*) became the first mayor of West Yorkshire in 2021. In 2021, an all-female shortlist for the new Labour mayor of Liverpool was scrapped. Probably in case there was a danger nobody called Andy or Dan would get the job.

It began to be okay for women (and men) to point out that the North of England was behind the times. 'Good God, how embarrassing is this?' said Greater Manchester Mayor Andy Burnham on seeing the conference press release, while Donna Hall, Chief Executive of Wigan Council, said, 'Holding back women holds back everyone and the whole of the North!' A positive outcome of this focus was that Donna and a group of inspirational women held an alternative conference in Doncaster, kicking off a movement called The People's Powerhouse. This was very much about giving more people a voice, particularly those who traditionally didn't have a voice in politics; having more balanced representation; and building 'strong places not just buildings' by drawing community groups together. It was more about trying to galvanise a horizontal approach to making things better from within the North, rather than a top-down approach led by politicians and businesses. It also put more emphasis on change coming from towns rather than the usual big cities such as Manchester, Liverpool, Leeds and Newcastle.

There are, and have been, Northern female politicians, of course, but they were generally outliers amid a sea of Oxbridge-educated men. In fact, many Northern female politicians seemed to gain popularity and respect in inverse proportion to how much of a contrast they provided to those establishment men. The public is primed to be receptive to this. It probably partly explains the massive popularity of the Jackie Weaver meme in 2021. As chief officer of the Cheshire Association of Local Councils, Jackie was parachuted in to chair the meeting of the troublesome Handforth Parish Council. The subsequent Zoom meeting went viral for the moments where annoyed male councillors hysterically shouted 'You have no authority here, Jackie Weaver!' and 'Read the standing orders. Read them and understand them!' It feels like every Northern woman has been Jackie Weaver to some aggravated mansplainers at some point in their lives – and that they would all hope to handle them with her calmness, aplomb and willingness to say, 'But you can call me Britney Spears.' That has certainly been the case for the female MPs I want to tell you about, women whose position was made possible of course by the efforts of the suffragettes from our previous chapter. Thanks to them, Nancy Astor became the first female MP to take up her seat in 1919 (the first elected MP was Constance Markievicz who, as a Sinn Fein member, didn't take up her seat), and the second was a remarkable Yorkshirewoman named Margaret Wintringham.

### Margaret Wintringham

Margaret was born in Silsden, West Yorkshire, very near where I grew up, and went to Keighley Girls Grammar School, near where I lived for the first ten years of my life. I have constantly been surprised in my research for this book. All the women I didn't know about. Then I think that maybe it's unreasonable to expect that every woman is memorialised. There is so much we have to learn and think about. I mean, at school we urgently needed to know about intensive pig farming in Jutland, peak-time traffic patterns in Skipton and the correct way to ask how to get to the town hall in French. Apparently. However, I would love to have known that I was growing up in the same place as one of the first female MPs. She's a woman I could have identified with because she was born just down the road. I'm not suggesting we should have had dictator-style pictures of local politicians looming down at us from the school walls (or maybe we should, given the relative paucity of female MPs) but it would just have been nice to have had more female role models.

There are things you might want a husband to pass on to you — a favourite shirt, an heirloom watch, the keys to the Jaguar. Margaret Wintringham, a headteacher's daughter born in 1879 (who went on to become a headmistress herself), got her husband's seat in parliament, making her the third elected female MP and the first to be born in England (and the North at that). She had to fight for it, though, but she had already proved her mettle in local women's suffrage societies. After her husband, Thomas, died in 1921, the Liberal Party invited her to stand for his seat in the subsequent by-election. (She and Thomas had no children. I'm guessing if they did, she wouldn't have been invited to stand, as the party would have believed she should be looking after them instead.)

She was backed by the National Federation of Women's Institutes who called her 'our institute MP' and unofficially coordinated the group of eight women MPs elected in 1923 to work cross-party on issues. She got on well with the Conservative Lady Nancy Astor and, in an interesting image of North/South, posh/not posh differences, said, 'I felt she went about her task like a high stepping pony, while I stumbled along like a carthorse, but we both had our uses and worked in complete harmony together.' Probably they bonded over the fact that the House of Commons was in no way set up for them — there was no women's cloakroom or toilet; in fact, they had to walk nearly a mile down a corridor from their offices to find one they could use. Margaret asked a lot of questions in parliament related to social issues affecting her rural constituency, or raised by the grassroots WI groups who backed her. She spoke up for women being allowed to vote at 21 instead of 30, women to be in the House of Lords, girls to be eligible for educational scholarships as well as boys, equal pay for men and women, and for female police officers to be kept when there was a move to get rid of them in 1922 (they had been allowed into the force during the First World War).

She and Lady Astor tag-teamed on the issue, with Astor pointing out that female police officers did preventative work, particularly with girls and young women in danger of a life of crime, that male police officers just couldn't do.

Astor pooh-poohed a suggestion that policemen's wives could do this instead, noting that, as with lawyers and politicians, policemen tended to marry their wives because they liked them, not because they were good at stopping women from falling into criminal behaviour. They succeeded in reversing the axe on women police officers in 1923, and fifty women officers were re-sworn, this time with proper powers of arrest. Perhaps, as the posher and more high-profile politician, it is inevitable that timelines of women in the police force seem to mention Astor's intervention but not Wintringham's. The high stepping Southern pony will always take more spotlight than the Northern carthorse . . .

### Ellen Wilkinson

*We are fighting the party of the rich! The party of*
*the powerful! The party of big business. That controls*
*the industries, the cartels, industry and the press!*
*These are our enemies!*

This is a slightly more (okay, a lot more) confrontational tone than Margaret Wintringham's, who, in the end, only had three years in the House of Commons, losing her seat to a Conservative man in 1924. That was the same year the firecracker of a politician who uttered the words above – at a Labour Party conference in Blackpool – entered the Commons. She became the first in a line of strong, charismatic Northern female MPs, mostly from the Labour Party, who achieved national recognition and affection. I felt ashamed when I was researching my show not to have heard of her before. She was a force of nature – a powerful speaker, much-loved constituency MP, journalist and writer, the first female education minister, and was tipped to be a future leader of the Labour Party. She was 'Red' Ellen Wilkinson. Perhaps I would have wondered who she was if I had passed the block of flats in Jarrow named Ellen Wilkinson Court, or drunk 'Red Ellen', a 'rich, ruby red ale' brewed in Jarrow, the town where she was MP and had her finest hour leading the Jarrow March. Or if I'd seen the humanities building named after her at the University of Manchester, where she studied on a scholarship – which were still only rarely awarded to working-class women when she graduated with a degree in history in 1913. Her greatest achievements, alongside her involvement with the Jarrow March, were implementing the 1944 Education Act which included the raising of the school leaving age to 15, and getting milk into schools (which made her literally the opposite of Margaret Thatcher, who became known as 'Thatcher the milk snatcher' for getting rid of it in 1971).

As a child, she was a clever, confident reader and talker who devoured every book put in front of her by her father, a self-taught intellectual who passed on his love of thinkers like Darwin and Huxley. He was a passionate Methodist and socialist, concerned with equality above all. Despite frequent childhood illnesses, Ellen won a history scholarship to the University of Manchester, where she learnt the research skills that stood her in good stead as a journalist, writer and politician.

She joined lots of the radical reform groups active in Manchester at that time, from the suffragettes, to the Fabians, Communists and the Labour Party, and became absolutely instrumental in leading meetings and talking with others and, in public, about a new, fairer world they could create. In 1924 she became one of the first women in parliament, representing Middlesbrough for the Labour

Party. The other three women who entered parliament that year had, like Margaret Wintringham, inherited their husbands' seats. You can see both Ellen's incongruity and her panache in photographs from her early political career.

There is one picture where all four-foot-eleven of her is captured in full flow, one arm outstretched, pointing, and the other fist clenched. She is wearing a sort of black beret over her mop of curly red hair (she was known for her red hair, hence the nickname 'Red Ellen', as well as being nicknamed the 'Fiery Particle', the 'Mighty Atom' and the 'Pocket Pasionaria', reflecting her keen sense of the dramatic). A sea of faces, as far as the eye can see, are looking up at her, transfixed. The vast majority are men – in flat caps, bowler hats, trilbies, and suits and ties. She must have been used to making herself heard as there's no microphone.

But the Jarrow March was the moment where she came into her own. She chronicled the march and the plight of Jarrow in her book *The Town That Was Murdered*. Only 100 out of 8,000 skilled manual workers were left with a job in the wake of the Great Depression and the closure of the town's shipyards and steelworks. She was instrumental in organising the march in which two hundred men set off on foot for parliament on 5 October 1936, carrying a petition signed by 12,000 of Jarrow's residents. It said they 'humbly prayed' that the house would recognize the 'urgent need for work to be provided for the town without delay'.

Although the march has become an important part of Labour Party history, it was not actually supported by them or the Trades Union Congress, and, in fact, Ellen made a trip up to the Labour party conference in Glasgow to try to persuade them that this was not a political matter, but a national scandal: people were starving because of lack of employment. She pointed out that they had widespread public support and said, 'So many people have raised their hats to me, I am beginning to think I am a monument.' When the marchers got to London, in the pouring rain on 4 November, Prime Minister Stanley Baldwin wouldn't take their petition and it seemed like the whole thing was a failure, which would really miff me off after walking 300 miles. However, in the long term it had more success as both a historic symbol of the hunger of the thirties and of people's capacity to stand up to their government. Ellen's writing, speaking, and behind-the-scenes organisation was a big part of ensuring that this was the case.

During the Second World War, Ellen was a junior minister in the coalition government, notably establishing the women's guard of fire watchers during the Blitz. Then, in the Labour landslide of 1945 she was made minister of education in the cabinet, the first woman to take the position. She presided over the landmark Education Act, which saw the school leaving age raised to 15 and free milk distributed in schools. She came to the job as someone whose own against-the-odds access to education opened the doors that enabled her to succeed as a woman and a politician. The Act opened doors for many more clever girls in the future to stay on at school, and eventually go to university.

Her health, never good, and which had always worried her friends because of her relentless pace of work, worsened and she died of an accidental overdose of bronchial medication in 1947 at the age of 55 when she still had so much left to do. She never married or had children but had long-term relationships with political cartoonist Frank Horrabin and politician Herbert Morrison. This fuelled gossip that her overdose was deliberate. Her friends and colleagues had no doubt of the magnitude of what she could have gone on to achieve. Perhaps, with her energy, verve and ability to connect to ordinary people, which inspired her constituents to call her 'Our Ellen', she could have become the first female party leader, as some tipped her to be. And I'm pleased to say the people of Middlesbrough will soon be tipping their hats to an actual monument of a woman who always fought for the poor and voiceless.

### The 'Double B' Battlers: Bessie Braddock, Betty Boothroyd and Barbara Castle (née Betts)
### Bessie Braddock

My next three women exemplify different facets of the strong Northern woman archetype. I mean, just picture Bessie Braddock (known as 'Battling' Bessie Braddock) who looked like everyone's idea of a nan: firm jaw, big rosy cheeks, breast like the prow of a ship. Imagine her in 1956, shooting three air rifles she had confiscated from juveniles into the ceiling of the House of Commons, while the speaker calls her 'out of order'. She riposted that you had to be out of order, or do something unusual, for anybody to notice you in that place. To be fair, I think they did notice her, given that the vast majority of MPs were still posh blokes in suits. She spoke up fiercely for the rights of the poor and for her home city of Liverpool, which made her popular there, and nationally. She even rejected a ministerial post because, like her husband, council leader Jack Braddock, she wanted to make sure she could stay focused on the needs of her city. (She was less popular in Wales, however, because she once voted in favour of flooding a Welsh valley in order to turn it into a reservoir for Liverpool, which you can see might have annoyed the residents slightly.)

She is commemorated in her home city with a bronze statue at Lime Street station in which she is shown walking, handbag in one hand, egg in the other. The egg is because she was the politician responsible for putting the lion standard mark on British eggs. Standing opposite, as if walking towards her, is a statue of the comedian Ken Dodd, cheerfully holding his tickling stick (I do wonder what Freud would make of their respective props). Sculptor Tom Murphy made them as a pair called 'Chance Meeting'. He had been inspired by the fact that Ken Dodd said he really enjoyed travelling down to London with Bessie as they headed to their respective performance arenas – he to his theatres and she to the House of Commons.

With her forthrightness and eccentricity, she stood out in the theatre space of the House. She had honed her skills as a councillor in Liverpool, where she admitted calling one councillor 'a blasted rat' and saying of the Tory councillors, 'I'd like to machine gun the lot of you.' To be fair, she was often frustrated because she felt her concerns about slum housing and poverty were not being taken seriously. She once famously made a speech through a two-foot megaphone in the council chamber for this very reason.

She had attended her first political meeting aged just three weeks old in 1899, taken by her mother, union organiser Mary Bamber, who is also commemorated with a sculpture in Liverpool and was called the 'finest fighting platform speaker in the country' by Sylvia Pankhurst. The pair of them made a formidable mother–daughter team campaigning against injustice. Mary instilled her values in Bessie when they served soup to unemployed people who had 'blank, hopeless stares and thin blue lips' during the hard winter of 1906–7. Mary became a Labour councillor herself in 1919, and was still speaking at campaign meetings two weeks before she died in 1938; she would have been desperately proud of her daughter's career as a Labour MP, which spanned from 1945 to 1970.

Teetotaller Bessie, who didn't wear make-up and holidayed in Scarborough every year, became popular with constituents because they saw her as one of their own. She looked like their grans, with her knitted tea-cosy hat – with her impressive 50, 40, 50 measurements she once took part in a fashion show for larger women – but she was a savvy and dedicated politician as well. One of her greatest contributions came after she was asked to sit on the Royal Commission on Mental Health by Sir Winston Churchill – no political ally, but one who recognized her abilities. The commission led to the Mental Health Act of 1959. Bessie was ahead of her time in supporting unpopular causes, such as mental health in prisons and asylums.

Her name still most often comes up in an anecdote in which she says to Winston Churchill, 'You're drunk,' and he ripostes, 'And you're ugly, but in the morning, I'll be sober.' Apart from the fact that the story may be apocryphal, and a similar generic joke had been doing the rounds for years, I think it's clear that what Bessie should actually be remembered for is her fierce dedication to the cause of improving the lives of poor people, and for using her formidable charisma and savvy to make it as one of the first working-class female MPs without compromising who she was and what she believed. Bravo, Battling Bessie.

### Barbara Castle

Thank goodness for YouTube. On it, you can see a small, neat woman with big, well-coiffed red hair and a cream blouse (which, with its double-breasted buttons and embroidery down the front, is somehow a deeply feminine version of military dress) absolutely take apart a room of Oxford students in penguin suits in 1975. Then you understand why Barbara Castle was regarded as one of the most effective speakers and politicians of her age. Talk about a smiling assassin. She starts off pointing out that when she was a member of this ancient university, women were not allowed to be members of the union, let alone speak. A ripple runs through the audience. Here she is, seizing her chance to speak now and pointing out that 'It should hardly be surprising that the establishment should score in this black-tie debate. In this university union, the cadet club of the establishment.' Oof. She's said it. Named the elephant in the room. Called out the existence of the establishment right in the heart of the establishment itself. You can see the slight smile on her face – she's revelling in the power of her voice and her platform. The bow-tied audience gasps, laughs, there's a ripple of applause. The students are loving her confidence, her audacity, her charm. You can see why she was nicknamed the 'Red Queen'. Though one of her friends said it should have been the 'Red Empress'.

Her course as a politician who wasn't afraid to court controversy and opposition could be charted from when she walked arm-in-arm with her friend round the schoolyard at Bradford Girls Grammar school, both of them proudly wearing big red Labour rosettes, knowing the coal merchants' daughters were annoyed. 'They thought we were going to put bombs under their desks or something. You could feel the hatred,' she said years later. She became Head Girl and then took the tried and tested path to politics of studying Politics, Philosophy and Economics at Oxford. If many men before her trod that route, she didn't see why she as a woman shouldn't too. There was some core of steel in her, though, that propelled her through all those gates she was not supposed to pass through, some of it doubtless instilled by her parents, who had strong socialist beliefs and lived them. She had been born Barbara Ann Betts in 1910 to Frank, a tax inspector, and Annie, a Labour councillor, who were socialists who lived the equality they believed in. Unlike many of her fellow Oxford PPE graduates, though, there was no network of contacts and family friends to smooth her path into politics.

Her path to becoming the most important female figure ever produced by the Labour Party stuttered for a while after she graduated. She moved back to Bradford and got involved in local politics, then during the Depression she had to sell dried fruit in Manchester from a mobile store. (Speaking as someone who had to work as an entertainer in an all-inclusive hotel in Tunisia before I could train as a journalist, I feel her pain.) Her way into politics, however, opened up once she moved to London and became part of a group of left-wing movers and shakers. She fell in love with the much older William Mellor, editor of the left-wing magazine *Tribune*, who became her mentor and gave her the introduction she craved to the London political world. He was twice her age when they got together and their relationship continued for ten years, although he wouldn't divorce his wife. He and Barbara were part of the left wing of the Labour Party and, alongside others including Ellen Wilkinson, established the Socialist League in 1932. Castle supported him through his bids for election and made several attempts of her own. However, in order to be seen as 'respectable' enough to gain political office she needed to be married, and after Mellor died, she wed journalist Ted Castle before finally winning a seat for Blackburn in 1945, which she held until 1979.

She had some lessons to teach us in how to know your own worth. In the middle of an interview with a documentary maker, she renegotiated her fee upwards (literally DURING the interview. I bow down to the Red Queen, it's hard enough to ask for more money before you start doing a job), saying, 'I'm on such good form and you're covering much more ground than I expected'. She was chuffed that a biography of Prime Minister Harold Wilson started with the line 'Barbara Castle was bullying the Prime Minister again,' although she alleged he was able to get her to take on the dirtiest jobs in cabinet by pointing out to her that she'd be the first ever woman to do whatever it was. There were persistent rumours that they had an affair, but she laid that firmly to rest, saying they just engaged in mild flirtation, adding he might say she had nice legs or that he'd dreamt about her last night but 'I don't think he's unusual in that'. This was obviously not the modern era – we're talking the sixties and seventies here. She was alternately frustrated and sanguine about the fact that female politicians were judged on different criteria to men. She said it was vital for a female politician to look nice and that the secret of Margaret Thatcher's hold over her party was her sexual attractiveness (I know that for some people that's like saying Hitler did so well because he had a nice moustache).

Barbara was indeed a female politician who achieved many firsts – becoming only the third female cabinet minister in 1964 – and was widely tipped as a future prime minister. Her biggest achievements included the Equal Pay Act (immortalised in the film *Made in Dagenham*, which followed the fight of female car-factory workers to be paid the same as men) and, when she was transport secretary (despite not being able to drive), introducing the 70 mph speed limit, breathalysers and car seatbelts. She said it was very satisfying to know she'd made such concrete achievements in her career. The breathalyser had been estimated to save 200 lives a year but it had already saved 1,200 by the end of the first twelve months. She served three terms under Harold Wilson, being dumped out of the cabinet by her political opponent Jim Callaghan when he took office in 1976. She said one of her other big achievements was managing not to retort, 'Well, you could start with yourself then, Jim,' when he said he wanted a younger cabinet. After losing her seat she became an MEP and then a peer, still speaking out on issues of the day, and was indomitable until she died in 2002 at the age of ninety-one. A statue was finally erected to her in Blackburn's Jubilee Square in October 2021 after earlier attempts at tributes in the eighties and in 2004 didn't attract enough support. She's striding along, clutching the Equal Pay Act, and is on the ground, as she would have wanted, rather than on a pedestal. At its unveiling, sculptor Sam Holland (a rare female sculptor) said the hardest thing was getting the pose right: 'It's all about capturing her energy and determination.' Thanks to this memorial, her qualities will be far harder for future generations to forget.

## Betty Boothroyd

'Order! Order!' bellowed the bouffant-haired woman in the white waterfall cravat and black robe who was the first woman ever to become Speaker of the House of Commons. She had checked that it was okay to stop wearing the wig, but otherwise her outfit was the same as the one worn by the men who had held the post for hundreds of years before her. Her beautifully projected, clear, strong voice – with the Yorkshire accent still detectable – was, however, new. With the charm and cheer that characterised her manner, she had also requested that while all previous speakers had been addressed as Mr Speaker, she wanted MPs to 'call me Madam!' Betty Boothroyd still stands out to many as the best parliamentary speaker of the modern era. She saw her role as being a servant of the House of Commons and was the first speaker to be elected by MPs from both her own party and the opposition, which indicates how well she was regarded as someone who would do the job fairly and with authority (and with unprecedented applause from MPs when her election was announced). She made 'I speak to serve' her motto as speaker because, she said, 'I think being from Yorkshire – we speak directly. No nonsense.' ('No nonsense' is clearly not the speaking style of many of her colleagues in the House of Commons. Not naming any names, but she has said she wouldn't trust Boris Johnson 'to run a bath'.) When she ran for the position in 1992, she knew it was important to win by a large majority, and she did. She said she told herself during the campaign to 'Just go for gold Betty, go for gold.' (I will offer some tips later on how to get an inner monologue like Betty Boothroyd's). In accepting the position, she said she had wanted to be picked for what she was, not for what she was born – a woman, a child of working-class textile worker parents, born in a terraced house in Dewsbury in 1929, who would never have been expected to rise to one of the most important offices in the land. She said her proudest day as speaker was when Nelson Mandela came to address the Commons as president of South Africa in 1996. They walked down the steps to Westminster Hall hand-in-hand, after he expressed some fear about the steepness of the descent. They were both politicians who knew something about the steepness of the ascent to power too.

Betty was born on Ellen Wilkinson's birthday — 8 October — and two days after Barbara Castle's birthday on 6 October, which means nothing of course, though I'd have loved to have been at their birthday tea party. Her mum took her to political meetings as a girl, where she would hear the likes of Bessie Braddock and Barbara Castle speak; her hero was Labour leader Clement Attlee. Part of Betty's drive came from wanting to change the conditions in which her mum, a weaver, had developed emphysema from her work in the mills. Betty failed the eleven-plus and her dad wanted her to get a steady job in the town hall. She wanted something more than that, however; after going to Dewsbury Technical College to learn typing, French and bookkeeping, she had a brief unusual interlude with the Tiller Girls dance troupe. Her time high-kicking on the stage always loomed large in later writing about her, but she was keen to play it down, saying, 'For something like three months I was a dancer. If you paid any attention to the media, you'd think I'd been a dancer for thirty years.'

Her main focus (back to her youthful passion against injustice) became politics and she picked up work as a secretary to Labour MPs, including Barbara Castle (Betty described her as a 'true friend and mentor' after she died). This experience of the political fray then inspired her to travel to the US to work for congressmen, with just a return ticket and £200 in her pocket. She ended up helping out on John F. Kennedy's 1960 presidential campaign and attending his inauguration, which she said was 'like a fairyland'. She certainly had to keep that Yorkshire grit handy, though, when it came to making her own career in politics as it took her FIVE goes at standing for election; she was on the verge of giving up when she was finally elected as the member for West Bromwich in 1973. Her later election as speaker meant all the more to her because of how difficult it had been to become an MP in the first place. In an early recognition of her ability to assert her authority in male-dominated environments, she was appointed as a Labour whip a year later.

She never married or had children, and she devoted herself to her job, saying that she was a loner but never lonely. She famously took up paragliding in her sixties while on holiday in Cyprus. She had given it up by her eighties though, saying it had become boring: 'I've done it a lot of times and when you are swinging over the coastline you have seen it all before. There's no one to talk to, no sweets to suck and no ice cream. Put me down please!' Her career in politics has continued into her nineties in the House of Lords, with one of her speeches on Brexit going viral and featuring as much of her no-nonsense Yorkshire directness as ever.

I did say I'd give some tips on how to do an internal monologue like Betty. I think calling yourself Betty would definitely help. As would a deep voice (she said she got hers by smoking a packet of cigarettes a day – obviously I don't recommend that . . . ) and flat Yorkshire vowels. Be encouraging but to the point. Advocate resilience and ambition. Betty said when she'd sometimes get a scared feeling in the pit of her stomach looking at all the men she had to go and speak in front of, or the ceremonial duties she had to conduct, she'd say, 'Go on, Betty. Put some Polyfilla on, get out there and do the job.' Exactly.

## Mo Mowlam

We've met many women whose achievements have only been recognized long after their era – but we've also seen how quickly women can fade from view. Take the redoubtable Marjorie 'Mo' Mowlam. She was one of the architects and negotiators of the Good Friday peace agreement that finally brought peace to Northern Ireland after years of conflict. However, twenty years on, when this achievement was being commemorated in 2018, a magazine cover showed a line-up of men in suits. Mo was literally out of the picture. As her stepdaughter Henrietta asked, 'Where the fuck was she?' saying she missed Mo more in that moment than she did on the anniversary of her death in 2005 or on her birthday. Tony Blair made a commemorative speech in Belfast which also didn't mention her, although at the time he had credited her with a crucial role in the process: 'It is no exaggeration to say she transformed the politics not just of Northern Ireland itself but crucially of relations between the Republic of Ireland and the United Kingdom, and it was this transformation that created the culture in which peace-making could flourish . . .'

Mo was born in 1949 and raised in Coventry by her telephonist mum and assistant postmaster dad. She was the only one of her siblings to pass the eleven-plus, and she became head girl at Chiswick Girls Grammar School. Both popular and academic, she went on to study sociology and anthropology at the University of Durham, then, after working for the legendary socialist MP Tony Benn, she moved to the US to take a PhD in political sciences. After four years in the States, she moved back to the UK to lecture at Newcastle University and Barnsley College, before becoming the MP for Redcar in 1987. She joined the Labour shadow cabinet in 1992 as minister for women and equalities, then minister for national heritage, before becoming the first female Northern Ireland secretary when the Blair government took power in 1997.

Blair said she was one of the most extraordinary and distinctive politicians to ever enter the Commons. One journalist recounted how she would drink from strangers' pints in pubs and working men's clubs in the North East and Belfast and get away with it because she was funny and charming. He asked her if it was true that she had once bullied a journalist to give her the bangles from her wrist – and Mo shook her arm to show the bangles sliding down.

Many people remember the story of her throwing her wig down on the meeting table during her treatment for a brain tumour and disarming po-faced politicians. Warmth and honesty and irreverence were part of her personal style. A civil servant recounted how, in a meeting in which she impressed him by confirming that the Labour government would have a constructive relationship with the Irish without following a simple Nationalist agenda, she first presented British and Irish officials with a 'Snog Kit' from that year's Comic Relief campaign containing a lipstick and a logbook in which to record their romantic adventures.

She recognized the need to visit and include all communities in the peace process, and to make sure that women from all sides were at the heart of it. Her controversial and unprecedented visit to the Maze prison following the murder of a Republican prisoner by Loyalist inmates put the peace process back on track. She made a success of the job, which had been seen as a 'poisoned chalice', but by the time US President Bill Clinton visited, she felt she was being sidelined and muttered on being introduced to him, 'I'm just the tea lady round here.' She felt that misogyny played a part in how she was being treated, and getting a standing ovation during Tony Blair's speech at the party conference in 1998 may have sealed her fate – she was too popular (though not among the Unionists). Peter Hain was given the job of Northern Ireland secretary in 1999 and Mo retired as an MP in 2001, spending the last years of her life in Kent with her husband, Jon.

Like Ellen Wilkinson, she died at the age of 55 with so much still left to do. Jon said after her death that she had insisted on steroids and radiotherapy to treat her brain tumour, rather than surgery, in order to be able to carry on her career, against the advice of her cancer specialist, and didn't let on to Tony Blair how serious her health condition was. At the time, newspapers speculated about why she had suddenly put on weight and was wearing a wig, so she was forced to speak out publicly.

The most poignant tributes to her came from her step-children, Henrietta and Freddie. They said she always had a childlike, eccentric streak – enjoying hiding a remote-controlled fart machine when self-important people came to stay, or making a game of stealing things from restaurants, once coming away with a haul of four seat tassels from the posh London restaurant Quaglino's. They recalled the private, celebratory funeral she had, where John Lennon's song 'Working Class Hero' was played on an out-of-tune piano, and spoke positively of the 2010 Channel Four film *Mo* starring Julie Walters as an accurate portrayal of her. Hopefully, Mo's legacy will be carried far beyond living memory as more inclusive histories continue to be written.

## *Jo Cox*

I don't want to be writing about this next politician, because she should be just one of a crop of bright, capable women from the North of England who are currently working diligently in the House of Commons to make the region and the country a better place, building on the legacy of the women who have gone before them. But Jo Cox, who described herself as 'a Yorkshire lass', is famous for her call for togetherness in the face of political hatred when she said, 'We are far more united and have far more in common than that which divides us.' Tragically, her name blazed across the public consciousness when she became the first MP to be killed in office for more than twenty-five years, during the brutal, divisive Brexit campaign in 2016.

She grew up in Heckmondwike in West Yorkshire, in a close family, and was shy at school at first, but became head girl at Heckmondwike Grammar and went on to study at Cambridge, the first of her family to go to university. The stories told of her life talk about how, coming from a working-class Northern background, she initially found it difficult to fit in and was lonely at first until she made friends and began to succeed academically. Both anecdotally and from research, this sense of being a 'fish out of water' is common among Northern students at Russell Group, and especially Oxbridge universities. Strange customs like dining at high table, wearing academic gowns, and layers of social etiquette can feel intimidating.

Nonetheless, like all of our Northern women who passionately wanted to change the world, she resolutely set about using her skills and gaining the experience she would need to enter a world that was utterly alien to her. Jo had wanted to be an MP since visiting parliament aged 15, and after graduating in 1995 she became an assistant to Labour MP Joan Walley before moving to Brussels to become political advisor to MEP Glenys Kinnock. She then joined Oxfam in 2001, leading on humanitarian campaigns such as Make Poverty History and the Maternal Mortality Alliance, as well as working on issues connected to the devastating conflicts in Darfur and the Democratic Republic of Congo.

Jo saw her chance to become an MP for her home constituency in early 2015 when the incumbent retired. She was elected from an all-women shortlist, an innovation Labour originally introduced in 1997 to help address the fact that since 1918 less than a tenth of MPs elected have been women. The timing hadn't been great, as she had two young children with Brendan, the husband she had met in 2009, but she was making family life work – even doing the 10 p.m. votes in the House of Commons in her cycling clothes so she could get home for the children's bedtime. Jo made a big impact in her short time in parliament and campaigned on national and international issues, including educational equality, education for autistic children, loneliness, and protecting civilians in conflict. She was also passionate about the issue of gender equality in political representation, joining the 50:50 campaign for equal numbers of men and women in parliament.

Her murder on 16 June 2016 sent reverberations around the world. She was the first sitting MP to be killed in the UK since Ian Gow, who was murdered by the IRA in 1990. She had been on her way to hold a surgery at her constituency office in Batley, after visiting a school and a care home, when a lone right-wing neo-Nazi sympathiser shouting 'Britain first,' shot and stabbed her multiple times. She urged her assistants to 'get away and let him hurt me, not you,' as he attacked her.

After the unthinkably shocking news of her death broke, her husband Brendan immediately called for people to 'fight against the hatred that killed her'. There is now an annual Great Get Together event in her name, where picnics, street parties and concerts are held with the purpose of encouraging unity and dialogue between different groups. A street in France has been renamed 'Rue Jo Cox' and a square in Brussels called 'Jo Coxplein'. When Britain's withdrawal agreement from the EU was approved in 2020, European Parliament president David Sassoli ended his speech by referencing her quote 'More in Common', the saying which adorns a commemorative coat of arms designed by her children as a permanent memorial to her in the House of Commons. Jo Cox continues to stand as a symbol of unity and togetherness, and of hope in the face of the destructive forces of division and hate which led to her death.

### What a Performance: Northern Women in the House

Although it feels premature to write about contemporary female politicians who have not yet fully achieved their legacies, looking at the careers and public images of some of these women reveals that 'being Northern' (or from a particular place in the North) is still a quality that forms an important part of a politician's public persona. It can be a vote winner, it can give you a certain sort of political capital based on perceived qualities of honesty and down-to-earthness, but, worryingly, as several Northern women politicians have attested, it can also make you a target for abuse and prejudice, both inside and outside the House of Commons.

South Shields MP Emma Lewell-Buck has spoken up against MPs who openly mocked her North East accent when they said she sounded like the North East comedian Sarah Millican. She won her seat in 2013, taking over from the incumbent Labour high-flyer, former leader Ed Miliband's brother, David. In contrast to him, she was a local lass, having spent all of her life in the North East, studying politics at Northumbria University and gaining a master's in social work at Durham University, before becoming a social worker in South Tyneside and their youngest ever councillor at the age of twenty-four.

Emma's fellow Northern MP Pat Glass, who represents Durham West, backed her up when Emma was shouted at in the commons during a debate on water bills, saying that she was appalled by the way that men who had gone to public school made the Commons macho and gladiatorial. She said they behaved especially badly towards women, particularly Northern women, saying, 'Generally if you are a woman, they target you and if you have a Northern accent they go for you . . . they start shouting about it to put you off.' Lewell-Buck said she wants her constituents to be represented by someone who looks like them and sounds like them, and that she doesn't care if the posh Tory boys don't understand her.

Angela Rayner, who became deputy leader of the Labour Party in 2020, grew up in Stockport and says she faces a barrage of trolls calling her 'thick' and uneducated because of her accent every time she appears on the telly or radio. She has emphasised how her working-class background, growing up on a council estate, and becoming a parent in her teens makes her just the sort of 'real person with real life experience' who should be in the Commons and said in her maiden speech that she was proud of herself and for her family, her party and the people she represents. She also said she would carry on doing things in 'her little Northern way'. Which, since it includes attaining the second-highest position in her party, suggests that's actually quite a big Northern way.

A politician's Northernness is likely to be used as a marker no matter what else they're talking about, and no matter what other facets of their identity they highlight. Described as a 'no-nonsense Northerner' by *The Telegraph* newspaper, Lisa Nandy – brought up in Bury and Manchester, now MP for Wigan – came third in Labour's leadership election in 2020 and was widely seen as a soft-left figure who could unite the party. Her dad is an Indian-born, Marxist academic, her mum a Granada TV producer. When she entered parliament in 2010, she became Wigan's first female MP and one of the first female Asian MPs. She is a strong voice for the North, pointing out the long-term inequalities in infrastructure between the North and the South, while also having a strong grasp of wider issues and currently serving as shadow foreign secretary. She has told of how after the Brexit vote a man shouted 'f***king traitor' in her face outside parliament and says 'all Northern female MPs are targets'.

It's not often that politicians get to deal with this stuff with humour, but one of the most brilliant stand-up performances I've ever seen came from a Northern Tory Muslim baroness – and that's not a sentence most people would expect to be saying. When Baroness Sayeeda Warsi went on Channel 4's *Stand Up to Cancer* special in 2021 – in which comics taught non-comics how to perform stand-up

– she turned out to be the star performer of the series. She finally got to resolve all the contradictions of her life as a working-class Muslim woman from Dewsbury who rose up through the ranks to become chair of the Tory party, and eventually a baroness in the House of Lords trying to fight Islamophobia in her own party. With the encouragement of stand-up Nick Helm, who had started out deeply unimpressed at having to tutor a Conservative politician, but was won over by her honesty and by the fact that she was clearly as much of an outsider as him, she ended her set with a triumphant 'I'm the baroness, bitches!' which she says she now uses as a mantra to cheer herself on. She threw off the high heels, neat jackets and buttoned-down emotions of her political speeches and let rip on the stand-up stage, saying that her mates in the Conservative Party had been doing some 'batshit things' and talking about how she'd tried to keep up with her posh Etonian colleagues by marrying her cousin, getting a double-barrelled surname and going hunting 'though I don't know if you know how difficult it is to get a gun licence with the surname Hussein-Warsi'. A moment for me that beautifully encapsulated how it is perfectly possible to express a Northern English identity and an ethnic minority identity at the same time came when she said, 'Hello, or as my people say, 'ey up.' She has said that she is often asked whether she is British or Muslim first but will say she is Yorkshire before both, a brilliant way to show how Northern identities can be used to help build solidarity rather than create divisions.

We can also see the dual themes of Pakistani identity and Yorkshire identity in the life of Bradford West MP Naz Shah, whose dramatic life story surely merits a film treatment (er, not Maxine Peake this time ... my vote would go to *Doctor Who* actor Mandip Gill here). She was born to a working-class Pakistani couple who settled in Leeds. Her dad refused to pick her up because she was a girl, and he beat her mother. After he left, she and her pregnant mother and younger brother lived in a series of unheated, rat-infested homes. Shah caught tuberculosis but had to become her mother's interpreter at the age of just six. Aged 12 she was sent to Pakistan for her own safety to escape her mother's violent new relationship, then was ordered to marry her first cousin when she returned aged fifteen. She left him after he beat her so badly he permanently damaged her ear. Meanwhile, her mother poisoned her abuser with arsenic and was sentenced to twenty years in jail, having been too ashamed to tell the court about the abuse she had suffered for years. Shah, still only 18, brought up her younger brother and sister, and despite having left school aged 12, then built an impressive career as an NHS commissioner and chair of a mental health charity, and eventually campaigned success-fully (alongside Southall Black Sisters) for her mother's release. Her experiences shape her politics, and since enter-ing parliament in 2015 she has campaigned passionately to make sure Muslim women in her mother's position have the support they need.

Her political career has been turbulent, encompassing a bitter election battle with the previous MP, George Galloway, for her seat, suspension from the Labour Party for anti-Semitism, doubling her parliamentary majority, and an apology from the Leave.EU campaign for calling her a 'grooming gangs apologist' (they were referring to gangs of Asian men convicted of abuse of young girls in Northern towns). They acknowledged she was in fact a vociferous campaigner against abuse. To be honest, as I look at all the obstacles and opposition Naz has faced, I think 'how on earth does she manage to be so resilient?' She and the other politicians I have written about must be absolutely tough as nails with triple-cured shellac and gel layers. Are they super-human? Then I realised that something they all have in common is a passionate dedication to causes which they see as more important than themselves, and the belief that they can work with others to make a difference. Naz talks about how proud she is to be a Bradfordian because, at a time when asylum seekers and migrants are demonised, Bradford is a City of Sanctuary where different communities come together to help others who are less fortunate. She and all the politicians in this chapter have actually helped create a different world, one in which it will be easier for other women like them to follow in their impressive footsteps.

# 5

# Sportswomen

I confess I generally think of the sports section of the newspaper as 'those wasted pages at the back' and have no idea of the difference between Rugby Union and Rugby League or Muay Thai and a Thai curry. I can probably explain the offside rule but that's only because I'm fed up of people saying girls don't understand the offside rule. It was only while making my show that it occurred to me that maybe, just maybe, some of my lack of interest was because this was all blokes doing blokey things, sometimes while drinking lager and blackcurrant, vomiting it up and then drinking it back down again (sorry, that's what the rugby lads used to do down the bar at Loughborough, the ridiculously sporty university I went to. Come to think of it, maybe that was what actually put me off sport). Anyway, once I started uncovering all these stories of sporting Northern women, I was gripped. They had to battle against so many odds, be ridiculously resilient (my quest to overcome the cliché of Northern grit is not going very well), and have achieved world-class success but – whaddya know – are often under-rated or under-remembered in their fields.

As Leeds boxer Nicola Adams said when she explained why her boxing career couldn't get started until the ban on women boxing was finally lifted in 1996: 'Women have had to fight for everything: they had to fight for the vote and they had to fight to compete in the marathon. It's always been a fight.' We know, by now, that Northern women are fighters, some of them literally.

## Lottie Dod

As I write this, I've just read that in 2020 a blue plaque was unveiled in Newbury, Berkshire, celebrating the Cheshire woman that the *Guinness Book of Records* named as one of the most versatile sporting stars there's ever been. About flipping time, I thought. There had previously been no marker of her at all anywhere, and she was such a talent – at pretty much everything she tried.

Certainly, she had a fortuitous start in life. Her dad had made a fortune in cotton, and she and her siblings grew up in a mansion in Bebington in Cheshire, with handy private tennis courts down the road. Lottie started entering tournaments aged 11 and was marked out as a rising star. In 1887 she passed the other five competitors to win the Wimbledon ladies' finals when she was just 15 years old, making her still the youngest ever person to win the tournament. She won the second set 6-0 against the gloriously named Blanche Bingley in only ten minutes. Given that women had to dress as uncomfortably as possible in the olden days, she had to play in a metal and whalebone corset that pinched her ribs and made her bleed. She retained the title in 1888, but she clearly didn't have the pressure today's stars face of sponsors and coaches breathing down her neck or getting her to model whalebone corsets on telly, because she didn't enter Wimbledon again the year after due to the fact that she fancied staying in Scotland on a sailing holiday with some of her chums (can you imagine the flak Andy Murray would get if he said he'd prefer to go to Center Parcs rather than faff about with all that practice or look another strawberry in the face?). Still, she resolved to come back and win the title three times in a row, which she duly did, beating Blanche Bingley each time. She also beat some of the top male players of the day.

Excelling in one sport is enough for most people but Lottie then took up several others – being only the second woman to pass the St. Moritz men's skating test and toboggan down the notoriously scary Cresta Run. She captained a ladies' hockey team in Spital – who only ever lost when she wasn't playing. ('We couldn't do it without you, Lottie. No, I mean, we literally couldn't.'). Next, she won the British Amateur Golf Championships in Troon in 1904. She then got interested in archery, and what would have been a passing sporting fad for anybody else (in which they'd clear out their unused bow from under the stairs a few months later) actually led to her competing in the 1908 Olympics and winning a silver medal. The First World War marked the end of her sporting achievements, though she did get a medal for giving a thousand hours of service to the Red Cross. This incredibly versatile sportswoman was still attending Wimbledon in her late eighties, and died in bed at the age of 88 while listening to the championships on the radio.

### Lily Parr

Move over George Best, David Beckham and Ronaldinho, Lily Parr was the coolest footballer there ever was and she was a Northern woman. She sometimes played while smoking a Woodbine, pretended to sell off the match ball for a laugh, and lived openly with her female partner. Obviously the FA supported her goal-scoring talents and appreciated the fact that, as her manager said, she had the best left foot in the world not just for a woman, but full stop, didn't they? No, of course they didn't. They banned her and all the other brilliant working-class female footballers enthralling massive crowds during and after the First World War from FA grounds in 1921. They suddenly said the game was 'quite unsuitable for ladies'. This had more to do with their annoyance that the revenue from these high-attendance games was going to striking miners, rather than any pretence that women lacked any of the essential parts for football, like feet or legs or brains. At least Lily Parr has now become the first female footballer to be commemorated with a statue. It was erected at the National Football Museum in Manchester in 2019, and presenter Clare Balding is one of the people who has brought her story, as well as that of the other women footballers of the time, to overdue public recognition.

St Helens-born Lily was almost six foot tall, had 'a kick like a mule' and had started off kicking a ball around on waste ground with her brothers. She was discovering football at just the right time, as women's teams were starting up everywhere because of the First World War: with no men around, it was deemed okay to watch women. Lots of factories started their own teams too. Lily began to play for St Helens Ladies, and then, aged 14, was scouted by the legendary Dick, Kerr Ladies team – the best women's team in the world at that time, founded at a munitions factory in Preston. She became a goal-scoring machine, netting a hat-trick in her first match there and forty-three goals in total in her first season.

Audiences loved to watch her and the rest of the team, flocking to matches such as one in which they beat the French national women's team 5-1 (all five goals scored by Lily). They played St Helens Ladies in 1920 in front of a crowd of 53,000 at Everton's Goodison Park. Even after the FA ban, the Dick, Kerr team carried on, touring the US in 1922, where they beat several men's teams and Parr was dubbed 'the most brilliant female football player in the world'. However, it was hard for them to carry on for long when they couldn't play in front of big home crowds anymore, and when the factory was taken over, team members, including Parr, were laid off. Their coach, Alfred Frankland, opened a grocer's shop and continued to manage them as Preston Ladies, and they were still by far the best women's team in the country – having won 643 out of their 652 matches by 1950. Parr finally retired at the age of 45, having scored well over 900 goals for the team she loved.

Lily started working at Whittingham Hospital after being laid off from the factory (note how, even as the best female footballer in the world, she still needed a day job, as did male footballers in those days), becoming a ward sister eventually. She bought a house and lived openly as a lesbian with her partner Mary, a fellow nurse, which was of course highly unconventional at a time when most gay people had to hide their sexuality. She got breast cancer in the late Sixties (though still asked friends to bring her Woodbines) and said of her mastectomy, 'It's taken me sixty-two years to get these and now they want me to get rid of them!' She died in 1978, but did at least live to see the repeal of the FA's ban on women playing in men's grounds in 1971, although as we'll see later it is only in recent years that the women's game has begun to regain anything like its former popularity.

### Three Ages of Cycling: Beryl Burton, Mandy Jones and Lizzie Armitstead

At least nobody could ban cycling for women – or could they? Actually, lest I get too caught up in the boundaries of the North of England, it's currently banned in Iran because it 'provokes men', and also in Saudi Arabia. And here in the UK, according to a study by transport charity Sustrans, 50 per cent fewer women than men get in the saddle more than twice a week, citing concerns about sexual harassment, safety and confidence on the roads. Which is a shame when you remember cycling symbolised freedom for the suffragettes. For one of the greatest cyclists of all time, Yorkshire-born Beryl Burton, it was simple. She said to herself, 'anything lads can do, I can do', then proved it by getting on two wheels and riding to victory again and again and again.

Beryl's Yorkshire grit had been honed through a tough childhood – at 11, as well as unexpectedly failing the all-important eleven-plus that would have got her into gram-mar school, she had a bout of rheumatic fever so severe she was in hospital for nine months and convalesced for a year. She was told never to exercise because of her heart arrhyth-mia. She was strong, though, through working on a rhubarb farm (she actually worked twelve-hour shifts there through the winter and kept it up during her cycling career. She never had sponsorship so she needed the money), and when her boyfriend got her a bike she began to feel free again. Speeding down the Yorkshire hills, the wind at her back, her heart pumping its own rhythm, she discovered a natural talent.

She broke records at all distances, won two world road race championships, five world pursuit titles, seventy-two national time trial championships and another twelve national pursuit titles. The record she set for a twelve-hour women's time trial in 1967 stood until 2017. This led to one particularly iconic incident when she showed she could go up against the lads. She set off from her home in Morley, near Leeds, to the twelve-hour time trial hosted by Otley Cycling Club. The men were due to start first at one-minute intervals, then the few women. Beryl prepared for her ride with food that sounded worthy of a *Famous Five* picnic and might be sufficient to get me to take up cycling. Give me her 'fruit salad, peaches, rice pudding, fruit and honey cake, peppermint and blackcurrant, coffee, glucose, malt bread, bananas, four bits of steak and some cheese' any day. The haul of food included the Liquorice Allsort that Beryl famously passed to Mike McNamara, one of the best men's cyclists, when she sped past him with two hours to go. Beryl won the major endurance race under exactly the same conditions as the men. She'd probably have won a world time trial championship too but her career was over by the time the governing body allowed women to race against the clock. She was 47 when women cyclists were finally admitted to the Olympic Games in 1984, so that was too late as well.

Fascinatingly, when her 20-year-old daughter followed her into cycling and beat her to the national road race title in 1976, Beryl was unable to congratulate her, due to her competitive jealousy. They didn't even shake hands on the podium. But six years later they shared a ten-mile tandem record. Tragically, Beryl died of a heart attack while out on her bike delivering invitations for her 59th birthday party.

I first heard of Beryl Burton when I was Poet in Residence for the Tour de Yorkshire, the slightly surreal event in which the Tour de France was held in Yorkshire in 2014. Beryl's name was once again on everyone's lips thanks to Maxine Peake's play *Beryl*, which had been commissioned for the event – though I did point out the irony of the race itself still being all men. I was doing this in quite a naive way at a very posh Tour dinner in Ripon Cathedral with tables laid with white linen and decorative yellow bikes festooning the naves ('Is there really not a women's race? It's still all just blokes on bikes then, isn't it?'). This led to an even more surreal moment in which cultural chief, Henrietta Duckworth, who had booked me for the poet job, carried a napkin round the tables which had our 'memorandum of understanding' scrawled on it about how there would be a women's race in future years. I remember that the charming Christian Prudhomme, head of the Tour de France, signed it, as well as Gary Verity, who had been responsible for getting them to bring the Tour to Yorkshire. There actually was a women's race the year after and it's happened every year since, apart from 2020 and 2021 due to coronavirus.

———————

Who wins a world championship cycle race and calls it daft? The great cyclist Mandy Jones, from Rochdale, did just that at Goodwood in 1982, aged just twenty. 'I won by accident. It was just plain daft. We were going downhill and I just rode past them. Then I looked back, saw I had a gap and kept going. I was praying my legs wouldn't collapse. But with around half a lap to go, I started thinking, "Hey, I could win this!'" She followed in Beryl Burton's footsteps, becoming the first British woman to win the championship since Beryl triumphed fifteen years earlier. Afterwards she had to ride her cycle back to her hotel down parts of the same track and kept stopping to let the men's race past. A policeman tried to tell her she couldn't go down there and the crowd were waving at him, frantically telling him she'd just won the women's world championship.

Her unofficial cycling career began when she was a young girl – her dad joined the West Pennine Cycling Club and they would go away on camping and cycling weekends and she would enter the odd race. The club has been called the beating heart of British cycling in the days before it became corporate. People would escape the grind of their jobs in Northern industrial cities and get out into the fresh air of the countryside. By the early eighties they would go to escape the grind of unemployment too.

Mandy said she was competitive when she got on a bike, though otherwise not that bothered. Things stepped up a (bike) gear, though, when her boyfriend, professional cyclist Ian Greenhalgh, started coaching her. She said he would sometimes push her so hard during training she would be left crying at the side of the road. This was before the days of sports psychologists. And as for finance? Mandy said her sponsorship was basically the dole. There was the odd council and sports grant but very little help in place – the only kit available were the same shorts and tops worn by the men. Sometimes men openly refused to join events if she was racing, saying they didn't want to be beaten by a woman.

After winning that championship she said she was burnt out and didn't really understand what was happening to her. She still managed to win some distances at the nationals a year later, even with an undiagnosed calf injury. (Her doctor said she shouldn't have been able to ride at all, never mind win anything – hadn't they heard of Northern grit?) After a few years off, during which she had a son, she began to make a comeback, but she picked up a back injury and then that was it. Mandy's cycling career was an example of a brief flare of phenomenal success in which her natural talent shone through – but then, because women's sport lacked infrastructure, she didn't get what she needed in terms of development opportunities or physical and psychological support. There's only a short window in which sports people are at their physical peak and for so many women it's been squandered due to a lack of expertise that could keep supporting them to the next level.

---

On the other hand, the era of super-professionalised sport has brought about its own hazards, not least extreme pressure. Our third cyclist, Lizzie Deignan, is very much a product of the modern era, with sponsorship, coaches, psychologists, the whole lot. But also drugs testing, which led to the greatest challenge of this outstanding Yorkshire cyclist's career. Under her maiden name of Lizzie Armitstead, she followed in Beryl Burton's and Mandy Jones's wheel treads by winning the UCI Road World championship. She had been discovered by British Cycling, who came to her comprehensive school in her birthplace, the West Yorkshire market town of Otley, looking for new cycling talent when she was 15 (pulling her out of a maths lesson – bonus). They found her to be a natural: exceptionally strong and fast. She didn't enjoy being seen in Lycra and bright yellow tops, though, saying that she was embarrassed when she started:

'It was an old man's sport, it wasn't cool.' She says it has become cool in the past ten years – in no small part due to cyclists like her. But when she was just 17 she would drive herself to Belgium for the junior world championships, her teacher mother and accountant father leaving her to it. Even then she says she saw it as a job.

Gold medals and professional road racing teams followed, and she even managed to win bronze in the 2009 UCI Track Cycling World Championships points race while injured. She was the first Briton to win a medal at the London Olympics in 2012, claiming silver when she came second in the road race. Lizzie has described the strategy of making a move in a cycling race as like 'chess on wheels'. She was eventually diagnosed with a hiatus hernia but still managed to win the British National Road Race Championships in Glasgow in 2013 during a flare-up (which puts my 'I don't think I'd better go for a walk, I've eaten a tad too much cake' into perspective). Then more medals followed, including a gold at the 2014 Commonwealth Games, the British National Road Race Championships for the third time, and that World Championships road race, winning in a thrilling sprint to the finish line. Her coach, Brian Stephens, wasn't even there for that because he had prioritised the men's junior team. Despite its higher status now than in Beryl and Mandy's time, it just goes to illustrate how women's sport is usually still the poor relation.

Lizzie's biggest challenge, however, came as she was building up to the Rio Olympics in 2016. The UK Anti-Doping Agency swooped in because she had missed three tests. Athletes have to provide an hour window of where they'll be every day so they're available for testing. She had plausible explanations for all of the missed occasions, but in the scandal-hit world of UK cycling, the allegations were devastating. Other cyclists weighed in to say how irresponsible she was to miss the tests (including Bradley Wiggins, who would be involved in his own doping scandal in 2018 over a Therapeutic Use Exemption of asthma medication when he won the 2012 Tour de France). Lizzie came fifth in the road race in those Rio Olympics and had to fight (successfully) to clear her name. She said the hardest thing was the impact on her family and friends back in Otley.

She documents all this in her memoir *Steadfast*, alongside the systemic sexism that still exists in British cycling – which includes women having to borrow helmets from men (forty years on from when Mandy Jones could only get men's shorts as kit) and a lack of experienced coaches. Not to mention the fact that the prize money was so much less for women – her 2015 world championship win netted £2,000, as opposed to £20,000 for the winner of the men's race. That, at least, has now changed and the pots are equal. She still rides all over Europe for a Dutch team but says that as she winds down her cycling career she would like to have a more balanced life and have children. Tellingly, she has said that if she has a daughter, she would prefer her to go into tennis rather than cycling because there would be more equality of opportunity for her . . .

### Three Women of Water: Anita Lonsbrough, Eileen Fenton and Charmian Welsh

Sometimes you've just got to find your thing. I'm still half-convinced that there is some sport I've never discovered that I could have been world champion in. Could it have been darts? My eyesight's a bit poor. Maybe water polo. It was always my favourite part of the day when I was an Airtours entertainer in that all-inclusive hotel in Tunisia, mainly because I could spend time under the water and pretend the guests weren't there. Perhaps it was pigeon racing. I just never had my own pigeon. Anyway, these next three women all found their thing in the water in the 1950s and received great support from their local communities, despite a lack of professional facilities and coaching. Whether they were cleaning cockroaches from a pool, wearing motorcycle goggles in the water or diving into coal dust, I'd like to introduce three strong Northern women who all made do and mended and succeeded in spectacular style.

Eileen Fenton was the first woman to complete the Cross Channel swimming race in 1950. Not only was she one of only nine out of the twenty-four people competing who made it across the channel from France to England, but she did the last few miles of it one-armed. In yet another example of ridiculous resilience, she carried on, even after she injured her arm while throwing her mug back into the support boat after taking a drink. She was in agonising pain and could hardly move it. Her coach Robert Betts begged her to stop but she refused, saying, 'I'm not coming out. I'm not giving up, I'll do it!' Her navigator tried to keep her going by singing her favourite song 'The Mountains of Mourne' through a megaphone. Whatever floats your boat I guess, literally. Her attachment to her home town of Dewsbury kept her going. She said later, 'I couldn't let all those people back home down. Especially the kiddies who were banking on me making it.' In the end, fifteen thousand locals came out to meet her when she came home after her swim. The townspeople, it seems, had always had faith in her – even when others had not. They had raised the money for the 21-year-old religious instruction teacher to compete in the race via a subscription fund, though one councillor said that some thought 'Eileen was such a slight, quiet sort of girl she wouldn't stand a chance.'

Little did they know that you can't tell just by looking at someone whether they've got the dogged determination needed for long-distance swimming. And probably as he spoke, implacable eight-stone Eileen was off practising for ten hours at a time in the town's old baths, or the mill dams, or in the sea at Scarborough. She only had one swimming cossie but her Uncle Tom stitched velvet into the arm holes so it wouldn't chafe; she raised a laugh by wearing motorcycle goggles when she was told she had to have swimming googles to enter one competition; and, as there was still post-war rationing, her dad grew vegetables in the garden so she could eat well. Everybody's faith in her paid off. Her sponsor, Horlicks, offered to pay her to go straight to the US to promote the drink, but she refused, knowing it was more important to see the massive crowd of people from home who had supported her. (Incidentally, 'Horlicks!' was possibly what she exclaimed when she injured her arm . . . )

The public took the tiny teacher with the cheerful grin to their hearts and she became a much-loved figure in Dewsbury itself. An oil painting of her hangs in the foyer of the town's baths, and Kirklees Council still has the black bathing costume in which she swam the Channel – which still fitted her at the age of ninety. She said that since the people of Dewsbury had made it possible for her to do the swim in the first place, it was important to give something back. She did that and more. One swimmer she mentored, Wendy Brook of Ossett, broke the world record for men and women swimming the Channel in 1976 at the age of twenty.

Eileen's impact continued to be felt as a coach and teacher long after she'd got out of the water.

———————

Our second woman of the water also went on to inspire other young people in a lifelong career as a coach but first she had to overcome a recalcitrant wasp, splitting swimming hats and her own fear of heights. Charmian Welsh was just a 15-year-old girl from a County Durham pit village when she represented Britain in diving at the Helsinki Olympics in 1952. She's a great example of what someone can do without proper facilities or coaching, simply by using their talent and determination. And a little ingenuity.

She practised for her crack at Olympic diving success in the pit pool (where water was stored to cool the coal) at Dawdon in County Durham, where her father was the manager. The pool had thick black coal mud at the bottom. Her mum would stand by her side, helping her get the moves right using diagrams from a diving manual. It wasn't easy, mind. Charmian actually hated heights. Once, she landed so badly in the water the impact took the skin off her hips and left her with two big bruises on her thighs. For years afterwards her hands would sweat whenever she thought of that dive. But she carried on. When she went into the water from the 10-metre board, the pressure would split her swimming caps, so she simply stopped wearing them.

She was as ready as she could be for those Olympics, so what were the chances that during her dive the Olympic judge would be stung by a wasp and accidentally record her a zero? She came fifth in her heat in the end, though it should have been fourth without that pesky insect. Villagers at Thornley, where her dad was pit manager, made a presentation to her when she returned from Helsinki, which filled her with gratitude, and her mum bought her the Anderson Tartan skirt she'd promised her – it cost twenty pounds! This brave, self-taught diver thankfully had more success in the Commonwealth Games in Cardiff in 1958, netting two gold medals. She was expected to compete in the 1960 Olympics in Rome but quit diving altogether the year before, saying there was too much politics in the sport. In 2013 she received a lifetime achievement award for her coaching of young people and was also given the freedom of Durham Baths. I imagine that means free entry for life, rather than licence to ignore the rules on not running, petting or bombing. Though if she ignored the rule about not diving, then the lucky pool users would have been in for a masterclass.

———————

For nearly fifty years from 1960, Yorkshire's Anita Lonsbrough was the only British woman to win an Olympic gold medal in the pool until Rebecca Adlington in 2008. You'd think Huddersfield Council, her employers, would be a bit more chuffed about having one of the country's top sportspeople working for them, processing people's rates, but instead they docked her wages when she took time off to train, and would only give her unpaid leave to go to the Olympics. Just to add to the contrast with today's Olympians, who have sponsorship deals, coaching and time for training, she didn't even get preferential treatment at the pool where she trained every morning before work. She'd have to wait for the boiler man to open up, then clean out the cockroaches before she could start training. Nice. She would go back for a lunchtime session, and an evening one as well if she could get in.

Born in York in 1941, Anita learnt to swim when her parents lived in India, then joined the local swimming club when they moved back to England. What if someone hadn't dropped out of a race one day which meant she had to do breaststroke instead of freestyle? Doing breaststroke saw her go from being a pretty good swimmer at Huddersfield Borough Swimming Club to being world class. Though in the winter of 1959, aged 19, she had no idea she was going to make her breakthrough in the next summer's Olympics, since she'd had gastroenteritis, gastric flu and an attack of shingles that left her nearly too weak to walk when she came out of hospital.

When it came to standing on the starting blocks in Rome in August 1960, she saw a fly swimming round and round in the water below and was afraid she might swallow it. Unlike Charmian's fatefully unhelpful wasp, the insect proved a useful distraction from pre-race nerves and she won the 200-metre breaststroke in world-record time. She came back a celebrity, to a 1200-strong crowd in Huddersfield (and a poem in her honour read by their mayor: 'Put out the flags and bunting/and let the bells be pealed/in honour of a grand young lass/who hails from Huddersfield'). She went on to add the European Championship to her Olympic and Commonwealth crowns and became the first woman to be awarded BBC Sports Personality of the Year in 1962. She is still the only swimmer ever to have won it.

*Fast Women*
### Dorothy Hyman
Modest 78-year-old Dorothy Hyman from Barnsley was surprised to hear her name on the telly. It was 2019 and young runner Dina Asher-Smith was being interviewed in

a sports stadium in Doha, saying that she wanted to get a medal at the world championships and become the first woman to do so since Dorothy Hyman, fifty-nine years earlier.

Was it really fifty-nine years ago? Dorothy thought to herself. Time passes too quickly. She was pleased to see Dina taking silver in the 100-metre final, then gold in the 200 metres. She's a lovely runner, thought Dorothy, and she comes across as a really, really nice person.

People thought the same about Dorothy too. She was named BBC Sports Personality of the Year in 1963 after her miracle year of 1962 when she won gold in the European Championships and the Commonwealth Games. She was the fastest woman in the world then, adding that accolade to the 100 metres silver medal she'd won at the 1960 Rome Olympics, where she had also taken a bronze in the 200 metres.

Dorothy thought back to the packed stadiums of Rome and the cheering spectators. She'd been interviewed for one of those Pathé news reels and filmed getting her GB uniform. As the reporter said, her Olympic place had also won her 'a blazer and a smart little hat'. There she was in black and white, with her mum and dad greeting her at the airport as she carried her two medals in her arms. There they were again at the National Coal Board headquarters in London, which was throwing her a reception, a proud moment for her father, a former coal miner. She was honest, though, when she said to the reporter that it would be 'a nice change to get back to work' at Ardsley Hall, in Barnsley, where she traced maps, also for the coal board. She worked there for thirty years until she was made redundant and then got a job in a care home.

The Pathé reporter didn't ask her about the races, though she would talk about them often enough in years to come. He asked her if Rome was romantic. She'd said yes, it was at night. Then he asked if she'd thrown three coins in the fountain. She said she had, though she'd done it wrong the first time – with her left hand over her left shoulder – so she'd had to do it again.

The fuss wasn't for her, not really. It was a lot to give up all of your life, to be in the condition you needed to be. She said was glad she wasn't in the modern era, with all that pressure. She couldn't compete in the Olympics anyway after her autobiography *Sprint to Fame* came out in 1965 and she got a bit of money from it, which meant she no longer qualified as an amateur athlete. Which was a pity because she did come into the best form of her life a few years later, but she wouldn't have been allowed to compete internationally, so what was the point? She did win another Amateur Athletics Association title at home in 1969 to add to her eight others, though. Now the sports stadium in Cudworth bears her name, and people stop her in the street if they hear her name on the telly.

## Diane Modahl

A theme with many of our sportswomen has been how the place they came from sustained them. Diane Modahl, one of Britain's most successful middle-distance runners, says that Manchester made her and enabled her to become who she is (the only thing she would change about it would be the weather . . . I'm with her there, I originally thought *Fifty Shades of Grey* must be a book about Manchester's climate patterns).

Growing up in Longsight to hard-working parents who had emigrated from Jamaica, her mum a nurse, her dad a labourer, Diane was scouted aged 11 by a volunteer coach when he saw her running at Sale Harriers. She said, obviously referring to being the only black athlete there, 'There was no one who looked like me in that club, but they were very welcoming, very positive.' She remembers 'parading around at a beauty contest' aged 15 and being asked what she wanted to do when she grew up. Having been running seriously for four years at that point, she said she wanted to compete in the Olympics. The room erupted into a big burst of laughter. But, as she points out, she competed in four of them in the end.

Her proudest moment, however, was winning a gold medal for the 800 metres at the Commonwealth Games in 1990. She also won six Amateur Athletics Association titles and a silver and a bronze in other Commonwealth Games. She held the English, British and Commonwealth record for the 800-metre and 600-metre distances. But, really, it seems likely her medal haul and her records should have been even greater. In yet another instance of a sportswoman falling foul of the flaws of the sporting establishment, the devastation wreaked on her life and career after a false-positive doping test lingered for decades. She was sent home from the Commonwealth Games in Canada in 1994 and banned by the British Athletics Foundation after her urine sample tested positive for performance-enhancing drugs. It was later proved that her sample had been kept in a room at a temperature of 35°C for three days, which would result in a false positive. She was entirely exonerated, but the trauma meant she never returned to the track as what her husband calls 'a fully committed athlete.' Ongoing legal battles with the BAF for compensation led to the couple losing their house and being on the verge of bankruptcy, at one point only having twenty pounds to live on for ten days.

In 2004 she took part in *I'm a Celebrity Get Me Out of Here* (the season when Jordan and Peter Andre fell in love, as I remember it) and still runs two or three times a week. Now she and her husband – her former coach, Vicente – help other kids in deprived areas (she has pointed out that Manchester is actually the fourth most deprived local authority) to realise their potential through their Diane Modahl Foundation, which includes raising funds so talented athletes can compete outside Manchester. Diane now plays a key leadership role in her city, on the boards of organisations that help the sort of kid she used to be. As she says, she wants them to feel they too can 'dream big'. As with so many of these sportswomen, the obstacles and setbacks Diane suffered in her career have been channelled into a public life helping others achieve their full potential.

### Tanni Grey-Thompson

Tanni Grey-Thompson is many things. As well as being one of the greatest sportspeople Britain has ever produced (she retired with an enormously impressive haul of eleven Paralympic gold medals, four silvers and one bronze. Plus five golds, four silvers and three bronzes at World Championships, thirty world records and six wins of the wheelchair London Marathon). But one thing she isn't, at least according to her birth certificate, is Tanni. Because her sister called her "Tiny" when she was born, Carys became Tanni.

She was born with spina bifida, which means she has always used a wheelchair, and it took a long battle for her parents to get her into a mainstream school. She said her dad knew how inaccessible the world was because as an architect he'd helped design it, but he told her, 'I don't care if you're in a wheelchair. You've just got to get on with it.' She recounted how her parents knew it was important for her to be included in activities. Once, a cinema refused to let her in with her friends when they were aged 9 or 10 because she was in a wheelchair, and her mum told her to go back and tell them she had never spontaneously combusted – which she duly did, and was allowed in. By the time she was at school, she knew she was competitive and wanted to get into sport. She chose wheelchair racing after seeing the London Marathon wheelchair race on telly, at a time when there was very little disability sport. She won a junior national 100 metres and then joined the British Wheelchair Racing squad aged seventeen.

Her first Paralympics was at Seoul in 1998 where she took bronze in the 400 metres, then after that it was mainly golds – a giant haul of eleven over the years. Basically, she needs a really, really big trophy cabinet, though when a journalist went to interview her in her home at Eaglescliffe on Teesside in 2014, her husband couldn't find them, trying first a big drawer in the kitchen, then suggesting they might be in the loft.

She was made a dame in 2005, and a crossbench life peer in 2010 (she chose to be Baroness Grey-Thompson of Eaglescliffe, which is near Middlesbrough and is where she has lived for the past ten years, so is very much an adoptive Northerner) and is now a forthright and funny campaigner and disability advocate, using her platform in the Lords. It is astonishing to hear about the ignorance she faces. She tells a story of how, when she was pregnant with her daughter Carys, a woman stopped her in the street and asked,

'How did you get pregnant?' Tanni replied, 'I had sex with my husband,' and the woman said, 'That's disgusting!' Tanni riposted, 'I think he's quite good-looking actually.' She says the first thing she was offered at her scan was a termination because medical professionals were concerned about how she would cope. In answer to their questions about what she would do if her baby was disabled, she said she'd make sure they had a really cool chair because the chair she had until she was 15 was horrible. She tells another story about how at an airport her wheelchair had gone missing on the baggage carousel and a member of staff put their hands under her arms and suggested she might give walking a try. Thank goodness she is now putting the resilience and power she showed in her athletics career into speaking up for others who face such ignorance.

## Queens of 2012

Yorkshire came eleventh in the overall medal table for the 2012 Olympics. If it were a country, that is. Seven golds, two bronze, two silver. And it's a list with undeniable woman power.

### Nicola Adams

It is half dance, half fight, as our blue-helmeted battler skips round the edge of the ring, jabbing again and again at the opponent she has dominated over the previous three rounds, still looking as fresh when she started. She didn't go in as favourite by a long way, having lost two of her three previous bouts with this opponent, but there is some magic in her now. She is channelling her hero, Mohammed Ali – the skips and shuffles, the sheer unbridled power and confidence. The arena crowd are roaring, they know what's coming and join in the countdown – 'Ten! Nine! Eight!' – not just to the end of the match, but to the first female boxer to win an Olympic gold medal. 'Three! Two! One!' Nicola Adams has done it. She smiles and smiles as she takes off her helmet, her gloves, her mouthguard. She's been waiting for this since she was 12, now she just wants to take the medal home to Leeds.

She had always been an innovator. Nicola, born in 1982, decided she wanted to be Mohammed Ali after her dad, Innocent, showed her videos of fights like his 'Rumble in the Jungle' against George Foreman. Unbelievably, the ban on women in boxing was only lifted in 1996, the year of Nicola's first bout at the age of 13 – though it would take another four years of hard graft, including an England training camp, before she was called up to box for her country. She was hampered at first, though, by the fact that women's boxing was only just beginning and she fought funding problems and lack of opportunities along the way. It was hard to find fights and coaches until the IOC decided to put women's boxing into the Olympics in 2009, meaning boxers could start preparing for the 2012 games. She supported herself with stints as a builder and as a TV extra, featuring in the background in soaps including *Corrie*, *Emmerdale* and *EastEnders*. (She said she most enjoyed being in *Corrie* and *Emmerdale* – the Northern ones of course . . . )

After her 2012 triumph, Nicola went on to win Commonwealth Games, European Championship and World Championship golds before making a triumphant return to the Rio Olympics in 2016, becoming the first female boxing double-gold medallist and, as she said, 'the most accomplished amateur British boxer of all time'. She has also made a stir in reality shows, most notably when she became half of the first same-sex pairing on the BBC's dance show *Strictly Come Dancing* in 2020 and received a rapturous response for her dances with professional Katya Jones, until they had to quit the competition when Katya tested positive for Covid. Nicola, who is gay, had asked for the pairing because she said she knew it was time for the show to change. This exceptional dancing fighter proved herself a fighting dancer and was once again at the vanguard of a revolution in what women were allowed to do.

### Barbara Buttrick

There was a tiny, four-foot-eleven, grey haired 83-year-old Yorkshirewoman cheering Nicola on that day at the Olympic final. Nicola thanked her afterwards, even amid all the congratulations coming her way. Her grandma, perhaps? No. Barbara Buttrick from Cottingham in East Yorkshire who, in her day, delivered twelve knockouts with her killer left hook without ever being knocked out herself, broke three noses including her ex-husband's (in training), and went undefeated in thirty matches between 1950 and 1960. This incredible woman, known as the 'Mighty Atom' and 'Battling Barbara', had to learn her skills by taking on all-comers in fairground booths, since female boxing was illegal in the UK in any other context. She had in turn been inspired by reading a newspaper article about a Lancashire prize fighter called Polly Fairclough who became Women's World Boxing Champion in 1900 and who replied 'do it, do it, do it' when the young Barbara wrote to her and asked if she should take up boxing.

In the end, Barbara had to move to the US to get the fights she needed, and took the women's world title in 1957. She quit in 1960 to raise two children, became a ringside photographer, and founded the Women's International Boxing Federation in the nineties, helping future generations of women into the sport she loved. She still lives in Miami, which designated the day she became the first woman to be inducted into the International Boxing Hall of Fame in 2020 as 'Barbara Buttrick Day'. I wouldn't fancy anybody's chances against this indefatigable woman, even now she's in her nineties . . .

## Kat Copeland

People who watched the 2012 Olympics might remember the huge incredulous smile that came across Kat Copeland's face as she and her rowing partner Sophie Hosking crossed the finishing line, two seconds clear of their rivals, taking the first ever GB gold for lightweight women's rowing. It was another triumph on what would later become known as Super Saturday.

It was only Kat's second season in the squad. She had been on the Start programme, based on the Tees, to find and develop new talent, after being spotted rowing at Yarm School (a private school in a beautiful setting with the River Tees running alongside it. I've swum there. Though at my school we didn't do rowing. Or only in the sense of arguing). I was astounded to read an interview where she said she was overweight and unsporty at school. She came second to last in the cross-country and could only do one and a half sit-ups in a fitness test at secondary school. (This is me! I am now convinced I too could become an Olympic rower. Apart from the fact I'd have to do . . . rowing.) After a friend asked her along because she didn't want to do it alone, she fell in love with the escapism of being on the river – and their coach made training fun. She says now that being on the river on her own when the mist is rising, the sun is coming up and it's completely still is very much her happy place.

## Jessica Ennis-Hill

When I think of school holidays, I mainly remember hanging around the park with friends, nicking pick-and-mix from Woolworths and waiting until *Countdown* came on (it was the days before YouTube, what can I say?). Jessica Ennis made rather more productive use of her time when, aged 11, she went to an athletics taster session at the Don Valley Stadium in Sheffield near where she lived. Her easy progress over the hurdles made a big impression on the coaches, including Tony Minichiello, who would end up coaching her to Olympic glory fifteen years later.

It's hard to imagine – having watched her sweep all before her on that Super Saturday, when the nation held its breath while she powered to victory in event after event – that when she was spotted at that stadium she was getting seriously bullied at school for being small and skinny.

She said doing sport was part of how she fought back, though people told her she was too small to succeed. She soon showed them when she took up the heptathlon and won gold in the World Junior Championships in 2005.

It was Jessica's face that beamed out from the posters welcoming visitors to London in 2012, as Britain's most famous athlete at that point and brightest medal hope. No pressure. She said she would sometimes be physically sick before competing. She had trained over ten thousand hours for the games and when it came to it, she treated an ecstatic nation to the show they were desperate for. Her coach looked out at the packed stadium before her first event (which is normally sparsely attended in a heptathlon) and said, 'There's 80,000 of your mates here to watch you.' She broke the British hurdles record, did a personal-best 100 metres and performed well in the high jump and javelin. Then, without even needing to win the 800 metres to take the gold, she powered from the middle of the pack to sprint home first. She raised her arms to the sky and looked up. She said she'd never celebrated across the finish line before but, 'In that moment, I had no control, I was finally free . . . I felt like I'd been holding my breath through the whole two days.' So had we.

She got married, and gave birth to a son, Reggie, in 2014 (which she said benefited her performance because she now had less time to dwell on how things were going in training) and took another world title in Beijing in 2015, going to the Rio 2016 Olympics a favourite to retain her heptathlon crown, but eventually took the silver. She retired after that and is still encouraging other youngsters into sport.

## Hannah Cockcroft

She whizzes down the track, head dipped, determined: a blonde Yorkshire warrior queen in her chariot, metres ahead of the other wheelchair sprint competitors. Again. Powered at the last minute by one of her favourite strawberry laces taken as a talisman, a treat after all those healthy power foods and all that training. The training is not what interests her – she's all about the winning. She looks up to see her mother waving the white rose of Yorkshire from the stands. Halifax's council leader had given it to her himself – it was the flag from above the town hall. What better use for it than to be cheering on one of the town's most successful daughters to yet another victory. And so it was – the spoils of war, another gold medal at the Paralympics in 2012. There would be three more in 2016 at Rio, more world records, twelve world titles, more flashes of carbon fibre and silver as Hurricane Hannah did it again.

In the postponed 2020 Beijing Paralympics she cut her hand on her wheelchair, too soon before her 800 metre race to get stitches, but still zoomed ahead of the rest of the racers on a rain-soaked track to her second gold of the games -and closer to her target of catching up with Tanni Grey-Thompson's record. 2020 was a vintage Paralympics for Northern women - seeing Leeds-born multi-tasker Kadeena Cox adding two more golds in sprinting and cycling after becoming the first Briton to top the podium in two sports since 1984 when she took her first two golds in Rio in 2016, while cyclist, Dame Sarah Storey, who was born in Eccles, Manchester, picked up her seventeenth gold to become Britain's most decorated Paralympian ever. She got her first gold (for swimming) aged fourteen in Barcelona and says she hopes to win three more cycling golds at Paris 2024 when she'll be forty seven!

## Beth Tweddle

I read somewhere that Britain's best gymnast is known for her 'uneven bar and floor routines'. I thought it was very impressive to have achieved so much while carrying pints across a bumpy carpet. Or by only occasionally being good. But of course it turns out that the uneven bars are actually bars of different heights, which gymnasts swing on and leap between, like a cross between trapeze artists and squirrels. Beth, who grew up in Bunbury in Cheshire, has in fact managed to be the only British athlete to pick up medals in the World and European Championships as well as the

Olympics (scooping fourteen gold, eight silver and six bronze medals in total, far more than any other British gymnast).

Beth's bronze at the 2012 Olympics was the culmination of years of working and hoping, after starting her competitive career aged seven at the Crewe and Nantwich Gymnastics Club. In the final, the crowd noise was so loud she couldn't hear her coach's final words of advice to her, just her teammate shouting at her to 'keep calm' as she'd asked her to. One of her moves was her signature 'the Tweddle', in which she catches the bar with her hands crossed. The 'double double' was a new dismount she put in to impress the judges and in the end it cost her the gold. She said she wasn't disappointed though: 'I can walk away with a medal in my pocket and it's the one that ends my career.'

### The future, football and fells

There feels great reason to be optimistic about the future of women's sport generally, though it still boggles my mind that it's only really in the past decade that professional women's sport has seen investment and audiences.

There are hundreds of women practising their skills on the fields, tracks, roads and waters of the North of England right now, and some of them will become household names in the future. But to end, we're going to look at some who have a lot in common with all the women featured in this chapter. It feels like they also illustrate the unspoken life cycle of being a sportswoman: compete against boys who feel annoyed about being beaten by a girl; get help and support to take your sport to the next level, although you lack the opportunities that sportsmen at an equivalent level have; overcome injuries and other obstacles; feel gratitude to the people and places that nurtured your talent; win some stuff; retire; and be absolutely determined to inspire girls to follow in your footsteps but with more backing and professional infrastructure.

### Football: Lucy Bronze and Steph Houghton

How many North Easterners know that Sunderland has produced one of the greatest footballers in the world today, as well as a current England captain?

Steph Houghton and Lucy Bronze stand out as beacons for other footballers to follow. A hundred years on from when the FA banned women's teams from their grounds, there is once again a buzz around the game and its players.

Former England women's team manager Phil Neville has said of Lucy: 'She's the best player in the world without a doubt, with her athleticism and quality. There's no player like her in the world.' She is undeniably regarded as the best female right-back in the world and was the first defender to win UEFA's Player of the Year trophy in 2018–19. She was also the first female footballer to be nominated for BBC Sports Personality of the Year, in 2015.

Lucy, who grew up on Holy Island for the first seven years of her life, started off playing mixed games in the school yard and, satisfyingly, her first footballing memory is of playing with the boys and one of the boys on the other team laughing at playing against a girl: 'Needless to say, he came off the pitch crying at the end.' (I would like to think he now cheers her on, on big screens in pubs while wearing a 'Male Feminist' T-shirt and weeping into his beer.)

She was signed for Liverpool in 2013 when it became England's first full-time women's team, then picked up international plaudits at Manchester City and Lyon before coming back to Man City in 2020. The next step for her depends on the fortunes of the England women's team and their upcoming tournaments. She says that as well as being a good leader on the pitch and for her team, she would like to change the game at FA and UEFA level because 'I want to help. I've played it, I know everything about it, and there are so many things that could be changed that aren't that hard. Or I might just retire, then buy a bar in Spain.'

The hopes of England's women's football rests in her hands and those of players like Steph Houghton, born in Durham in 1988, who also started off with Sunderland, going to their youth camp in the holidays and loving the opportunity to play football for five hours a day. She credits her parents for supporting her and taking her to games on wet and windy Wednesdays when, as a nine-year-old, she trained with Sunderland's Under sixteens. She said her heroes growing up were David Beckham, Steven Gerrard and Kevin Phillips (no female role models for her at the time of course, unlike up-and-coming girls now who have the likes of her and Lucy Bronze to look up to), and remembers the bell going at break time and running up to the top yard. If you were first, you'd play until you got beat, and she'd say to herself, 'Right, I'm going to stay on here for fifteen minutes and not get beaten.'

Steph says she couldn't believe it when she was called up to play for the England squad in 2005, aged just seventeen. She says she wants to continue to captain England's team to international glory and sees it as her job to continue challenging perceptions about women in football and inspire the next generations of footballers.

She says she's seen both sides, at Sunderland where they had to pay for their own kit and get on a bus at 5 a.m., and at Manchester City where there are facilities, nutritionists and coaches and it's possible for 21-year-olds now to be far ahead of where she was able to be at their age. She sums up something that is perhaps the case for all the sports covered here, and which means women gain so much more than just the sport itself by being involved with it, when she says that it gives you 'confidence, friends, alliances'. Something the women embroiled in the world of professional sport also emphasise is that so many more women can benefit from physical activity than just professionals like them. We can see that in one of the most ruggedly individual of endeavours, one deeply entwined with the landscape of the North. Let us end at the top of the world, with some fell runners who are humbling and astonishing in their sheer Northern grit.

## Fells: Wendy Dodds, Jasmine Paris, Nicky Spinks and Helene Whitaker

These women are not household names but perhaps they should be. Each feat seems more amazing than the last, performed against greater odds. But how to describe the sport of fell running? It seems that, basically, people run up and down a lot of mountains while eating a lot of food. These multiples of mountains are called 'rounds' and always have a man's name. In one instance (the Paddy Buckley), the man it was named after has never actually done the round himself. It is the opposite of a shiny corporate sport with branding. There is a lot of celebrating in pubs, and camaraderie, with previous winners of races coming back the following year to cheer on their successors. I imagine there is also probably a lot of Kendal Mint Cake.

Women were only allowed to start competing in these races in the early eighties, and immediately started winning things. Harrogate physio Helene Whitaker (then Diamantides) won the inaugural Dragon's Back Race in Wales in 1992 in a mixed pair with Martin Stone, beating all-male pairs. It was such a tough race that only sixteen people finished out of the fifty-five who started, and it wasn't run again for ten years (even Olympians only need four years to recover). It's been called possibly the toughest race in the world – 200 miles of mountains, with over 45,000 feet of ascent and descent (even typing this has made me feel tired). When the race was run again in 2002, Helene was the first woman to cross the finishing line (and fourth overall). She was also the first woman to run all three classic British rounds in one summer in 1989.

Nicky Spinks, a cattle farmer from Glossop, celebrated ten years as a breast cancer survivor by being the fastest person ever to do the Double Bob Graham Round in 2016. The single round is forty-two peaks. With the double, you turn straight around and run all forty-two again. That's 132 miles of mountaineering. She knocked a whole hour off the previous record holder Roger Baumeister's time. Until 2016 she held the record as the fastest woman across all three classic rounds. Even more impressively she stopped for fish and chips halfway through. Now that is my kind of sport. Apart from the running up hills aspect of it.

Then, along came Jasmine Paris, a small animal vet (that is, a vet to small animals, not a tiny lady), who was born in Manchester and went to the University of Liverpool. She now holds the overall record for two of the classic rounds. But she grabbed international headlines in 2019 when she won the 268-mile Spine Race, a non-stop mountain run from Edale in Derbyshire to the Scottish Borders. It took her eighty-three hours, and she smashed the men's course record by twelve hours. (Let me just repeat that. TWELVE hours. Again, let's take that moment to remember how she wouldn't have even been allowed to enter it thirty years before . . . ) She was breastfeeding her daughter Rowan at the time and had to stop in order to express milk. She said it slowed her down a bit at one checkpoint, but it didn't slow her down as much as she'd feared. The only thing more impressive than this might be if she'd actually been carrying Rowan under her arm and breastfeeding her as she ran, though that wouldn't have surprised me at all. As well as being a vet and giving birth to a child during training, Jasmine was also studying for a PhD in leukaemia. She said she would get up at 5 a.m. to run. This puts into perspective the days when the most impressive thing I do is singlehandedly unwrap a Lion bar. She also comes across as a lovely person.

Finally, so many fell runners have been passed by 70-year-old veteran Wendy Dodds during her forty-plus-year running career that it even has its own verb: being 'Dodded'. The now-retired GP from Kendal has completed more two-day Original Mountain Marathons than anyone else, with 43 to her name and the most wins overall. She ran sixty races in her sixtieth year and, at 61, was the oldest competitor to complete the notorious five-day Dragon's Back Challenge in Wales (yes, THAT one. I'll do it if they install a stairlift). She has also been a sports physio and Team GB doctor at four Olympic games, as well as a volunteer doctor at the 2012 Olympics. Giving up her professional commitments allowed her to finally become a full-time athlete and reproduce some of her best times from twenty years earlier.

This seriously impressive and resilient woman, who is getting even better with age, seems to be a fitting person to end a chapter that could have contained even more Northern sportswomen – many of whom have never quite had the recognition they should have. So many obstacles overcome, so many achievements earned. But so often with an eye on the future of their sport and its participants. These motivational women's best legacy will often be to have had their achievements superseded by those they inspired to come after them.

# 6

# Writers

There is a classic 'Northern writer' photo beloved of news-papers illustrating their articles. It is very closely related to the 'Northern musician' photo. It consists of a man standing against a brick wall. Perhaps we actually see the terrace stretching off into the distance, or maybe even the cobbled street. The writer should not be smiling, but instead wearing an expression that says something like, 'Look, I grew up against these bricks and cobbles, but still I managed to hold a pen instead of a shovel. Marvel, soft Southern people at my simultaneous Northern grit and clever, but rough-hewn, mind. Do not think for a minute that I use moisturiser.'

Occasionally the bricks can be replaced by a moor and a windswept look. We have seen Ted Hughes in this pose, and Tony Harrison, Simon Armitage and all the Angry Young Men who emerged in the fifties – Stan Barstow, John Braine, Keith Waterhouse . . . Some of them began to carry their own brick walls on their backs if they knew they were having a photoshoot just to save time (this may not be true).

The North of England has produced dozens of amazing writers and I would contend that it is in writing that the true complexity of the North is revealed, and in which stere-otypes of Northernness can most effectively be combatted, including ones about gender. At the same time, in order to get your book into the hands of readers you have to over-come the facts that the publishing industry is (even now) overwhelmingly London-centric; that you somehow need to be able to afford to live while writing your book; and that when you're promoting it, London-based journalists will ask you whether your characters will need subtitles when it gets turned into a film.

We will see during this chapter that a sense of place and a feeling of being far from the centre of power impacts the writing that comes from Northern women. It is part of their strength and attraction (look how the Brontës are one of the North's biggest cultural exports) but has also been a factor in making it harder to get published in the first place. Personally, I have been more inspired by writers than by anybody else, particularly those that wrote from, and about, places I knew and in a voice I recognized — women like the Brontës, A. S. Byatt, Jeanette Winterson and Sally Wainwright. In fact, they're why I'm writing this book rather than conveying it to you via the medium of contemporary robotic dance.

I wish I could mention every woman who has ever writ-ten from the North, but I can't, so I will just be picking out some of those who have stood out in the history of literature (or really, just the past four or five hundred years), and hope-fully you will be encouraged to read and reread, or watch their work and make your own discoveries. The wonderful thing about writing is that no matter how long ago someone put words on a page, they can still speak directly to your mind now. You can have conversations with dead writers, no Ouija board required. Let us start then, with some pioneer-ing women who were writing at a time when not only were women not encouraged to have these conversations, they were actively shut out of the rooms where they were happening and told to shut up and sew instead.

### Pen Pioneers

Margaret Cavendish, the Duchess of Newcastle upon Tyne, was a self-taught scientist, philosopher, novelist and poet. She also wrote, arguably, the first science-fiction book, *The Blazing World*. In the seventeenth century, a time when women were responsible for only 0.01 per cent of all books published, she managed to write 23 of them. Her mind was so busy she would sometimes wake her scribe in the middle of the night to get her latest thoughts down (although it goes against my socialist principles, I can't help now thinking I would really, really like a scribe I could wake up in the middle of the night with ideas for this book. Trying to get Siri to understand my Northern accent just isn't the same).

Margaret was suitably apologetic – in a brilliantly passive-aggressive way – about having the temerity to speak up when it was seen as deeply unseemly for a woman to do so. For example, she wrote in one of her book introductions: 'Since all Heroick Actions, Publick Employments, as well Civil as Military, and Eloquent Pleadings, are deni'd my Sex in this Age, I may be excused for writing so much.'

Despite her innovative output, it's unlikely you have heard of her. She was one of my discoveries when she featured in a display at a Newcastle museum during the Exhibition of the North in 2018 and I immediately wondered why she wasn't more known. Perhaps one explanation is to be found in the British Library's comment on her: 'Critical opinion has gone back and forth in the years since Cavendish's life as to whether she was really to be taken seriously as a writer and philosopher, was merely an eccentric, or something in between.' This is a tactful way of saying, 'Basically, some people thought she was a batty old posh woman living in Newcastle, who made her own eccentric outfits like some sort of seventeenth-century Lady Gaga, and wrote a weird, thinly veiled autobiographical fantasy in which she ruled over a race of little creatures who lived on the moon and was best ignored.'

The Stanford Encyclopedia of Philosophy is less dismissive, saying that she was important because her theories anticipated philosophical and scientific arguments about the nature of matter by several decades. Basically, she believed that everything in the universe, including human beings and their minds, was material, and that matter itself could think. I don't have time or space or brain to explain why this is important, and why it is particularly resonant with some of the most cutting-edge quantum physics of today.

Reading the encyclopedia's substantial entry on her, I am left a bit heartbroken by one poignant detail. Margaret's husband, William Cavendish, who she met while a maid of honour for Queen Henrietta Maria (a position she took at the age of 20 so she could have independence from her family who thought she should sit quietly and sew and spin), was pretty encouraging of her work – at least, we can deduce that, since most husbands of the time just wouldn't have let her publish it at all. They met at a traumatic time – when the court had gone into exile to France during the English Civil War. Once back living in London, Cavendish ran a discussion group called The Cavendish Circle and together they met figures like René Descartes and Thomas Hobbes. These thinkers wouldn't engage with her directly in print (because she was a woman), so she dialogued with their ideas in the form of a correspondence between herself and a fictional third person. It's so sad to think of her eagerness to converse with her intellectual equals being rebuffed – but so impressive that she found ways to get a word in anyway.

After publishing several influential books on natural philosophy, it became harder to ignore her, and the Royal Society (a circle of posh men discussing cutting-edge ideas, and which included her middle brother, John – a scholar who had actually always discussed things with her in private) made her the first woman to be invited to one of their meetings in 1667.

Margaret recognized the limitations she and other women faced, but saw the imagination as one way to transcend the obstacles, and writing as a way to be free. In the introduction to her novel *The Blazing World*, which has been described as the first science-fiction novel written and published by a woman, she made this poignantly explicit:

> Though I cannot be Henry the Fifth, or Charles the
> Second; yet, I will endeavour to be, Margaret the First:
> and, though I have neither Power, Time, nor Occasion, to
> be a great Conqueror, like Alexander, or Cesar; yet, rather
> than not be Mistress of a World, since Fortune and the
> Fates would give me none, I have made One of my own.

She encouraged others to join her in her world, or, if they didn't fancy being subjects, to write their own in which they too could be free to live in a way that they couldn't amid the social constraints of their time. As we will see, that is an invitation accepted by many women in the centuries to come.

———————

Mary Astell was born in Newcastle in 1666, the year that Margaret Cavendish published *The Blazing World*. She is often regarded as a less radical precursor to Mary Wollstonecraft, who was born 93 years later, but both of them have been called 'the first feminist'. Astell came from a middle-class family, the daughter of a coal company manager, and all the family finances went to educate her brother after their father died when Mary was twelve. She was educated informally by her uncle, though, who was connected to a Cambridge philosophy school. Later, one of her most important proposals concerned the education of women. In the book *A Serious Proposal to the Ladies for Advancement of their True and Greatest Interest*, which she wrote in 1694, she suggested there should be all-women colleges.

Mary's own life exemplified how educated women could gain independence by making the brave move to London, just as she did to make her living as a writer, aged just 22, after her mother and sister had died. (Even then, there was a brain drain to London for people in the creative industries!) She got involved with influential women she met in Chelsea, and the Archbishop of Canterbury also provided support, including through contacts with publishers. One of her most famous lines came from her book *Reflections on Marriage*: 'If all men are born free, how is it that women are born slaves?' Had there been T-shirts at the time, this surely would have been a bestselling slogan. As an Anglican Conservative using rational philosophy as her weapon,

Astell was very different to the left-wing Mary Wollstonecraft (whose family lived in Beverley, near Hull, in the 1770s), who advocated revolution and political change, but many of their conclusions about women's liberation were the same. Daniel Defoe, John Locke and John Norris said Astell's ideas were impractical, even though it was difficult to argue against the solid reasoning behind her arguments. She retired as a writer in 1709, after founding a school for the daughters of Chelsea pensioners, and died in 1731, a few months after having a mastectomy to remove cancer in her right breast. There is a plaque to her in Chelsea and one in Newcastle Cathedral. Although not as 'sexy' as the direct action advocated by Wollstonecraft, her words and ideas introduced the then radical idea that women were equal to men, and influenced other thinkers in turn, including, eventually, some early suffragettes. 'Who was first?' debates seem quite willy-waving, but I now certainly make sure Mary Astell's name is mentioned too when it's suggested that Mary Wollstonecraft was the first feminist thinker. As Margaret Cavendish said, imagining other worlds has real power, and Mary Astell had the courage to do that.

### The Brontës and Beyond

I read Charlotte Brontë's greatest novel, *Jane Eyre*, at the ridiculously young age of seven and grew up five miles from the parsonage where the three famous writing sisters were brought up in Haworth. I can't be objective about them. They were somehow entwined in my life from the beginning.

There's lots of stuff I didn't know about until an embarrassingly advanced age – how to keep a plant alive, the name of the hole your wee comes out of (it's your urethra, not your vagina – who knew? Oh. Everyone) and how to pronounce

Alnwick ('Annick', fact fans). Also, I didn't know about feminist pioneers like the aforementioned Mary Wollstonecraft and Mary Astell. But because of the Brontës I was actually deeply acquainted from a young age with the idea that not everybody would take women writers seriously, but that women should jolly well ignore that and get on with it anyway. I visited Haworth and saw how lots of tourists from all over the world came to the small village with the steep cobbled street, endless tea shops and businesses named things like the Brontë Balti House, the Jane Air B&B and the Branwell Woman Clinic (I might have made those last two up . . . ). They visited because of the words that came out of the minds of these three intense sisters, which are still remembered and read, and felt more alive to me than many of the words I heard around me.

With Emily and Charlotte, the two best known of the sisters, it's not either/or like Macs and PCs or like being a cat person or a dog person (okay, it is – and I'm a Charlotte person). The moment where Jane Eyre stands up to Mr Rochester and tells him she's just as worthy of love and respect as him is a piece of writing I carry with me to such an extent that it is part of what makes me who I am. I keep this inside usually, though now I'm thinking I should have quoted it on Tinder dates:

Do you think, because I am poor, plain, obscure and little, I am soulless and heartless? You think wrong! I have as much soul as you and full as much heart. And if God had gifted me with some beauty and much wealth, I should have made it as hard for you to leave me as it is now for me to leave you. I am not talking to you now through the medium of custom, conventionalities, nor even of mortal flesh – it is my spirit that addresses your spirit; just as if both had passed through the grave, and we stood at God's feet, equal – as we are.

The Brontës' story is so familiar it has passed into myth, and I'm meant to be writing about forgotten women here, but it is still worth recounting as it highlights the context for so many other important voices. The sisters were born to Maria and Patrick, an Irish curate who preached in a small village in Bradford. They had six children – five daughters and a son. Shortly after moving to Haworth, when Charlotte was five, Emily three and Anne not yet two, their mother Maria died, possibly of uterine cancer. Her sister, Aunt Branwell, came to help look after them and stayed with the family for the rest of her life. More tragedy struck the Brontës when the eldest sister, also called Maria, and second daughter Elizabeth contracted tuberculosis in the unsanitary conditions at Cowan Bridge, the boarding school where lots of Yorkshire clergy sent their children, and they died in 1825 at the ages of just ten and eleven. Young Charlotte and Emily were brought back home from the school and the three remaining girls and their brother developed the intense imaginary life that would become their training ground as writers.

Legendarily, they began imagining their own fictional worlds (thanks again, Margaret Cavendish), filled with soldiers and battles and romances, writing them down in tiny books in cramped handwriting. Charlotte and Branwell had the land of Angria, Emily and Anne had Gondal. Alongside the landscape of the moors outside their house, these imagined worlds became more important to them than their real lives. But real life and the need to earn a living interrupted their escapist alternative universes. After disastrous forays into the world of being governess for exploitative employers and horrible children (summed up in one letter by her plea, 'Am I to spend the rest of my life in this wretched bondage?' teaching 'these fat headed oafs'. She was no Maria von Trapp . . . ), Charlotte formulated a plan: they would set up their own school so they could be their own bosses. Their father agreed to send her and Emily to school in Brussels so they could brush up on their teaching skills. Charlotte fell in love with their teacher, Monsieur Heger, (which eventually led to her book *The Professor*) and Emily got fed up and came home early. Meanwhile, Anne and Branwell took teaching jobs for some posh people near York, though it all ended disastrously when Branwell had an affair with the mistress of the house, Mrs Robinson (no relation to the one in the Simon and Garfunkel song).

When Charlotte took in the reality of the situation in which all her siblings were unemployed and their great hope for keeping them above water – Branwell – was mainly drinking and taking opium, and generally auditioning for his own ninetheenth-century version of *Withnail and I*, she decided the only plan was for the three girls to make a living from their writing. This was a leap of faith because there was not exactly much encouragement for them to do this. Charlotte had written to the Poet Laureate, Robert Southey, in 1837, enclosing some of her poems, and he presumably wasn't auditioning for a job as a motivational coach as he responded with lines like 'Literature cannot be the business of a woman's life and it ought not to be'. Undeterred, Charlotte gathered some of their poems together and, with a legacy from their aunt, paid for them to be published under the title *Poems of Currer, Ellis and Acton Bell* in 1846. Emily and Anne insisted on anonymity. I think this was almost the first fact I knew about the Brontës – that they had pseudonyms beginning with the same letters as their real names so people believed they were men. This self-published volume sank like Instagram poems from somebody without many followers, but still persistent, Charlotte decided the way forward was novels, not poems.

The girls walked round and round the oak dining table in the parsonage night after night, reading sections of their work aloud to each other. And what works they were. Anne was writing *Agnes Grey* – arguably the first portrayal of an ordinary woman in fiction as the main protagonist – a heavily autobiographical tale about a woman who is governess to two selfish children until her brother has an affair with the mistress of the house. It critiques class relationships and education, and tends to be underrated compared to the novels her sisters produced. Emily wrote *Wuthering Heights*, a dark, Gothic story of the doomed love of Heathcliff and Cathy Earnshaw, which was eventually recognized as a masterpiece (Emily was brilliantly depicted in the 2018 spoof musical *Wasted* as the first goth). Charlotte's first novel was actually *The Professor*, but that was rejected by several publishers. She then sent them another governess novel with a plain heroine like her sister's – this one was of course *Jane Eyre* – and it was that book which went on to be a runaway bestseller in 1847, eventually seeing her sisters' novels published shortly afterwards by a publisher eager to cash in on the mysterious 'Bell brothers'.

Charlotte took a published copy of *Jane Eyre* into her father's study at this point and said, 'Papa, I have been writing a book.' I would expect nothing less understated from a Yorkshirewoman – she wouldn't have been able to go in and say, 'Look, this is my bestseller, it's going to save us all and also become one of the most loved books in the whole world.' He called the other girls in after a while and said, 'Girls, Charlotte has been writing a book and I think it is better than I expected.' Thanks, Dad.

However, just as things could have been looking up for the Brontës, Branwell died of tuberculosis in September 1848 at the age of thirty-one. Emily became ill too but refused medical attention and died in the December. Anne then also became ill, and Charlotte took her to her beloved town of Scarborough for some healing sea air, but she died there in May 1849 aged just twenty-nine. (She is buried in the graveyard on the clifftop, unlike the other siblings who are buried at the parsonage. People lay flowers there on her birthday and on the anniversary of her death. I went once and it was beautiful and peaceful and you could see the sea.) A family servant later recounted that Charlotte poignantly still kept up the siblings' nightly ritual of pacing round the oak table on her own, because she couldn't sleep otherwise.

She gave up her anonymity and embraced life as a famous author, making connections with other writers, visiting London, travelling with her publisher and continuing to write two more novels – *Shirley*, which exposed working conditions in the North's mills and factories, and *Villette*, which was set in Brussels. She married her father's curate, Arthur Nicholls, in 1854 and was unexpectedly, quietly happy with him. Go on, give her a break life, you can't help thinking. Just let her be happy. But when Charlotte became pregnant, her fragile body couldn't deal with the strain and she died at the age of 39 in March 1855. In an illustration of just how easy it can be for women to be erased from history by how they are described in legal documents, Charlotte's profession was given as 'wife of curate' on her death certificate, Emily was described as 'daughter of Patrick Brontë, incumbent' and Anne was put down simply as 'spinster'.

Patrick had lived to see his wife and all six of his children die, but set about preserving their literary legacy, commissioning the writer Elizabeth Gaskell to write a biography of Charlotte and carefully keeping and labelling mementoes of their lives, which are still part of the Parsonage Museum collection today. Their books are all still in print, they have inspired countless other literary works and screen adaptations (and Kate Bush's most famous song) and, at a time when there are still so few public memorials to women, the whole town of Haworth is basically a Brontë theme park (sorry, Haworth – it is more than that, but also that). They are, perhaps, the women people think of first when they think of Northern women and, given the sophistication of their writing, the varied and layered portraits they made of the social and cultural context they lived in, the love and resilience they showed in sticking together as sisters, and – led by Charlotte – finishing and getting their wonderful books published against all the odds, I am deeply proud to think they are our ambassadors.

## Elizabeth Gaskell

For a long time I knew Elizabeth Gaskell only as Charlotte Brontë's biographer, but actually she was one of the most important chroniclers of the Industrial Revolution, and the North, in her own right. Not to mention the fact that her biography of Charlotte Brontë has been described as the first modern biography because it focused on her subject's personal life and not her accomplishments. It was of course also written about a woman, by a woman. One slight quibble is that although she usually presented a nuanced picture of the North in her own novels, her biography presented Haworth as a 'wild rough place' where the Brontës were 'castaways'. This literary licence, presenting the Brontës as aliens whose writing had bloomed in an inhospitable place, erased the fact that Haworth was a well-connected trading town with plenty of access to music, art and culture, and links to the outside world. Yes, the moors are wild and it's quite rainy, but heck, Elizabeth Gaskell was based in sunny Manchester for goodness' sake.

She was born there to an upper-middle-class family in 1810 and grew up to be, according to an 1897 anthology of essays celebrating Victorian novelists, a pre-eminent writer alongside Charlotte Brontë and George Eliot, 'possessing a genius which time, fashion or progress cannot dim or take from'. However, as we have seen in this book, time, fashion AND progress can all very much take their toll on how women are viewed at any particular moment in history, and her brand of realist writing gradually grew out of fashion over the course of the twentieth century. Plus, the fact that she has a less dramatic life story than either the Brontës or George Eliot has perhaps made her a less compelling figure at a time which particularly values stories of women's rebellion. However, her house in Manchester was restored in 2014 and is now somewhere her work and life are remembered and celebrated. It has been recreated to be, as far as possible, like the home Charlotte Brontë visited and described as 'a large, cheerful, airy house, quite out of Manchester smoke – a garden surrounds it, and as in this hot weather, the windows were kept open – a whispering of leaves and perfume of flowers always pervaded the rooms'. Popular telly adaptations of her novels *North and South* in

2004 and *Cranford* in 2007 helped bring her work back to consciousness, as did a 2018 book by Nell Stevens called *Mrs Gaskell and Me*, which blends memoir with an imagined account of her falling in love with the writer Charles Norton in Rome.

Elizabeth really did take a trip to Rome in 1857 with her daughters and loved the city and the chance to get away from the controversy created by her biography of Charlotte, which had just been published. Writing it had been a difficult balance – Charlotte Brontë's depiction of the passionate Jane Eyre led to her being called unchristian and unwomanly; the cultural critic Matthew Arnold said it was 'one of the most utterly disagreeable books I've ever read' and the *Quarterly Review* said it 'violated every code human and divine', although many people defended the book too. Gaskell set out to show that Charlotte was a respectable sister and, briefly, wife and - having died with her unborn child - a mother. Basically, she sanitised her, by not including, for example, the love letters she sent her married Belgian teacher. The first edition sold out quickly, but the second edition was only available for a month because various people objected to their depictions in it – including the woman Branwell had the affair with, Charlotte's widower, and relatives of the headteacher at the boarding school where the two oldest Brontë sisters died (who was clearly a horrible man. Sue me . . . ).

But back to Elizabeth. She was brought up by her aunt in Knutsford after her mother died when she was just eighteen months old (Knutsford later became the inspiration for the small country town of Cranford). She married Unitarian minister William Gaskell in 1832, when she was 22, and they settled in Manchester, where she supported his work – helping the poor, teaching reading and writing in Sunday School and doing general Good Work. Their daughters were born in 1834, 1837 and 1842, but after her son William died of scarlet fever in 1845, aged just nine months, her husband suggested she write as a distraction from her grief. (This was wise – good work, William.)

At this time, Manchester was the third largest city in the country and growing rapidly, with terrible slum conditions for workers accompanying the rapidly accumulating wealth of the mill and factory owners. Co-writer of *The Communist Manifesto* Friedrich Engels, who lived in Manchester at that time, wrote a precursor to TripAdvisor reviews when he called it 'hell on earth'. There was also a great deal of radical reform activity. Elizabeth saw all this and in the introduction to her first novel *Mary Barton: A Tale of Manchester Life*, published anonymously in 1848, wrote that she had wondered, 'How deep might be the romance in the lives of those who elbowed me daily in the busy streets of the town in which I resided? I had always felt a deep sympathy with the careworn men, who looked as if doomed to struggle through their lives in strange alternations between work and want.' As she had hoped, the depiction of the awful conditions workers lived in stirred the public conscience and contributed to debate about industrial and political reform. Charles Dickens then became an important figure in her transition to popular writer, asking her to write stories for his journals, one of which became her novel *Cranford*. They sometimes had a difficult working relationship, though, as he liked to edit what she wrote, once exclaiming to a sub-editor, 'Oh! Mrs Gaskell-fearful-fearful! If I were Mr G. Oh heavens how I would beat her!' Not cool, Charles.

Victorian convention meant her readers came to know her as 'Mrs Gaskell', which made her sound safe and respectable, though she was a lively, independent figure who liked to travel abroad and had a wide circle of literary and non-literary friends and correspondents, including John Ruskin, Charles Kingsley and Florence Nightingale. Sadly, she died suddenly of a heart attack at the age of 55 at a house in Hampshire she had been renovating in secret as a post-retirement surprise for her husband and family. As we have seen, her literary reputation has waxed and waned since, but she is currently once again being recognized for the value of her well-researched novels and – yes, let's give her her due – for being able to tell a really good story.

In a way, this period of writing set the template for how the North of England would be seen for years to come. It still shapes the imaginary landscape of the North (or what Phillip Dodd has called 'the Lowryscape') and, along with novels like Dickens's *Hard Times*, set up the idea of the North as full of 'dark, satanic mills' (actually a William Blake line about London), dirty-faced downtrodden workers in terraced houses, and cotton or wool barons rolling in money and muttering darkly about 'trouble at t'mill'. However, the North is rural as well as industrial, and middle class as well as working class. In years to come, publishing was sometimes receptive to, and sometimes resistant to, women who challenged the dominant clichés about the North, as we shall see.

## Isabella Banks

Isabella Banks, born to politically active Mancunian parents two years after the Peterloo Massacre in 1821, is most famous for her novel *The Manchester Man*, which was published in 1870. She's less known outside Manchester than the Brontës and Gaskell but her work was remembered in the city in the name of the iconic student pub Jabez Clegg until it closed in 2013. Clegg was the 'Manchester Man' whose life story is told from the Napoleonic Wars up until the Reform Act. The novel tells the story of the first industrial city in the world's first industrial nation. Isabella didn't start writing until she was 43, after five of her eight children had died and her alcoholic husband suffered suicidal depressions. She was writing to keep her family going, and produced twelve novels, three books of poetry and three volumes of short stories.

She had attended the magnificently named Miss Hannah Spray's Ladies Day School for Girls in the city, and her parents took her and her siblings to plays, told them stories, and sold lace caps that Isabella made in the milliner's shop and apothecary they opened downstairs in their house. At the age of 17 she did what the Brontës had hoped to do and opened a School for Young Ladies, which she ran for nine years until she married the poet and journalist George Linnaeus Banks in 1846. As was the custom at the time, her books were published under his name – Mrs George Linnaeus Banks. The stress of being her family's lone bread-winner and her battle with bronchitis contributed to her death at the age of sixty-six. It strikes me that despite the image of writers settling down in garrets, driven by a creative compulsion they can't control, several of the great novels of the Industrial Revolution (those by the Brontës and Isabella Banks, that is) were written because women couldn't rely on alcoholic men and had to earn their own living. These women were not working class, so they were educated, but they were not upper class enough to be able to sit back and not work. However, just to be perverse, I'll introduce us now to a writer who had a compulsive need to produce words, writing nearly five million in her lifetime, but who was an heiress with no need to work, or sell her writing, and in fact with every need to conceal the content of it.

## Anne Lister

Anne was an exceptional character, sometimes called 'the first modern lesbian', and a figure who has come to popular prominence again in recent years thanks to a television series about her life. The BBC's *Gentleman Jack*, written by Yorkshire screenwriter Sally Wainwright, sparked huge interest in her life story when it was broadcast in 2019. The heiress to Shibden Hall in Halifax, she was born in 1791 and wrote nearly five million words of diary entries chronicling her life, sex with women, and her travels, much of it in code that was only deciphered in the late eighties after a woman called Helena Whitbread started researching her. (The code was actually also cracked in the late 1890s by her relative John Lister, but he quietly hid her diaries behind wood panelling in Shibden Hall on realising that the code concealed her sexual encounters with women. He was also gay and didn't want to draw attention to the fact.) These diaries are not all *Fifty Shades of Grey*, though. Much of them involves an obsessive accounting of Anne's life, from how long she slept, to whether she had veal cutlets or pork for dinner, to what Greek she learnt that day. She said, 'I feel relief from unburdening my mind on paper.' The revelation of how many women she slept with showed that sexual relationships between women at that time were much more common than had been thought, leading the historian

Emma Donoghue to describe the diaries as 'the Dead Sea Scrolls' of lesbian history.

Shibden Hall was where we used to go on school trips when I was a West Yorkshire schoolgirl in the eighties. I remember its Tudor beams and cosy wood-panelled rooms. I remember sitting on a sloping grass lawn in front of the house and eating the plasticky slices of ham in sandwiches my mum made for a packed lunch with thick slabs of butter on white bread (I usually remember more about the food I've eaten on trips than anything else). I don't, however, remember any mention of Anne Lister. Apparently, that's because there wasn't any mention of her in the museum in those days, which is sad since she was another local writer who could have inspired me. To be fair, though, it was the eighties. Lesbians hadn't actually been officially invented until that kiss on *Brookside*. But she is certainly remembered there now. In fact, last time I visited, just before coronavirus hit (I may even have caught Covid-19 in Shibden Hall, but that's another story), there was due to be a 'Dress up as Anne Lister' day at the Piece Hall market in Halifax. She is very definitely Halifax's most famous daughter (well, today she might well have called herself Halifax's most famous non-binary person).

Since we're still in a section shadowed by the Brontës, I'll mention that it seems likely that Emily Brontë may have met Anne Lister when she worked at a nearby school. Pupils and teachers went to visit Anne at Shibden Hall and it's likely Emily would have been among them. As Shibden Hall has a 'red room', it's speculated that Charlotte Brontë included the famous red room in *Jane Eyre* because Emily told her about Shibden Hall. Even more speculatively,

Brontë scholar Nick Holland has suggested that Emily took the pseudonym 'Ellis' because of the middle letters of the name Anne Lister. Brilliantly, this is just one of those things that we'll never know – though if Emily did meet Anne, it's likely that Anne made an impression on her, as she was charismatic, seductive and unconventional. Having watched *Gentleman Jack*, I can really only now picture her as Suranne Jones, the actor who plays her. Strong and definite, with an aquiline nose, dressed in elegant black suits that led to her nickname in Halifax – 'Gentleman Jack' – and utterly unapologetic as she persuaded yet another young woman to have sex with her, assiduously recording the number of orgasms they had with X's in her diary.

As her fellow writer Jeanette Winterson points out, in the early nineteenth century it was perfectly okay for women to have close, passionate friendships, to share a bed (if a friend was coming to stay, a husband might vacate the marital bed so the friend could sleep in it) and touch and kiss. There wasn't really a sense of understanding that these might be sexual relationships. What was not okay, however, was for a woman to act like a man. That was seen as threatening the whole power structure that relied on men being men. Anne Lister absolutely violated this, with her efficient running of the Shibden Hall estate and remodelling of the house and gardens; with her clothing and masculine manners; with her running of a coal mining business alongside her partner, heiress Ann Walker; and with how they (secretly, though) exchanged wedding rings in a ceremony in a church in York in 1834 and lived together as man and wife. This led to mocking letters arriving at Shibden Hall wishing 'Captain Lister' good luck with 'his' new life, but Anne refused to rise to the bait. She was used to ignoring mockery of her non-conformity. For the last several years of her life, Anne and Ann travelled across Europe. Anne loved adventures and mountain climbing, and chronicled her travels in pages and pages of writing. Her travels led to her death in 1840, however, when she caught a fever in Russia, possibly from an insect bite. Poor Ann Walker had to bring her body back to England, then was dragged out of a room in Shibden Hall by her relatives, after holing up there with a loaded pistol refusing to leave. They declared her insane and sent her to an asylum for a while.

In a bit of a gothic twist, Dr Belcombe's asylum was the same asylum that Eliza Raine, Anne's first lover (who she got together with while they were both 15-year-old girls at boarding school in York), had been sent to. She had suffered a breakdown because of Anne's dalliances with other lovers. The great love of Anne's life at that time was Dr Belcombe's daughter Mariana, who Anne hoped to live with one day but who had ended up marrying a man called Charles for his money (Anne called this 'legal prostitution'). He then slept with a servant, leaving both Mariana and Anne with venereal disease for the rest of their lives. I'm almost wondering whether Anne added to her business ventures by being on commission to send women to Dr Belcombe's asylum. Anyway, it's an odd detail in a wonderfully odd life, though perhaps her newfound lesbian iconography should not let us ignore how the fates of some of her lovers highlight how very dangerous it was to be a woman who defied convention at that time. Part of Anne's genius was to ensure that she used her personal power, wealth and business sense strategically to make sure she was always the one who ended up on top (probably quite literally).

## Beatrix Potter

Beatrix Potter is hardly a forgotten voice, you may say. But as well as being the writer and illustrator behind some of our best-loved, most enduring children's characters – Peter Rabbit, Mrs Tiggywinkle, Pigling Bland and Jemima Puddleduck – Beatrix Potter had an often overlooked role. She was also a brilliant businesswoman. She designed and created the first Peter Rabbit doll herself once the stories took off in 1903, making it the world's oldest licensed literary character. I had an idea in my head of an eccentric old lady happily living in a Lakeland cottage making up stories about talking animals, but actually she was an extremely canny operator, running farms in the Lake District, becoming a nationally renowned expert breeder of Herdwick sheep, and restoring cottages and preserving land. She gifted fifteen cottages she had saved from developers and more than 4000 acres of land to the National Trust on her death in 1943, which still forms a vital part of their Lake District holding. Her house, Hilltop, is preserved as a museum, just as she lived in it, and thousands of visitors enjoy her stories coming to life at The World of Beatrix Potter in Bowness-on-Windermere. She still sells two million books a year all around the globe.

It had all started with her parents encouraging her to draw from an early age, including cute illustrations of her pet rabbit Benjamin Bouncer, who enjoyed buttered toast (don't we all?) and going for walks on a lead (less so). She and her enterprising brother sold Christmas cards featuring their pets. It wasn't that her family needed the money – they were really well-to-do. Her dad had studied law in Manchester and trained as a barrister, and her mum was the daughter of a cotton merchant and shipbuilder from

Stalybridge. Beatrix was also absolutely fascinated by fungi, and ended up publishing some important research on the subject, which she wasn't allowed to present to the relevant society because she was a woman (they issued a posthumous apology to her for not taking her work seriously). She struggled to break free of her family at first – they disapproved of her planned marriage to her first love, an editor of her books, because he was 'in trade', though tragically he died of leukaemia a month before their wedding. She then bought Hilltop Farm in the Lake District, where she had enjoyed wonderful childhood holidays, and there she seemed to come into her own, living the life she wanted to live, in a place that suited her. She married a country solicitor (who her family also disapproved of), got very involved with his extended family, though they didn't have children of their own, and together they farmed and conserved the place where they were so happy, all while she became one of the most popular and successful children's authors of all time, whose part of the Lake District has become as synonymous with her and her work as Haworth is with the Brontës.

**Frances Hodgson Burnett**
Our final writer as we look beyond the Brontës took inspiration from *Jane Eyre* for her most famous book, a children's book that I loved but didn't recognize for its Brontë resonances when I read it. Frances Hodgson Burnett was born in Manchester in 1849. Her dad, an ironmonger from Doncaster, died when she was four and her mum took over the running of his shop in Manchester. Frances therefore spent a lot of time with her grandma, who gave her a book called *The Little Flower Book*, which she always said had a great influence on her writing. Something else that

influenced her were the people and places of Manchester as it slid into decline during the Lancashire Cotton Famine. She would watch young women on their way into the Ancoats cotton mills and observed the extreme poverty and dirt in the streets. One of her schoolteachers said she was a born storyteller who held the other children spellbound with her tales in the playground. She used this ability eventually, remembering those times and places after her mother had sold up and the family had emigrated to join her mum's brother in America – in Knoxville, Tennessee – when Frances was fifteen.

Frances began sending short stories to magazines when she was 19 to help earn money for the family. She called herself a 'pen driving machine', but had earned enough by 1869 to move the family into a bigger house in Knoxville, the year before her mother died. In 1874, now married to a doctor called Swan Burnett (who sounds like he should be a character in a children's book himself), and living in Washington, she published her first novel *That Lass o' Lowrie's*, about a pit brow girl called Joan Cowrie who ended up being abandoned by the mine owner's son (who was clearly untrustworthy because he had 'fine London ways'). Joan was a prime example of the trope of the strong Northern woman holding her family together and coping in the face of poverty, somewhat like Frances's mum. We would see these terraced-street-dwelling Women Who Coped again and again in the family sagas that were to come in the twentieth century. Sagas by women like Catherine Cookson, Josephine Cox, Barbara Taylor Bradford, Marie Joseph, Audrey Howard, Olive Etchells, Shelagh Kelly and Elvi Rhodes. At one point in 1999, six of the 139 books published in Britain with sales of over 100,000 were sagas set in the

North West of England. Two books by Josephine Cox alone had a sales value of over £3.8 million.

These resilient women turn me back to thinking about the writers themselves. Again, it's not all airy floating about in a nightie and wafting words onto a page. There is a certain need to appeal to a market of readers. Frances did that with her children's books too, which were runaway successes. *Little Lord Fauntleroy*, *The Little Princess* and *The Secret Garden* are classics. *The Secret Garden* has never been out of print since she published it in 1911, though its success was slower growing than some of her other work that is now forgotten, such as the play *Esmerelda*, which was the longest-running Broadway play of the nineteenth century.

Until researching this book, I had no idea of the circumstances in which *The Secret Garden* was written. Frances wrote it during her many visits to a manor house at Buile Hill Park in Salford. By 1890, she had been spending a lot of time back in the UK, in London and Manchester, still writing prolifically and burning herself out doing so, but convinced she needed to keep her family afloat. In that year, her eldest son died of tuberculosis, which devastated her and had a massive effect on her life and writing. She did charity work in London, including starting the Drury Lane Boys' Club, and wrote a play with a starring role for a surgeon, anti-vivisectionist and actor called Stephen Townsend who she'd met on a previous trip and had been spending a lot of time with. Her marriage was effectively over, though wasn't officially ended until her youngest son left Harvard University. The *Washington Post* called her a 'new woman' at that point and said her divorce was because of her 'advanced ideas regarding the duties of a wife and the rights of a woman'. She then married the ten-years-younger Townsend in 1900, realising quickly it was a terrible mistake and that he wanted to control her and her money. After suffering a collapse and entering a sanatorium, she divorced him two years later. Burnett then moved permanently back to the States in 1907 and spent the final seventeen years of her life splitting her time between a summer home she'd had built on Long Island and a winter home in Bermuda. All a long, long way from being the little girl who peeped through the mill gates in a dark and smoky Manchester.

*The Secret Garden* is now the most enduring and resonant of her works. Her main character, a spoiled posh girl called Mary Lennox, obeys Margaret Cavendish's exhortation to create her own world to escape into when she discovers a secret walled garden at the Edwardian Yorkshire manor house she has been sent to after her parents and their servants died in a cholera outbreak in India. She encounters a young boy there, Dickon, who has an almost mystical ability to communicate with the birds and animals in the garden. In his affinity with nature and wandering on the moors he is a proto-Heathcliff – the book has been called '*Wuthering Heights* for children', though there is also an echo of *Jane Eyre* in how she hears mysterious crying behind locked doors in the big house. In contrast to the realistic commentary on class divisions of her first novel – *That Lass o' Lowrie's* – this is more magical realism in which hierarchies of class, gender and ethnicity are thrown into question by the healing power of the garden.

Perhaps audiences cannot bear too much reality when it comes to hearing about inequalities, whether between the classes or indeed between the North and South of England. But for a time, in the mid-twentieth century, three women writers from Yorkshire took up a platform to write about them.

*Getting Real*
**Storm Jameson, Winifred Holtby and Phyllis Bentley**

I could almost call this 'the section of realist Northern women writers, famous in the mid-twentieth century, but not as remembered as they should be, that I'd not really heard of until I started researching my show, but there again, it's not like I actively went looking for Northern women writers to read.' That would have been a very long title for the section, though, so it's a good job I've not called it that.

I think the moment when I thought, 'Oh, I've got to read more Storm Jameson' was when I saw that she preferred to live in hotel rooms rather than be responsible for a house and said, 'My hatred of settled domestic life was, is, an instinct, and borders on mania.' It's good, therefore, that the block of flats that bears her name – Storm Jameson Court in Leeds – is actually student flats (which describes itself as a 'stunning hotel-style building' in order to entice students to spend their loans there, though to be fair looks like a very slightly nicer version of any other set of student rabbit-hutch rooms). She is celebrated by the University of Leeds, where she earned a first-class degree in English Literature in 1912 after growing up in Whitby in a family of shipbuilders. Her mother was ambitious for her and had sent her, aged 16, to the Municipal School in Scarborough, assuming she would qualify for one of three North Yorkshire scholarships to enable her to go to university. With the relief of a bookish girl who has been teased and is now appreciated for being clever for once, she said she liked Municipal because she no longer felt like 'a freak'. She described herself as 'self-absorbed and undisciplined' as a student (further identifying with her there) but went on to produce a seriously impressive body of work: over forty-five books and many articles. Perhaps the most outstanding was her two-volume autobiography *Journey from the North*, published in 1969–70. Her lyrical, multi-layered reflection on her outward-looking life is beautiful. I identify with so much here too. As someone who lives on the North East coast, I can feel this exactly as she describes it:

> I could not live in Whitby again, but in a sense I live
> nowhere else, since only there and nowhere else except in
> the lowest level of my being, do I touch and draw energy
> from a few key images, sea, distant lights, the pure line of a
> coast, first images and last, source of such strength as I have.
> Source, too, of my talent for happiness.

She was a deeply politically committed writer right from the beginning, joining the Women's Pilgrimage to Downing Street in 1913, which marched on Downing Street to show the strength of feeling in favour of women's suffrage. She even says she bit a policeman during the demonstration when they arrived at Hyde Park. Storm Jameson married her husband and gave birth to a son in 1915 and commuted for several years between Whitby and London. She found leaving her son difficult, which prompted her to say in her autobiography that the split between writing and parenting was much easier for men and that 'any woman who wishes to be a creator of anything except children should be content to be a nun or a wanderer upon the face of the earth ... the demands made on her as a woman are destructive in a particularly disintegrating way – if she consents to them'. It feels like Storm managed to achieve some sort of balance, though, all while also contributing to shaping the sort of world she believed should exist – through both words and activism.

She became a committed pacifist after the First World War, in which her father was interned in a prison camp and her brother was killed in action. After the war she joined the International Women's League, then later the Institute of Revolutionary Writers, who set up a Marxist journal in 1934. She burned many of her papers in 1940 in case they led to her fellow anti-fascist and anti-Nazi activists being put in danger, and also abandoned pacifism at that point, saying she had been 'absolutely certain that war was viler than anything imaginable but I don't think that now' (after already losing her brother, her younger sister was killed by a bomb in the Second World War). With her second husband, novelist and historian Guy Chapman, she lived a cosmopolitan writer's life in London. Her books included a deeply feminist trilogy called *The Triumph of Time*, a chronicle of a nineteenth-century female shipbuilder from Whitby. She said later of her busy 1920s and 30s: 'During these years I came to know so many people that I almost died of it.' She was the first female president of the English section of the organisation for freedom of expression, PEN International, and helped many writers escape Nazi Germany and Eastern Europe both during and after the war. There was a catharsis there for her it seems, as Storm's mother had accompanied her husband, a shipowner, to many foreign ports before staying at home, restlessly, with her children. Storm said that what made her loathe fascism was having experienced the authority of 'my violently feared and loved mother'. Storm died at the age of 95 in 1986.

Winifred Holtby attended a peace symposium organised by Storm Jameson in the thirties and they would both ultimately be most recognized for their literature connected to this time. Winifred was born in 1898 in Rudstone in East Yorkshire to a farming family and, like Storm, became a feminist activist, socialist and civil rights campaigner as well as a well-regarded novelist. I must have first heard of her when her most famous novel, *South Riding*, was adapted into a television series in 2011 starring Anna Maxwell Martin as Sarah Burton, the brilliant headteacher who believed passionately in girls' education. It lays bare the effects of the Great Depression of the 1930s in one Yorkshire town.

Winifred was accepted into Somerville College, Oxford, at a time when 'farmers' daughters didn't go to Oxford' as one of her family members commented at a screening of *South Riding*. She left in her first year, though, to do war work, joining the Women's Auxiliary Army in France. She said she had 'the desire to suffer and die'. When she went back to Oxford, she formed a friendship that would become the most important of both their lives – with the writer Vera Brittain. Since lots of articles that I read during my research mentioned 'known for her friendship with Vera Brittain', I spent some time trying to work out whether this was a euphemism for a gay relationship. Basically, that isn't known (surely it's none of our business?) but they lived together for several years and their writing lives were entwined. They encouraged each other as novelists. Winifred's first novel, *Anderby Wold*, which explored the impact of radical politics and social change on an East Yorkshire farming community, was well received, whereas copies of Vera's *The Dark Tide* were burned because of her portrayal of Somerville College.

Winifred also wrote journalism and seems to have noted the phenomenon of 'mansplaining' many years ago in a 1929 article called 'The Man Colleague' in which she noted 'this passion for imparting information to females appears to be one of the major male characteristics'. Vera told Winifred that she took precedence over her husband, the academic George Catlin who she married in 1925, because 'you are more necessary to me because you further my work, whereas he merely makes me happy'. George said of Vera's closeness with Winifred, 'You preferred her to me. It humiliated me and ate at me.' Nonetheless, Winifred moved in with them when they returned to England after George had a spell teaching in America, which must have led to some awkward moments over the cornflakes. Winifred helped bring up Vera's two children, including the politician Shirley Williams, who later remembered Winifred's sense of fun and 'radiance' and how 'she was a ray of sunshine in the intense and preoccupied atmosphere of home life in my early years'.

In 1933 Winifred stepped in to appease Vera's husband who was annoyed about appearing in her autobiographical book, *Testament of Youth*. Then, in turn, after Winifred's tragically early death at the age of 37 in 1934, Vera made sure *South Riding* was published posthumously, despite the objections of Vera's mother Alice who was worried about the depiction of local politics, given her own position as a county councillor (she resigned when the book was published). Vera also wrote a biography of Winifred, *Testament of Friendship*, which was published in 1940.

Winifred's greatest legacy as a writer is *South Riding* – she herself recognized it as her best work. She was modest about her writing talents, noting she was unsure whether she was more reformer or writer, saying, 'I have no illusions about my work. I am primarily a useful, versatile, sensible and fairly careful artisan. This has nothing to do with art. It has quite a lot to do with politics.' Even while writing *South Riding*, on retreat in Withernsea in 1934, she broke off to hand out anti-fascist leaflets outside a meeting of Yorkshire Blackshirts. (I feel a bit guilty that I have just broken off this chapter to go get another latte and croissant from the nice café down the road). Perhaps *South Riding* is successful because it manages to fuse art and politics seamlessly. Somehow this combination was deeply unfashionable by the sixties; young male writers, such as John Braine, Alan Sillitoe and Keith Waterhouse, satirised the preoccupations of the regional novelists and made their questions about the future of a North whose industry was declining and which was subject to the economic needs of an increasingly powerful London and the South East seem irrelevant (at a time when they were actually more relevant than ever). We can also see the division between art and politics exemplified in the work of another forgotten Yorkshire female novelist, who was described as the most important regional novelist since Thomas Hardy. The *Inheritance* trilogy that made her name (and which was a television hit in the sixties) tells the story of a Yorkshire mill family up to and after the Industrial Revolution, but few people would know the author's name now.

---

Phyllis Bentley, who was born in Halifax in 1894, was inspired by her very different uncles, who were both mill heirs. Joseph was all about the brass and continued building up a mill empire. James believed in art and politics and he reformed secondary schools in West Yorkshire. When

Phyllis wrote about *The English Regional Novel* in 1941, she realised that she herself was a regional novelist, though later she also recognized their increasing irrelevance. Phyllis was another of these committed Yorkshirewomen galvanised into activism by the world wars – she said she was particularly proud that her books were banned and burned in Germany under the Hitler regime. She had been educated at Cheltenham Ladies College where she was teased for her Yorkshire accent. Then, back in Yorkshire, she was teased for her 'airs and graces'.

This is the classic between-two-worlds experience that afflicts most writers from the North at some point (while also being a bit of a writerly superpower). She loved the Yorkshire landscape but was frustrated by how Yorkshire people could stubbornly value brass over books. Later, as the Depression of the 1930s kicked in, she felt great sympathy for their resilience and wanted to make sure the struggles of the region were recorded. I went to school just four miles up the road from where Phyllis lived (well, up a big hill actually that sometimes strained the number 576 bus, especially in the snow), and once again I am annoyed that I hadn't heard of her. We had a house system at school where you would get merit marks for things like not openly shooting up heroin in the playground (not saying it was a rough school or anything), and she would have been a brilliant candidate for one of the luminaries after whom the houses were named.

---

The explosion in education after the war led to a great increase in the number of people writing, though, across all genres. As the women I am about to mention are still writing now, I am going to be optimistic that they will not be immediately forgotten. They include some of Britain's most loved and interesting novelists and, as far as I know, they are rarely written about all together as 'Northern women writers'. Probably many of them would dispute that that's what they are (though actually, many of them talk about the importance of the place, landscape and people they came from when they are interviewed).

## Northern Women Writing Now

Pat Barker is one of Britain's greatest living novelists. My personal favourite is her *Regeneration* trilogy about war trauma explored through doctors and poets, which won her the Booker Prize in 1995 for the final instalment, *The Ghost Road*. But she's continued to do fascinating work since then, exploring other aspects of identity in wartime – and most recently her Greek-myth inspired *The Silence of the Girls* and *The Women of Troy*. She says she started off trying to write 'sensitive middle-class lady novels' which didn't suit her because her own voice was more earthy and bawdy. Born into a working-class family in Thornaby on Tees in 1943, she studied history at the London School of Economics, then returned home to nurse her grandmother. She struggled to get her work about working-class women published after she started writing in her mid-twenties. She went on a course run by novelist Angela Carter, who said, 'If they can't sympathise with the women you're creating then sod their fucking luck' and advised her to send her work to the feminist press Virago. They published *Union Street* in 1982 and it remains one of their bestsellers. Finally having her voice recognized had its own frustrations, as she said in a *Guardian* interview: 'I had got myself into a box where I was strongly typecast as a northern, regional, working class, feminist – label, label, label – novelist. It's not a matter so much of objecting to the labels, but you do get to a point where people are reading the labels instead of the book. And I felt I'd got to that point.' (Which is of course a paradox of this chapter and of this whole book – so often Northern women are struggling against expectations of who they should be, and now I'm lumping them all back together under a 'Northern women' title.)

I remember once feeling sorry for a journalist I met who said he'd never read A.S. Byatt's Booker Prize-winning novel *Possession* because he started it and realised it was too middle class for him. As my class consciousness has grown, alongside the inverted snobbery chip on my shoulder, I wonder if I'd have missed out on it if I hadn't read it before the inverse snobbery happened. I was first given *Possession* by a student boyfriend who astonished me by doing things like making vegetarian stroganoff from scratch, listening to Radio 4 and having a really high quality record player. Anyway, the entwined stories of two literary academics and the Victorian poets whose romance they investigate, remains one of my favourite books of all time and has also fuelled my imagination on trips to the book's settings on the North Yorkshire coast – from Whitby, with its famous ammonite and jet (a hard black stone, not an aeroplane) to Robin Hood's Bay and the Boggle Hole.

A.S. Byatt is a novelist of big ideas and big feelings who was born into a family of four in Sheffield in 1936, her father a judge, her mother a frustrated Browning scholar turned housewife. She went to the Mount School, a Quaker school in York, and was an academic for ten years, before becoming a full-time writer.

Interviewers know not to mention her sister, novelist Margaret Drabble, and vice versa, since they notoriously don't get on – and I don't want to reduce either sister to a literary feud since I don't have much space to write about them here and they're both brilliant, important novelists. It is interesting, though, that their mother, Kathleen Marie, came from a working-class family, fought her way to the University of Cambridge and then had to give up her teaching career when she had a family. She was fiercely dissatisfied about this and was ambitious for her daughters, who both went to Cambridge themselves – it feels like one of those stories in which the socio-economic context of women can reverberate down the generations. Unfulfilled ambitions can be passed on to (even forced onto) children, along with trauma and anxiety. A.S. Byatt once said: 'I had a strong sense of not knowing how to behave socially, handed down from my mother's anxiety about having got herself right out of her class.' An overheated *Slate* profile of the sisterly feud pointed out that between them, Byatt and Drabble have published 57 books (fifty-eight, now), won eighteen major awards and received four royal titles. It added that Byatt had earned close to a million dollars for *Possession*. This makes them two of the most successful and feted novelists the North has ever produced.

That leads me to think I accidentally grew up in a sort of golden age of high-profile Northern women novelists when I was doing my A levels, while living in a damp bedsit above a brothel in Queensbury, up the hill from Halifax (this is obviously a story for another time). I read about Byatt and Drabble in the Sunday papers and heard Jeanette Winterson provoking and annoying people (mainly by having the temerity to be a clever, opinionated Northern woman. And gay) on my black and white portable telly, just as her lesbian coming-of-age classic *Oranges Are Not the Only Fruit* was turned into a brilliant BBC series, aired in 1990. She said later: '*Oranges* won the Whitbread Prize, but I discovered how tough it was to try and live honestly and honourably as a gay woman in Britain. I was trying to talk about books and art, the press just wanted to talk about sex.' Was Northernness important to her too? Of course it was – she has said, on accepting a professorship at the University of Manchester, 'I am from Manchester and the North is part of me; how I write, as well as who I am.' Winterson's brilliant 2011 memoir *Why Be Happy When You Could be Normal* de-fictionalises the story of her upbringing by her eccentric, overbearing adoptive mother in a Pentecostal community in Accrington, Lancashire, and she has won numerous awards for her twenty-two novels. She lives in the Cotswolds, while her partner, the psychoanalyst Suzie Orbach, lives in London. She urges: 'There are so many ways of managing love and life, be creative!'

Then there was Kate Atkinson from York, winning the Whitbread Prize for *Behind the Scenes at The Museum* in 1995, which featured a pharmaceutical supplies shop like the one her parents ran. It was inspired by a dream she had about walking round the Castle Museum in York and the exhibits in the street scenes coming to life. In a common theme for post-war writers, her dad wanted her to have the life chances he didn't have, and sent her to a fee-paying school in York. She has published five novels featuring the curmudgeonly detective Jackson Brodie, adapted into the TV series *Case Histories* featuring the (Northern) actor Jason Isaacs. I'm still utterly haunted by her 2013 novel *Life after*

*Life*, which won the Costa Novel Award that year. It features a central character who is born in 1910 and lives through the turbulent events of the century again and again. As she says: 'People move on, history remains.'

There is a joy and lightness and a surreality to Kate's work that conveys something I find is rarely written about the North and about Englishness generally. You can also find it in the work of the late poet and novelist Julia Darling who wrote two well-received novels set in Newcastle – *The Taxi Driver's Daughter* and *Crocodile Soup* – before her untimely death of cancer at the age of 48 in 2005. When I was first starting out as a working poet in Newcastle in 2004, I was so inspired by seeing her speak at an event where she emphasised that professional writers often burnt themselves out running workshops trying to make a living, but they had to remember to look after themselves because otherwise their time and inspiration to write would dry up. She was one of the most respected and loved writers on the scene and it was devastating reading the wise, calm blogs of her last days. Her last post was one of her poems in which she prefigured her own quiet death at home:

> Eventually, I was placed on a bed like a boat
> in an empty room with sky filled windows,
> with azure blue pillows, the leopard-like quilt.
> It was English tea time, with the kind of light
> that electrifies the ordinary.

*Guardian* critic Alfred Hickling said of her books:

> Darling is routinely labelled a 'Newcastle writer', as
> though literate people on Tyneside were a breed apart.

And though her novels of working-class life undoubtedly belong to the great tradition of Sid Chaplin, Tom Hadaway and Alan Plater, Darling herself is not a native Geordie at all . . . But the great strength of her writing is its sense of place.

Darling was actually born in Winchester, in the house where Jane Austen died, but never felt at home in the city and immediately fell for Newcastle when she moved there in the early eighties. I remember some of the groups of blokey, Geordie working-class poets being chippy about a Southern middle-class writer coming in and picking up plaudits. But she embodied something vital about a modern, cosmopolitan Newcastle that was open to migrants of all kinds.

Hickling says she often evokes place with a couple of well-chosen smells, and I think one of the things that both Atkinson and Darling capture is the smells and tastes of the North, not the dirt and smoke of those Victorian novels, though, but particular consoling sweetnesses. Cakes from Betty's tea shop, knickerbocker glories at the seaside on a cold day – the small (almost retro) treats that bring joy to everyday life.

That brings us perfectly on to Joanne Harris, who is half Yorkshire and half French. Born in Barnsley, the teacher who attended Wakefield Girls High School hit the jackpot with her book about a magical French chocolate shop – *Chocolat*. It was her third novel and she had to give up teaching at that point because there was so much publicity around her magical realism fairy tale, and its subsequent film adaptation, which invented a whole genre of 'gastromance'. It made her one of only four authors in the UK to earn a million pounds from a single novel, though she has now written many more bestsellers. She is also influenced by Norse mythology and a strong sense of place, with French villages and Yorkshire villages continuing to feature in her books, reflecting her dual heritage.

Meanwhile, fellow Wakefield Girls High student Helen Fielding, whose dad was the managing director of a textile factory in Morley, chronicled a woman who tried not to taste things because she was obsessively counting calories. Fielding went to Oxford, joining the Revue at the same time as Rowan Atkinson and Richard Curtis in 1978, and then became a journalist and documentary producer. She is one of the highest-earning authors of all time for her *Bridget Jones's Diary* series, which started as a newspaper column about a nineties girl about town then became four bestselling books and four high-grossing films (why am I talking about brass again, when I was talking about literature?). Satirical writing is hard but often leads to you being underestimated for daring to make people laugh, even more so if you're a Northern woman, so (biased as I am) I tend to think Fielding's writing is underrated, lost in discussions of just how much weight Renée Zellweger had to put on in order to play a size-twelve woman. I remember reading *Bridget Jones* with her obsessive recounting of her weight and her perpetual sense of not quite getting it right, and recognizing the pressures that were on women to look the part, act the part, and bag yourself a fairy tale romance.

A film adaptation of your novel is definitely not a sure-fire path to riches, though. Prolific Scarborough-born novelist Susan Hill said she was broke, even though her 1983 book, gothic horror ghost story *The Woman in Black*, has run in the West End for over twenty-five years and became a 2012 film starring Daniel Radcliffe which took fifty million dollars in the US and £20 million in the UK. She has Tweeted that film accounting is 'very weird'.

Let's shift the focus across the Pennines now (that has been A LOT of Yorkshire writers) and look to Liverpool. Beryl Bainbridge was one of the best novelists of her age and was made a dame in 2000. Born in 1932, she wrote eighteen novels, five of which reached the Booker Prize shortlist. She had a traumatic childhood with an emotionally abusive father, though said she wrote her neurosis away.

Her life story makes her sound like a character in a book. At Merchant Taylors' School she was known as 'Basher Bainbridge' for fighting, and had a relationship with a German prisoner of war she used to sneak out at night to meet. After being expelled from the school, she went to a drama school, then her father got her a job as an assistant stage manager at Liverpool Playhouse, which led to the book (and later the film) *An Awfully Big Adventure*. She wrote short books, distilling twelve pages of draft into one perfectly honed page and was darkly funny, exemplifying how, as she said in *Watson's Apology* (her 1992 novel based on an 1871 murder case in which a clergyman bludgeoned his wife to death), 'tragedy, though hard to contend with, was an affirmation of life'. Or in other words, miserable people are often having more fun than you think . . .

It's funny how rarely Liverpool is referred to as 'The North', in the way that Yorkshire or Lancashire are – as if it's a separate thing in itself (and it's such a distinct identity that perhaps it is). Another Liverpool novelist, Linda Grant, whose sharp-eyed contemporary tales move between Liverpool, London and Israel, says when she first started writing she struggled with where she might fit. She said in a 2011 *Guardian* interview: 'I wasn't part of any kind of Jewish world. Being from Liverpool was really important but I wasn't working class and the whole Liverpool identity was a working-class identity. If I tried to write in a neutral English voice it didn't feel like me at all, I felt completely alienated. I didn't really know what to do.' I would especially recommend the former journalist's memoir of her mother's dementia, *Remind Me Who I Am, Again*, or her Orange Prize-winning novel *When I Lived in Modern Times*, which recounts the creation of modern Israel through the eyes of a Jewish hairdresser in sixties London who goes to live on a kibbutz.

## Northern Noir

Crime novels often have a strong sense of place, though for a long time, that place in English crime novels was usually London. In recent years, though, the trend for Scandi-noir, in which Scandinavian detectives in lovely knitted jumpers solve crimes in windswept places while polishing off some pickled herring, has led to publishers and readers recognizing that they quite enjoy a windswept place. Tartan Noir picked up this craze with a spate of Scottish thrillers, then it sort of moved further south, to the North of England, and we now have Northern Noir (though that might just be marketing by publishers), which welcomes in new voices along with some authors who were already writing crime.

Ann Cleeves's work is often set in the North East and has reached the mainstream through her Vera novels. Sheila Quigley was a rare truly working-class writer from the North of England who hit the headlines in 2004 when her first crime novel *Run for Home* (set on Holy Island) was picked up for a six-figure sum. She was living on an estate in County Durham and had worked in a tailoring factory. She was a hugely popular figure on the talks circuit until her death in 2020. Mari Hannah was a working probation officer when she picked up an award in 2010 for her first book, *The Murder Wall*, the first in her Kate Daniels series, before she even had an agent. She's gone from strength to strength since, picking up the Crime Writers' Association's Dagger in the Library award in 2017 for her body of work. She lives in a small Northumberland village with her partner. LJ Ross (Louise) was born in Northumberland, went to London to work as a lawyer, then came back to write, and now lives between Northumberland and Edinburgh. She writes the DCI Ryan series of thrillers set on Lindisfarne. Her first in the series – *Holy Island* – became a number one bestseller when it was published in 2015. (I wonder if the people of Holy Island sleep a bit less easily in their beds what with all these thrillers insisting it's full of murders. I don't think there's been an actual one on the island for decades ... )

There is still a literary prize encouraging women writers over 40 in the name of North East writer Andrea Badenoch, who died of breast cancer in 2004 and who combined crime plots with a focus on the social conditions that created crime, in books including *Blink* and *Loving Geordie*.

Moving back to the North West, Cath Staincliffe, based in Manchester and born in Bradford, won a Crime Writers' Association award in 1994 and has since written the *Blue Murder* series for TV. Lynda La Plante, from Liverpool, has produced a huge body of books and telly work – most famously the *Prime Suspect* series starring Helen Mirren as DCI Jane Tennison, which burst onto our TV screens in

1991 and ran until 2006. Other Liverpool thriller writers worth checking out include Margaret Murphy, who writes as Ashley Dyer, and Mary Torjussen.

There are more novelists and poets living and working in the North of England today than there have ever been. There's work to be had running creative writing workshops in universities, schools and community groups; the cost of living is less than in London; and there's often a sense of writerly community and support. Since big publishers began to notice there was a world outside London and that if they wanted a greater diversity of voices they might have to actively go to where those voices are, there's even beginning to be some publishing infrastructure in the North, or at least in Manchester and Sheffield. The Portico Prize, run by Manchester's Portico Library, rewards the best book to evoke 'the spirit of the North', a phrase I discovered when I was on the panel in 2020, that we judges had a strong sense of, even if it's hard to describe. Jessica Andrews' stunning *Saltwater* was our winner, a still too-rare book by a working-class Northern woman writer, featuring a working-class heroine from Sunderland. The annual shortlists showcase the proliferating perspectives on what Northernness is and can be. As Anita Sethi says in her travelogue-memoir *I Belong Here* (written after she was racially abused on a train from Liverpool to Newcastle and told to go back to where she came from) writing is an act of 'reclamation' since she is from 'The Glorious North' and, as a brown woman, belongs here just as much as a white man. Some of the country's most relevant, exciting literature is emerging from the region - for starters, two of the most compelling lockdown novels come from Northern writers (*Burntcoat* by Sarah Hall and *The Fell* by Sarah Moss). Many others will already have been written but sit mouldering in drawers or dormant on hard drives, waiting for the right intersection of time, place, audience and opportunity that make up the rocky but rewarding path to publication and, perhaps like the Brontës' work, will help shape the identity this complicated, beautiful, multi-layered region.

# 7

# Women with Microphones

I once interviewed a comedian who said they didn't realise they were Northern until they went to university and everybody who wasn't from the North soon told them (this is the inverse of the joke 'How do you know somebody's from Yorkshire? They've already told you five times').

I realised I was Northern when I tried to get a job after university. Even when I applied for jobs at Northern radio stations, it turned out that with my Yorkshire accent, wanting to be a radio newsreader was as unlikely as Kojak being allowed to advertise shampoo. Essentially, because public schools approved and reinforced a certain accent, we are told that this voice is the only one that has the authority to tell us serious things. Regional accents, it seems, are for comedy. Until very recently, if you listened to the media you'd assume people with regional voices are just not as clever as those with posh voices. Luckily, Channel 4's *Made in Chelsea* has come along to disprove this once and for all.

During the Second World War, the BBC got a man from Halifax called Wilfred Pickles to read the news in order to 'confuse the Germans' (but actually because it was thought he would be harder for Nazi broadcasters to impersonate).

It didn't work, in that his flat vowels and his wishing people 'good neet' at the end of the bulletin outraged people from the South of England so much that he was taken off the air after only three days. Basically, British people would rather be invaded by Hitler than have a Northerner reading the news. No wonder I have a chip on my shoulder . . .

Eighty years on, BBC *Breakfast*'s business editor Steph McGovern often tells of how a BBC boss told her that she should consider losing her Teesside accent because it made her sound 'stupid', and a viewer offered her £20 if she would 'speak properly'. Meanwhile, when I tried to get my first jobs on the radio, I was given the same advice as Margaret Thatcher was given when she first started public speaking (not 'be nicer to people and don't start any wars') – lower my voice and practise speaking in a whisper, while flattening out my accent. It worked. My polished up 'newsreader voice' got me jobs on Newcastle radio stations Metro and Galaxy where I discovered something else about being Northern. It was a lot harder to get coverage in the national media if the story came from 'up North'.

In launching a new product or show or star, you could do exactly the same thing in Leeds and London, and only the London event would get capital-based journalists to come along. But why would they want to jump on a train to Leeds or Newcastle for a few hours with only overbaked pasties to eat and a probable eighteen-hour rail-replacement bus diversion? Funnily enough, national journalists were not up for this at all. Add to that a sense that the only things worth knowing about happen in London, and you have a situation in which Northerners feel they must either move to London to get themselves heard, or resign themselves to 'the under-rated' being part of their title. They might also be lucky, of course, and hit one of the periods when Northernness, or regionality generally, is cool. That's different to it being taken seriously. My litmus test of whether the stigma and prejudice that surrounds Northernness has been overcome will be when we finally hear someone with a Northern accent reading the national news. It doesn't rank high on the list of campaigns that feel very important to people, but it will show that something fundamental has changed.

Until then, something I am determined to do is to champion Northern voices wherever I find them. To champion them in their diversity and their difference and their outward-looking perspective. To champion even those who think it's parochial to be labelled as a Northern voice, because I know just how many cultural, social and economic barriers they face to being heard.

In many of the other categories I've covered, you can't easily find or follow the work of the Northern women in question. I mean, if you were a complete political geek you could probably look up Ellen Wilkinson's speeches in the Commons, or if you were a sports freak you could find the video of Mandy Jones cycling to glory in the World Championships. You could imagine Hilda of Whitby speaking at the Synod, or swim in a pool where Hilda James set a world record, but really you can't fully engage with their work in the way it was meant to be engaged with. The great thing about the creatives – the novelists (so many of them they had to have their own chapter), the musicians, the artists and the playwrights – is that you can. You should, you must! Here are some accounts of brilliant women whose words you might listen out for. As Northern voices they help shape and reshape perceptions of the North and give a wider picture of who we are.

## Comedians

I was always interested in comedians but it took me a long time to notice that most of them were men. I mean, the ones that loomed large on eighties telly when I was growing up were women like Victoria Wood, who seemed ubiquitous as well as hilarious, and Marti Caine who hosted *New Faces* in her sparkly frocks, and Cilla Black, whose singing career I didn't know about but who made us laugh asking 'ar Graham for a quick reminder' in her Scouse accent on *Blind Date*. All funny Northern women who were fronting shows built around their unique personalities.

It wasn't until I started doing stand-up on the comedy circuit myself that I noticed a definite lack of gender diversity. I was often the only woman on the bill at the open-mike nights I started doing around the Northern clubs in the late nineties. Truth be told, I wasn't very good at stand-up. Audiences liked me, I was funny-ish, but I hadn't worked out how to turn my quirkiness into something that audiences could either relate to, or find weird enough to laugh at. Things got better when I started adding poems into my set. If the audience don't laugh, you can just say it's because it's a poem. Plus, poetry audiences are very happy to laugh after listening to all those miserable poems about people's dead dads. Anyway, I put myself up for panels about women in comedy and started running events aimed at getting more of us on stage. Partly this was a selfish thing – the less time an audience were spending thinking that it was odd that a woman was on stage, the more time I would have to convince them I was funny.

At the first workshop I ever ran, in a studio theatre connected to the main library in Gateshead, a woman rang me up to ask about it first. It was a strange format, granted – participants would spend the whole day taking part in performance exercises, then take to the stage in the evening to show off their skills. I knew from my own personal experience how useful it was to develop my confidence in a workshop setting, because I'd been going to drama sessions since I was thirteen. In fact, drama workshops were where I learnt to be a normal person (relatively speaking). But at the same time I also knew that the best way to learn how to be on stage was in front of an audience. There was no substitute for just doing it. I couldn't have made the transition away from my physiological reaction of shaking and not taking in enough breath and my voice coming from high up in my throat (all due to adrenaline and cortisol flooding my system) if I hadn't kept going back on stage and gradually becoming more comfortable in front of an audience. The reason public speaking is such a big fear for many is that your body's fight or flight response kicks in because being exposed in front of people triggers a primeval fear that a lion will come and eat you (or something). The best way to overcome this is the exposure therapy of doing it again and again and again. It turned out that combining the workshop format with a performance opportunity at the end of it seemed to bring forward more women than usually participated in solo performance courses (and maybe it helped that I was a woman). It is less intimidating to know that your skills will be nurtured and taught in front of fellow amateurs, rather than turn up to a random pub and expose yourself to the drunks and lions.

So, the woman who rang me had just got divorced at the age of 29, and she talked about how she had written plays for the local Live Theatre in Newcastle but sometimes wanted to perform her own words rather than see other people mangling them. She had been to see Linda Smith, the late comedian, on tour and it was one of the only things that pulled her out of her post-divorce depression. It made her realise she wanted to make people laugh herself. I had a lot to say about how I felt that there should be more women on the comedy circuit, and how satisfying it was to speak your own words, and I remember the light in my hallway fading from light to dusk as we talked. It turned out that she had been born just two days before me and we shared a sense of humour but also a way of analysing the world. We had both always felt a bit set apart from the people around us. I knew I was looking forward to meeting her at the workshop.

There wasn't much time to talk to her on the day, what with the time spent standing in a circle introducing ourselves, playing scarecrow tag, shouting out lines from our sets, and helping participants give feedback on how they came across on stage. I did direct the camera crew from the local news programme her way because I thought a recently divorced woman who worked at the job centre and was trying stand-up for the first time was a good story. Later that evening, you could have powered a stadium with the amount of adrenaline backstage as the participants geared up to perform to the audience of forty or so friends and family sitting round cabaret tables. I can still see my new friend there under the spotlight: pale, her face a bit frozen, her dark blue jeans and plain top that screamed 'don't look at me', saying these lines which stood as funny and true and so sharply, beautifully written, capturing something about her experiences as a young woman, a young Northern woman, making comedy out of the marriage break-up that had devastated her. How she asked her husband for her curtains back and he said, 'But they're lined.' How her mam had said, 'I never liked him anyway.' How she said, 'You know when you lick a tear from the bottom of your nose . . . and it's not a tear?' Every word precisely placed. I knew, despite her nervousness, she had 'it'. Whatever 'it' was, she had it – and people would respond in their millions. I had a flash forward to her standing on stage at the Royal Variety Show. An audience cheering.

It came true, that flash forward, because the woman was Sarah Millican, who you've probably heard of given that she's one of the country's best-known, best-loved stand-up comedians. She went onto be a finalist in two of the big comedy newcomer competitions the following year, then won the Best Newcomer award at the Edinburgh Fringe in 2008 and the British Comedy Award People's Choice Award for King or Queen of Comedy in 2011 and BAFTA nominations for her TV show in 2013 and 2014. She appeared at the Royal Variety Show in 2010 and 2014 (saying, 'The third time you go on it, I think you win a member of the Royal family!').

I am so proud of all she's achieved – it was mixed with a complicated envy at first because maybe the reason I could envisage her future path so clearly from the very off was that it was what I'd wanted, and I knew perfectly well there was a space for her to step into it. (It's a bit like my dream of running a bookshop on a boat – I can see perfectly how it would work and be brilliant, but I'm just not the person to do it.) People very much wanted to hear Sarah's voice. A relatable, friendly, acute observer of everyday female life and love and body image insecurity that wasn't usually heard amid the flood of identikit models and stick-thin presenters that were on telly in the noughties. I think her Northernness was important in this. It did make her more 'one of us' for a mainstream comedy audience and it signalled that she was funny. She could have had another working-class regional accent – Brum or Cockney, say – but Northernness is also associated with warmth and coping. An Everywoman just cracking on with boyfriends who fart after curries and magazines who tell you your tummy shouldn't be a 'cake shelf'.

At the same time (and I'm going to have to be restrained here because I did a PhD on this subject, literally, and could easily bang on for a lot longer), Sarah's Northernness was consistently used as a 'marker' by reviewers. Basically, the posher the reviewer (in broadsheets like *The Times* and *The Telegraph*) then the more likely they were to comment disparagingly on Sarah's voice and also her body. (This focus on the voice and body also happened more to male comedians from the North. In the course of my research, I analysed hundreds of reviews and did pie charts and everything. Not those sorts of pies.) They also often commented negatively on her swearing and sexual content. Basically, the further away somebody is from the ideal of middle-class people who are slim and restrained and talk nicely and keep their bodily fluids out of sight and out of mind, then the more likely they are to have their skills underestimated. Sarah is, flat-out, one of the most talented comic writers and performers the country has ever produced, but doesn't always get the critical acclaim she deserves. I am biased, of course, but we can see the pattern with other comedians.

———————————

Victoria Wood has perhaps done more to shape a Northern voice than any other writer, aside from Alan Bennett. She also didn't get the critical acclaim she deserved, but the wave of love and sadness that swept across the country when she died of cancer of the oesophagus in 2016, aged just 62, reflected how important a figure she was. People shared their favourite clips – her 'Two Soups' sketch with Julie Walters; her Channel swimmer looking out to sea and bravely saying, 'I came fourth in geography,' as she sets off on her own while her parents go to London to take in a show; the girl with the yellow beret pleading 'I'm looking for my friend, Kimberley'; snippets from her surreal sitcom/soap spoof *Acorn Antiques* and her comedy series *Dinnerladies*; her climaxing the 'Ballad of Barry and Freda' song with 'Spank me on the bottom with a Woman's Weekly!'; and her television announcer character played by Susie Blake, who linked *Victoria Wood As Seen On TV* sketches together and memorably intoned, 'We must apologise to viewers from the North. It must be awful for them.'

She talked about her lonely childhood in Bury, where playing the piano and observing people gave her solace from a disconnected family and feeling out of her depth at grammar school. She was a contestant on the telly talent show *New Faces* in 1974 (she was beaten by Lenny Henry and Marti Caine), which led to her doing topical songs on the TV show *That's Life*. It took her a while to find her comedic voice, though, with her whimsical songs and shy patter not being hard-hitting enough for club stand-up, but she was also doing something quite different from the Footlights comedians from Cambridge and the alternative comedians like Rik Mayall, Tony Allen and French and Saunders, who were pioneering their own material at the Comedy Store in London.

Where you start off is so important in comedy, as I found out when I interviewed contemporary stand-ups based in the North. It's hard to get comedy scouts and producers to travel even as far as Manchester – you have to go to them at the industry showcase, which is the Edinburgh Festival, and hope you have ten grand to fork out putting on a show at a decent venue. Lack of contacts and confidence meant that despite national television exposure, Victoria spent several years being miserable and frustrated and watching telly in a Birmingham bedsit (the activity that became the basis of her entire future career).

Things really took off for her when she met fellow student Julie Walters when they both starred in a West End revue. Peter Eckersley, head of drama at Granada Television, commissioned a play from Victoria and she gave Julie Walters a starring role. He then commissioned a sketch show and Victoria insisted on Julie getting equal billing. *Wood and Walters* was a hit and introduced Victoria to other actors she would continue to work with over the years, including Celia Imrie, Duncan Preston, Susie Blake and Patricia Routledge. All those years of watching telly and learning the piano paid off.

Victoria did things her own way, in her own time, and it's astonishing, looking back at her career, what an innovator she was. Most stand-ups learn their trade on the live circuit with other stand-up comics. She basically taught herself, and eventually became one of the best in the country, winning a British Comedy Award in 1990 for Best Live Act and doing a record-breakingly long tour in 1993 that culminated in fifteen sold-out nights at the Albert Hall. Her comedy was the comedy of ordinary lives – big dreams punctured by ridiculous reality, captured in perfectly observed small details (no one knew the humour of a brand name better than Victoria). It wasn't working-class humour, it wasn't middle-class humour, it was in the land of the in between, where most people find themselves, so it struck a chord as very English, as well as very Northern. She said, 'The Italians have got opera, the Spanish have got flamenco dancing. What have we got? Weight Watchers.' Every word was precision engineered. It was specific but it was universal: 'I'm going North. It's a compulsion with me. Even in Tesco's I head straight for the freezer cabinets on the back wall.' And, 'My mother was trapped under a Blackpool tram for four and a half hours. She didn't get counselling. She got a cup of tea and two tickets to Charlie Drake.'

I can see how much I, and so many others, have been influenced by her as a comedian and writer. It's a mixture of the fact that she wrote comedy based on how the sort of people I knew talked, and her genius in capturing it so brilliantly. However, in common with Hylda Baker and Sarah Millican, having control over her material, her artistic vision and her career was vital to her. In recent years she had moved into writing and directing dramas. She leaves behind her a body of work that – despite being some of the most hilarious of modern times – deserves to be taken seriously as a commentary on ordinary lives, and a transformation of that ordinariness and tragedy into something beautiful. I'm sure Victoria Wood wouldn't let me get away with such a grandiose statement without deflating it, though – puncturing pretension was part of her genius, after all. As she said, 'Some of us drink champagne in? the fast lane and some of us eat our sandwiches by the loose chippings on the A597.'

———————

Nowadays there are more female comedians from the North than there were when Victoria Wood started, or even than when Sarah Millican set out in the mid-noughties. Acts like Sophie Willan from Bolton, whose TV series *Alma's Not Normal* found inspiration in her unconventional childhood growing up with a heroin-addicted mother and spending time in care. Or look out for Kiri Pritchard McLean, Mancunian comedian Rachel Fairburn, and Lucy Beaumont from Hull. All of these are stars whose comedy embraces their roots – without it being the joke at the centre of their act.

There are also memorials to female comedians. Mancunian comic actor and writer Caroline Aherne shot to fame in the nineties with her *Mrs Merton* chat show. In character as an ageing housewife, she would innocently ask guests devastating questions, such as when she famously asked Debbie McGee, 'What attracted you to the millionaire Paul Daniels?' But many would say her greatest achievement was the sitcom *The Royle Family*, co-written with Craig Cash, which she also directed and starred in. It was revolutionary for its bittersweet depiction of a working-class Manchester family. She died of cancer in 2016 at the age of 52, but a BBC bursary set up in her name to foster comic writing talent has so far been awarded to Sophie Willan, Amy Gledhill and Kiri Pritchard-McLean.

A statue of Victoria Wood was erected in her home town of Bury in 2019. It was sculpted by Graham Ibbeson who

has also sculpted a statue of Eric Morecambe. It was controversial at first because the preliminary model that was
unveiled looked about as much like her as I look like the
supermodel Naomi Campbell. But to be fair, the finished
piece, in which she's wearing one of her trademark long
coats, clutching a microphone and clenching her left fist as
she did when she needed to remember a line, is a reasonable
likeness. Much more so than the statue dedicated to Marti
Caine in her home city of Sheffield. 'Sheen' looks like a stone
waffle. Marti Caine definitely didn't, being renowned for her
glamour. But she was a lover of abstract art and was due to
unveil the statue two weeks before she died of cancer in
1995, aged fifty.

Marti – or Lynne, as she was born – grew up with a
mother who had a history of alcohol and drug abuse,
and her father died when she was very young. She married
at 17 and described herself as 'just another starry-eyed
wannabe . . . married with two babies, an ex-beauty queen,
stuck on a council estate with little hope of fulfilling any
dreams for a better life.' But then, aged 19 and stuck with a
bill of £19 for her mother's funeral expenses, she auditioned
at a working men's club and began a career as a cabaret
singer and comic, eventually winning the *New Faces* competition in the same series, as I've mentioned, in which Victoria
Wood was also a contestant. She went on to compere the
revived *New Faces* in the eighties, toured nationally, and
starred in a sitcom called *Hillary*, which was written especially for her. Her bestselling autobiography, *The Coward's
Chronicles* was published in 1990. She said she called it that
because she was fed up of being portrayed as amazingly
brave because she had cancer. (It does seem to me that bravery was a hallmark of her life, though, not just in the work

she did for cancer charities while she was ill herself, but in getting on stage and being funny as a woman at a time when there were so few on stage.) There were a few other female club comedians in the seventies and eighties – it's still possible to watch, online, a Tyne Tees documentary from 1981 called *Laughing at Life* about the North East comedian Pauline Petty, for instance. Pauline ran her own club nights in Whitley Bay, complete with pie suppers, but it was very much not the norm.

An achievement of all these women is to have made a craft, an art and a profession out of the ample practice Northern women have in turning their traumas, tragedies and everyday annoyances into the laughter you share on doorsteps, at the back of the bus, down the phone and on Zoom. They show us ourselves and we laugh right back with them.

### Musicians

I love that Victoria Wood's statue is holding a microphone. Microphones are phallic. Microphones must still be mainly for men. I can't think of any other explanation for why there are relatively so few female singer-songwriters from the North of England. Apart from the fact that it might also be something to do with parkas. If you look up photographs of Northern musicians and bands, they are nearly always wearing parkas. Perhaps they just don't make them for girls? Not only are they wearing parkas but they are also, like the Northern writers, leaning against stone or brick walls. This might be something they learnt in the playground as boys. I was busy putting make-up on a decapitated head (the sinister girls' toy known as a Girl's World) while the boys were perfecting their lean and parka technique. Bands who define the modern North – like The Smiths, Joy Division, New Order, The Stone Roses, the Arctic Monkeys, Oasis, Echo and the Bunnymen, or the Futureheads, and Maximo Park – have a very similar aesthetic (I am sure they would dispute this and point to differing hair lengths, taking us back to the monks at the Synod of Whitby). They are also nearly all blokes. Lists of 'The 100 Best Northern Songs' or 'Fifty Songs from Past the Watford Gap' or Greater Manchester Mayor Andy Burnham's inauguration playlist might as well be titled, 'All the Blokes, Leaning Against Walls in Parkas, Plus Lisa Stansfield'. This is mainly a Manchester dominance and there are exceptions, of course. Gillian Gilbert, for example, whose dad always said she was never the same after she saw Siouxsie and the Banshees on the television as a girl, and who joined New Order as keyboardist and guitarist in 1980, and Rowetta, who joined the Happy Mondays in 1990.

The sociologist Katie Milestone has researched Manchester's cultural sector and found that only 23 per cent of creatives working in it are women, compared to a proportion of 42 percent elsewhere in the country. She partly connects this to the way that 'laddishness' and 'creativity' are associated together in ideas of Northernness which are perpetuated by popular bands, among other things. I think this is fascinating and true and makes sense of how there's an almost invisible expectation at some level that women should be doing the parka sewing and the hair cutting, but not the actual talking or singing. As recently as 2014, I was commissioned as one of twelve artists for a high-profile Northern project and it wasn't until quite near the end that I, or anyone else, seemed to notice that the eleven other commissionees were blokes. It was pretty cold on that windswept headland in Sunderland – I could have done with a parka. Things have changed even in the past few years, though, because I don't think that would be allowed to happen now.

There was a point in that project where I did suddenly realise how my being a woman meant I was regarded in a certain way. I was stood with a group of schoolchildren about to perform a poem live on BBC One. The floor manager had told us there were thirty seconds to go. One of the girls, stood in the row in front of me, burst into tears and said she didn't want to do the poem. I was left to comfort her by rubbing her back awkwardly and persuading her that she did, after all, want to perform a poem live on national telly. I can't help feeling that someone would have given Liam Gallagher or Shaun Ryder some help at this point. Or possibly not left them in charge of the emotional wellbeing of some 13-year-olds. Anyway, she and the rest of the kids did brilliantly and, of course, the one child who messaged me a couple of weeks afterwards to say she wanted to do it all again? The very same girl. It's always the way. Performance feels terrifying but it can be addictive. Once you've seen people like you do it, once you've done it yourself, you can get hooked. It's just getting hold of that microphone or onto that stage in the first place, which is why I'm a great advocate of the new initiatives that actively encourage women into the spotlight.

I mentioned Lisa Stansfield, and it really did feel for a long time as if she was the only overtly Northern woman out there in the world of music. She was born in 1966 and got her start by winning a talent show called *Search for a Star* when she was fourteen. This led to her presenting kids TV music show *Razzmatazz*. Which, the more you say it, is a very weird word. And it really did suggest showbiz excitement, glitter and glamour in the eighties, but now ... doesn't. Her biggest hit by far was the now classic 'All Around the World', one of the defining songs of the late eighties. It came from the multiple award-winning soul album *Affection*, which went on to sell over five million copies around the world (all around the world – oh. Bet she's fed up of that pun). But she is also associated with one of the other best-known Northern female singers – Gracie Fields. This is partly because they are both connected to the Lancashire town of Rochdale and because Gracie's original surname was Stansfield (despite what's commonly thought, they are not actually related). It's also because they were both what the press might call 'unapologetically Northern' (this is code for 'has a Northern accent and has the cheek not to have had elocution lessons!').

Gracie Fields is from a much earlier era, of course. Born in 1898, she lived above her gran's fish and chip shop. She also got her start in a talent contest, aged just seven, and performed in local charity shows around Rochdale. At first she worked in the cotton mill half the week and went to school for the other half, before turning to full-time singing. She described her mother as 'stage mad' and when interviewed on the Michael Parkinson show in the seventies she said, 'My mother wanted me to be an opera singer but we couldn't afford it. We didn't have the brass. You did whatever you could do.' For her, this involved a career singing in London theatres once she moved there in the 1920s, selling over five million (yes, million) records with songs like 'The Biggest Aspidistra in the World' (which was written by her husband's mistress, adultery fact fans). Then it was the huge films of the thirties and wartime that made her a superstar and universally known and loved as 'Our Gracie'. She had a beautiful voice but was also funny and warm and a morale-boosting star of films like *Sally* and *Sing As We Go*, being paid a record-breaking £200,000 by Hollywood for four films, though in interviews she made it clear how much she much preferred sparking off a live audience. She was once described as 'the greatest entertainer this country's ever produced'. I think I fell for her when I watched a clip of her last ever public appearance – a surprise closing act of the Royal Variety Show in 1978, at the age of eighty. White haired, operatic voiced (her mother would have been proud!), in a glittery blue kaftan, she belts out one of her most-loved songs, 'Sally in her Alley', then as she gets to the line 'Marry me, Sally', she says in a perfectly timed aside, still in a broad Lancastrian accent, 'I've been singing a man's song all my life', causing the audience to absolutely howl.

She lived on the isle of Capri with her Romanian husband in her later years – a far cry from Rochdale – and continued working all her life, saying she enjoyed doing the housework so that her days consisted of either 'starring or charring'. She told Michael Parkinson that Capri reminded her of her Lancastrian home because the people were close and enjoyed 'tittle-tattle'. There's a theatre named after her in Rochdale, and in 2016 a beautiful statue of her was unveiled there (the first new statue of a woman in Lancashire for a century) – she's singing into a microphone and holding a trademark headscarf in her hand. She was joking in her comic, nostalgic song 'In a Little Lancashire Town' when she sang 'Where once t'rubbish tip used to be/they've bunged up a statue to me!' so it's rather glorious that this was a ridiculous prediction that came true. Perhaps she knew, at some level, because she absolutely worked her Northernness and her connection to her audience – both parodying

Northernness and embodying it with a knowing smile and a gorgeous trill of that voice which allowed her R's to roll in the Lancashire way.

## Shout Above the Noise: Kenickie, Pauline Murray, Louise Distras, Joolz, Kathryn Williams and Nadine Shah

In complete contrast, there is a small but strong counter-current of female punk in the North which overturns expectations of what women are supposed to be and sound like. The first I was aware of it was when the Sunderland band Kenickie burst onto the music scene in the mid-nineties with songs like 'Punka' and 'In Your Car'. They opened for the Ramones at the Brixton Academy in 1996 and impressed US singer Courtney Love, who said, 'I hope we're a good example to them, I hope this record's huge and then the big labels will start sniffing around and then those big fucking raw-boned sexy Newcastle girls will be huge and have Number Ones.'

As we are still in a world where a BBC weather map managed to place Newcastle in the North West instead of the North East, it's probably a bit much to expect the lead singer of Hole to distinguish between the completely different cities of Newcastle and Sunderland, but still ... Kenickie inspired other girl guitar bands but split up in 1998 after a gig at the London Astoria with the words – uttered by lead singer Lauren Laverne who is now one of the country's best-known TV and radio presenters – 'We were Kenickie ... a bunch of fuckwits.' It would be refreshing if more ousted governments would end their terms of office like this. I've since been quietly starstruck when encountering band member Emma Jackson in her new guise as a sociologist, and Marie Nixon during her time working for the Arts Council, and they were definitely not fuckwits.

Back in the earliest days of punk, another determined young woman from the North East noticed that it hadn't yet come to her town of Ferryhill in County Durham, so in 1976 this 18-year-old decided to start her own band. Footage of Pauline Murray and the rest of Penetration giving it their best leather and safety-pinned pogo-ing while the working men's club crowd looks on encouragingly, if a bit baffled, is gold. She said it was hard to start off there because 'men were men and women were women' and most people didn't like standing out. Sanguinely, she says they did get chased and have a brick put through their window but 'nothing we couldn't handle'. They set to work getting as many gigs as they could, supporting bands like The Fall (whose first female member Una Baines had a big impact on the band's direction with her feminism and politics, even though she was only a member for two years). Pauline worked with legendary Manchester producer Martin Hamnet to make her *Pauline Murray and the Invisible Girls* album in 1980, which is seen by critics as underrated and ahead of its time. As one of the few female-led punk outfits, Penetration is often left out of punk retrospectives and, on being asked about that, Pauline agreed they were often overlooked and said in an interview with *Penny Black* magazine: 'I don't know whether it was because we are true North, we're not part of the Manchester scene. We are Newcastle. People thought we didn't know anything ... I'm massively outnumbered by men and I don't know whether that's got anything to do with it as well.' Their song 'Shout Above the Noise' has become one of my favourite anthems because of her sharp, fresh voice and the great melody, but also because of the message of speaking your truth no matter what else anyone else thinks you should be saying. Pauline Murray is still recording and performing music and very much speaking and singing hers.

Other interesting punks to check out include Louise Distras from Wakefield, who was described by *Kerrang!* Magazine in 2017 as 'the most exciting voice in UK punk right now' and has been involved in social campaigns, including collaborations between punk and grime artists that supported Labour leader Jeremy Corbyn's campaign for re-election. Her West Yorkshire accent introducing the album *Dreams from the Factory Floor* with a spoken word piece about how 'you work, you work, you work, devoid of soul' reminds me of another West Yorkshire punk voice, Joolz Denby, from my home city of Bradford. Born in 1955, Joolz has been a punk poet and spoken word artist since the late seventies and was instrumental in setting up the punk band New Model Army. She says she was the first woman poet in the UK to get up on stage at rock venues in the eighties when men threw lit cigarettes and glasses at her, and spat at her so much she had to shower after the show. She had a flare of mainstream literary success in the noughties when her first novel *Stone Baby* won the Crime Writers' Association's Debut Dagger Award and her third, *Billie Morgan*, was shortlisted for the Orange Prize in 2005. As a Bradfordian school girl who spent much of my spare time at the city's library, she was the first female writer I ever saw reading her work live. I remember that she seemed to speak with my accent, and that she looked cool with her tattoos and coloured hair and nose piercings. But it seems to me that she resists definition within any one particular literary or cultural scene. One of the best ways for that to continue, of course, is to live far from the main cultural centre of London. It makes you at best exotic and at worst, incomprehensible to the mainstream media, but social media is helping facilitate a move towards artists being able to build and keep a fanbase wherever they live.

There are other acts who don't easily fit into pigeonholes or ideas of the North, and it's fair to say none of them would be seen dead with their hands in the pockets of a parka and leaning against a brick wall while kestrel poo slides majestically down their face. Kathryn Williams from Liverpool, who has lived a long time in Newcastle, was shortlisted for the Mercury Music Prize in 2000, has produced fourteen albums to date and is also a published poet and novelist. Kathryn Tickell was official piper to the Mayor of Newcastle by the age of seventeen (I'm guessing her careers adviser didn't have that on their list of possible jobs). She is regarded as the world's best Northumbrian piper and is also a fiddler, composer and educator who has released fourteen of her own albums and guested on over a hundred more. She traverses the genres of jazz, world and pop music as well as the traditional music she is helping keep alive. Nadine Shah is from the seaside village of Whitburn, near Sunderland, and was nominated for the Mercury Music Prize in 2018 for her album *Holiday Destination*, whose title is taken from holidaymakers in Greece bemoaning the arrival of Syrian refugees. She has been fiercely political and socially aware since her first album and, when it was revealed that arms producers BAE Systems had unwisely been brought on board as one of the sponsors of the Festival of the North (which was the organisation that commissioned the show that led to this book), Nadine was one of the first stars to speak out and to pull out, losing her own much-needed fee. I mainly just panicked and emailed people, threatening to tut. She has also spoken out against sexism in the music industry, pointing out that female artists at festivals get 'thirty per cent, if not 60 per cent less' than men in the same slot. And she has passionately called for more older women's voices, saying there are hardly any in the charts, whereas we hear plenty from men over fifty. Her father is Pakistani and her mother white with Norwegian heritage so she said that growing up she didn't belong anywhere. At Asian weddings she would be called a 'gora', an insulting term for a white person, while at school she would be racially abused for not being white. Nadine is a rare Muslim woman's voice in music, in the North and generally, so long may she continue to make her interesting post-funk, post-punk music and keep, as *The Guardian* said, 'gobbing off' to the media.

## Lady Be Good: A Playlist of Northern Female Musicians

I want to say more about all these singers, and musicians across other genres, but all of them have recordings available online. Sometimes remembering is just about enjoying again. Make your own Northern women playlist, choose your tipple – be it Yorkshire Tea, or Newky Brown Ale – and add a regionally appropriate treat – parkin, Yorkshire Brack, fruit cake with Wensleydale (some people who have gone along with all the statements in this book will leave in outrage now I've suggested fruit cake and cheese could ever go together), or a Greggs doughnut (Newcastle's finest) – and listen. Here are some tips:

Surely opera singers are fat Italian ladies, not Northerners? At school she had a big voice and was told to stand at the back of the choir and sing quietly – there's a symbol of being a woman if ever there was one. Kathleen Ferrier went on to become one of the most loved voices in the world. Born near Preston in 1912, she had no musical training and went to work as a telephonist. After entering a piano competition where she lived in Cumbria, her husband bet her a shilling she wouldn't also enter the festival's singing competition. Not only did she enter it, she won both the piano and singing competitions, was the toast of the whole festival, and began to be in huge demand to sing on the radio (take that, school choir mistress). She went on to win more singing competitions and became a wartime entertainer, a muse for Benjamin Britten and Mahler, and sang all over the world, touching people's hearts with a quality of humanity in her voice that people of all ages and classes responded and warmed to. People were absolutely devastated when she died suddenly of cancer in 1953 at the age of just 41, after a stellar ten-year singing career. Kathleen wasn't in my show, but she was the person who would be most mentioned afterwards by older people when I asked who I'd missed out. I should have listened to recordings of her before – I can understand how she lives on for them.

Showing the power a legacy can have, Lesley Garret's career took off when she won Decca's Kathleen Ferrier Prize in 1979, and since then the daughter of railway workers from Doncaster (her mum and dad both believed in the power of music and art to transform their lives, and her dad became a headteacher, her mum a school secretary) has sung opera and crossover music all over the world, receiving a CBE in 2002 for her services to music, which, for me, include demystifying opera and showing how it's something that can be for everyone. Whether she's popping up in *Countdown*'s dictionary corner or on ITV's *Loose Women*, she's working that Yorkshire warmth and down-to-earthness to full effect, even if next time you see her she's in a full opera gown belting out the national anthem at a sporting event.

In opera the male and female roles are very clearly defined, so female opera singers are not treading on anybody's toes (unless something's gone horribly wrong in a dance number), but female band leaders? Now that's a different matter. Ivy Benson, born in 1913 in Holbeck in Leeds, became one of the top band leaders in her 1940s heyday after starting her all-girl band in 1939 and was as big a national name as Vera Lynn during those years, even though she isn't as much remembered (I would say change the record, but that's just what we're doing). Ivy's main instrument was the saxophone, and she enjoyed how it was taboo for women to blow the brass, as it were – don't even mention the trumpet or trombone. She wanted to challenge the pay gap between male and female musicians and be in control of her own outfit, so made the bold moving of putting an all-female band together. She achieved a significant victory when Ivy Benson and her All Girls Band were appointed to the prestigious role of one of the BBC's three resident dance bands in 1943, even though it led to protests from male musicians in the so-called Battle of the Saxes. At least one male arranger deliberately placed wrong notes in printed music meant for her musicians, and a delegation of representatives from the Musician's Union even went to object to the BBC, to no avail. Ivy was a perfectionist and her band were handpicked 14- and 15-year-old girls from mining and factory brass bands in Northern towns. She said: 'I could have gone out with anything as long as we looked nice,' but the music was key to her. She told her girls: 'I want you to look like women but play like men.' Her band were booked fifty-two weeks a year, from the London Palladium to Covent Garden, and also got to tour the world. They included Gracie Cole, a County Durham miner's daughter, who Ivy paid £18 a week (as against £6 for a London bus driver), and who was recognized as one of the best jazz trumpeters in the world – she went on to play in a male dance band, which was unheard of for a woman in those days. Ivy carried on entertaining with her band until 1982, and when an interviewer asked her if she was a legend, she modestly said in her Yorkshire accent: 'I'm just an ordinary person doing an ordinary job.'

Spice Girl Mel C (a fellow Northern woman, of course, from Merseyside, alongside Mel B from Leeds) presented a radio documentary on Ivy Benson and her band and one of her interviewees said they were the original Girl Power. That was an epithet also applied to Mandy and the Girlfriends, one of the first all-girl bands, from Hull, who were formed in 1965 and, like Ivy Benson's band, entertained troops in Germany, albeit in 1967. I'd particularly recommend checking out their cover of 'Money'.

We should also have some folk on the playlist, and we're lucky with that in the North, so do add in folk innovators The Unthanks, or Rachel and Becky Unthank, from Ryton in Tyne and Wear, whose debut album *Cruel Sister* from 2005 was named *MOJO* magazine folk album of the year, and whose 2019 triple-album *Lines* commemorates some of the women from this volume, including Hull's Headscarf Revolutionaries and Emily Brontë. Or how about Barnsley's Kate Rusby, known as the 'Barnsley Nightingale', who is one of the few folk singers to have been nominated for the Mercury Music Prize and who has been a serial botherer of Radio 2's Folk Awards lists. And there's Eliza Carthy of the famous folkie Carthy-Waterson clan, who hails from

Scarborough and has twice been nominated for the Mercury Music Prize, as well as receiving both folk and world music nominations for her 2003 album *Anglicana*. She was awarded an MBE in 2014 for services to folk music.

Then some pop: Tasmin Archer (another voice from my home town of Bradford) and her number one hit 'Sleeping Satellite' from 1992 will always be a favourite for me. She had been a sewing machine operator, and a clerk at Leeds magistrates' court when she first left school, until a flare of pop stardom saw her win a Breakthrough Brit Award in 1993. Or there's fellow Bradfordian Kiki Dee, born Pauline Matthews in 1947, who became the first British female act to sign to the Motown label after her hit duet with Elton John, 'Don't Go Breaking My Heart', in 1976. It had taken her a while to achieve solo success after winning a talent competition when she was ten, then working in the Bradford branch of Boots (I used to buy my first Rimmel lipsticks there. I feel they should have had a plaque. To celebrate Kiki Dee, not where I bought my lipsticks), before signing with a Leeds dance band and becoming a backing singer for acts including Dusty Springfield through the sixties. She performed with Elton John at Live Aid in 1985 and has continued releasing singles and also achieved success in West End musicals.

For more voices for our playlist, we could jump across West Yorkshire to where Leeds's Corinne Bailey Rae has sold millions of records worldwide after starting out in indie bands in Leeds and wanting to be a girl with a guitar. Following a MOBO award, several Grammy nominations and an ongoing stellar international career as a singer and recording artist, one of her songs was chosen by NASA to celebrate the *Juno* spacecraft's mission to Jupiter. I'd also be listening to 6 Music playlisted singer-songwriters Beccy Owen and Martha Hill from the North East, and, well, so many more. But it's time to meet some radio women, some of whom are among those who get to share their own music playlists with the world.

## Queens of the Airwaves

I used to work as a radio newsreader and since I was told I was too Northern to work on Northern stations, I've listened out with an interested ear for other Northern voices. I think, at its best, radio can be your most intimate friend. Just one person whispering into your ear, anchoring you in a time and place, informing you, entertaining you, soothing you. But it's all about the voice, and, as we know, Northern voices are not a neutral topic.

Two of our most respected RP broadcasters are from humble Northern backgrounds and had elocution lessons at the start of their careers in order to enter the hallowed portals of your lugholes via the hallowed portals of the BBC. Joan Bakewell, born in Stockport into a lower-middle-class family in 1933, became head girl at Stockport High School for Girls, then won a scholarship to Cambridge to study economics. She started out as a studio manager, then moved into television, presenting on the topical and arts show *Late Night Line-Up* from 1965 to 1972 where she was often called 'the thinking-man's crumpet', which I think tells us pretty much all we need to know about attitudes in the sixties to women in the media. She went on to present groundbreaking and award-winning documentaries and was made a Labour peer in 2011. However, in 2020 she spoke out at a literature festival to say that she had been told she wasn't getting as much telly and radio work anymore because she sounded 'too posh', the Northern accent she lost to fit the standards of the day ironically now having become more acceptable on air again.

Jenni Murray was born into a working-class family in Barnsley in 1950 and is best known as the presenter of Radio 4's *Woman's Hour* from 1987 until 2020, where, as well as providing a probing and compassionate voice on how topical issues affected women, she also provoked huge listener response when she opened up about personal matters like her breast cancer, menopause and lifelong struggles with her weight. She studied drama at the University of Hull (where she recalled directing a production the local school children pronounced as 'Turd of Turd Hall') and had elocution lessons from the age of five because her class-aspirational mother didn't want her talking 'like the other kids on the estate'. She found her mother's expectations of her very onerous in some ways, saying in an interview with *Third Way* magazine: 'Her generation of women were so tightly laced . . . then suddenly here was this daughter with Dusty Springfield eye make-up and Cathy McGowan hair.' But that RP accent was her passport to working in local radio for the BBC, then presenting *Newsnight*, before going on to become one of the country's best-known and loved broadcasters, being made a dame in 2011.

In contrast to these two women who had to erase the Northernness from their voices to be acceptable as journalistic voices of authority, Liz Kershaw and Sara Cox's Lancashire burrs are crucial factors in their identities as presenters. They, of course, are music and talk presenters rather than journalists, so you could argue there's less of an issue with how much 'authority' they carry, and that the association of a Northern accent with warmth is a plus.

Perhaps so much so that it might obscure how skilled they are as presenters. Liz, originally from Rochdale, is the second-longest-serving female national radio presenter in the country (after Annie Nightingale), having started out on air in 1987 on Radio 1. She said she was groped there several times and it was an intimidating place to be as a young woman. She was instrumental in setting up the radio station 6 Music in 2002, then saving it when it was threatened with closure in 2010, and is recognized as a dedicated and knowledgeable advocate of new bands. She's an outspoken critic of BBC management and is well aware of presenters' subordinate position, saying, 'We're just like pawns in a game.' Her cheery voice is probably more familiar to me than that of some of my friends.

I'm also a huge fan of Sara Cox. She was born in 1974 and grew up as the youngest of five children on a Bolton farm (she's written a memoir about growing up in the countryside called *Till the Cows Come Home*), and was scouted for some modelling as a teenager and put on telly's *The Girlie Show* when they discovered she could (more than) string a sentence together. Along with presenter Zoe Ball, she was often pictured in the Nineties with a pint in her hand, coming out of a club, as the media discovered the surprising fact that some attractive young women like drinking and socialising too and coined a whole new word – 'ladette' – to cover this apparently new and exciting development. For me, the most interesting thing about her is that she's as funny as a stand-up comic and as lyrical as a poet when she's in full flow (though her full flow sometimes gets her into trouble, such as when Radio 1 issued an apology in 2000 after she wished the Queen Mother a happy hundredth birthday by saying, 'she smells of wee, bless her, but we all love her').

Sometimes when I hear her glorious flat vowels and rolling R's I'm reminded of how rare it still is to hear the proper Northern accents I grew up with on a national platform, and yet of how it will always in some way sound like home.

## Activist Voices

Because of this, I, and others, can fall into the trap of associating a Northern accent with warm, cosy homeliness and failing to notice when something new is being said. This can be an advantage, as we have seen with comedians like Sarah Millican and Victoria Wood, when their friendly tones can act as a Trojan horse for sharp social critique. (I've noticed that even when I think I've managed to sound really, really cross about bad service in a shop or a café, people will still respond to me as if I'm joking or making a cheerful observation.) Similarly, I have always loved reading the distinct Northern sensibilities of Guardian writers Lucy Mangan and Grace Dent, whose references to taking your coat off inside or you won't feel the benefit (when you go outside), Toby Taverns and proper gravy felt like they were subverting the London media world I was both fascinated, and repelled by, from within, but who are also both subtly sharp critics of Southern cultural colonialism. I will end this chapter by noting that there is now more opportunity than there has ever been for Northern female voices to be heard. The advent of social media means people can take the microphone into their own hands and carve out their own soundscapes. I still notice a relative lack of Northern women doing this (at poetry and comedy events, for example, or in political activism and online) and wonder if it stems back to historic issues of confidence and the association of 'laddishness' with creativity.

The world of spoken word can be a litmus test for the sort of things people want to say, as it can be a free-for-all space, literally. Most people start by getting up on stage at an open-mike night, or posting videos online. Toria Garbutt, for example, grew up in Knottingley in West Yorkshire, home of the last deep mine to close in Britain, and has supported legendary poet John Cooper Clarke on tour with her hard-hitting dialect poems of working-class female life: 'It's alrate being a Knottla lass/it's the other stuff you can't talk about/like your mum fucking off and your sister on smack'.

Other working-class women poets and performers in this generation include Louise Fazackerley from Wigan, Kirran Shah and Kirsty Taylor from Bradford, and Vicky Foster from Hull. There is now the possibility of spoken word artists like these getting Arts Council and broadcasting opportunities. This is a shift for a scene which has previously seen itself as 'grass roots', but I'm a fierce advocate of this professionalisation because it actually means creatives without a separate financial safety net can afford to take part.

Doing a lot of poetry gigs in the 2000s, I kept finding myself performing alongside amazing young black poets who were savvy, politically aware, and virtuoso performers. It turned out they had a lineage in common – two exceptional Northern women were mentoring new generations of voices, sacrificing the energy that a lot of poets put into making sure their own voices are heard and brands nurtured. Leeds Young Authors was founded by inspirational poet Khadijah Ibrahiim in 2003. Born of Jamaican parents in Leeds, with Jamaican grandparents of the Windrush generation who arrived to what she said was a 'cold' welcome in Leeds (in both senses of the word), she started the project to give young people in deprived areas of Leeds the chance to tackle issues like racism and poverty. Leeds Young Authors became the first ever non-US team invited to take part in the US's biggest poetry slam competition, and – spoiler alert – the six young people's triumphant performance against the odds is captured in the indie documentary film *We Are Poets*. Similarly in Manchester, Shirley May has worked with generations of young people through her Young Identity project and many of them are now taking up the microphone themselves for a living. Both Khadijah and Shirley are exceptional poets and performers themselves but it's only in very recent years that their work has been more widely published and shared by a literary establishment that has often been slow to take on board voices from outside the white, middle-class norm.

Similarly, disabled people are beginning to claim a voice. Rainbow-haired poet and comedian Jackie Hagan from Skelmersdale has become one of the biggest names in disability arts with her frank, hilarious one-woman shows – including in the hit show *Some People Have Too Many Legs* – tackling her working-class identity and mental illness as well as her physical disability, which stemmed from a leg amputation. I have also learnt far more about the world of LGBTQI+ activism by hearing poets talk and rhyme about it on pub and arts centre and festival stages. Tom Juniper from Sheffield has been open about their transition to a non-binary identity, as has AJ McKenna from Newcastle. Sometimes in mainstream discourse it can feel as if we're not too far away from the 1960s, when Liverpool's April Ashley became one of the first people in the country to have gender reassignment surgery but was outed by the *Sunday People* newspaper in 1961 while working as a model in

London. Her then husband was able to have their marriage annulled in 1970 on the grounds that she was legally a man (she was finally legally recognized as a woman in 2005). Although I can't claim spoken word stages are a utopia (there's far too much spilled beer and vape smoke and interminably long nights of young men rapping about their penises for that), I do think they symbolise a future in which more people are accepted for their complex, multi-faceted identities, including their beautiful Northernness and all the other things that make up who they are.

Some Northern actors also use their platforms in order to raise their activist voices. Cherrylee Houston, from Morecambe, who has played Izzy on *Coronation Street* since 2010, was awarded an MBE in 2021 for her advocacy of disability arts for young people and fellow disabled actors - having herself been told as a young aspiring thespian that no one would want to employ an actor who used a wheelchair. Merseyside's Liz Carr, who is best known for playing Clarissa Mullery in the BBC forensic series *Silent Witness* has spoken at many rallies over the past twenty years on topics like the right of disabled people to leave independently and on the potential discrimination of assisted suicide. She says she doesn't see why, as an electric-wheelchair-using woman, she can't act in dramas set in any era - and, during the pandemic, tweeted an injunction which holds for so many of our Northern speaker-outers:

'Survival is a deeply political act
Survival is an act of resistance'.

# 8

# Stage and Screen

Nowadays you might know someone is Northern if they open their mouth and Northern vowels fall out. They sound Northern. It's not likely to be because they are wearing headscarves or clogs or a pinny. They don't look Northern. In fact, we've had fashion shops for a while here in the North, along with aeroplanes and streetlights. This chapter will look at some women who have made us see the North in particular ways. Some of them are household names, some of them have achieved mainstream recognition, some of them were pioneers against the odds whose contribution is only now being recognized. But through their performances, their shows and their art, all of them have changed ideas about who and what the North, and a Northern woman, could be and can be in the future.

## Screenwriters and Playwrights

I think comedians and singer-songwriters have something in common, which is that they have the power to define a place in other people's minds. As with novelists, they can reflect and create new imaginative worlds, but they can also shape how we see and hear a region. Perhaps this is even more the case for these four women playwrights and scriptwriters, who have reached mass audiences in the post-war era and created characters who represent people of the North (particularly women) whose voices are not usually heard elsewhere. As we will see, this has usually been welcomed by audiences, but has provoked more complicated reactions from the establishment.

## Shelagh Delaney

I first encountered Shelagh Delaney's play *A Taste of Honey* in GCSE drama while badly acting out scenes from it; probably while Richard Dobson was throwing chairs around the room and I was wondering whether we'd get cornflake cake again for school dinners was not the best setting to discover it, or her. I am absolutely astonished, for example, to find out that she wrote it when she was just 19 years old. Nineteen! Just three years older than I was when I did that GCSE. She was one of very, very few working-class voices, and female voices (never mind the double whammy of the two), writing plays when it premiered in 1958. She had written it in two weeks on a borrowed typewriter after seeing a play by Terence Rattigan and realising she could write a better one. Her story of alcoholic single mother Helen, whose white daughter Jo has a relationship with a black sailor, becomes pregnant and is cared for by her gay friend Geoffrey, was a key example of the 'kitchen sink' dramas that became popular in the 1950s and sixties. It was radical in challenging the idea that women would find fulfilment in marriage and motherhood and was made into a film starring Rita Tushingham, the one we watched in GCSE drama.

Shelagh was mentored by Joan Littlewood but received some flak for the controversial subject matter of her play, and Salford Council thought it portrayed the town in a bad light. When the play became a massive success, though, they asked her for the original manuscript for their library. Brilliantly, Shelagh, daughter of a Salford bus driver, turned them down and gave it to Littlewood instead. *The Spectator* also slammed the play, saying it was 'the inside story of a savage culture observed by a genuine cannibal'. A genuine cannibal? I'm fairly sure Shelagh didn't actually eat people. Though maybe a patronising reviewer from London might have tasted nice on toast. With some honey. The *Daily Mail* blamed it all on the 1944 Education Act giving working-class girls like Shelagh ideas above their station. She knew exactly what sort of stereotypes she was up against, saying in an interview: 'Usually North Country people are portrayed as gormless, while actually they are very alive and cynical.'

Jeanette Winterson has argued that Shelagh would have had more subsequent success if she'd had some of the support and acclaim an equivalent man would have had. She said in a piece for *The Guardian*'s 'My Hero' slot: 'She was the first working-class woman playwright and we let her go.' Shelagh's obituary in *The Guardian* calls her subsequent writing career 'mercurial and chequered', though she kept writing until she died in 2011 and had some more successes, including the cult film *Charlie Bubbles* in 1967, starring Albert Finney as a writer having a breakdown, and the screenplay *Dancing with a Stranger* in 1985, which was about Ruth Ellis, the last woman to be hanged in Britain. (It seems to me rather that she didn't have much inclination or interest in pursuing a creative career in a nice, responsible, linear, middle-class way and tended to write what she wanted when she wanted.) Famously, Morrissey was obsessed with Shelagh Delaney, his fellow Salfordian writer, and featured her photograph on the covers of 'Girlfriend in a Coma' and *Louder than Bombs*. He said, 'At least 50 per cent of my reason for writing can be blamed on Shelagh Delaney', though we shouldn't hold that against her.

## Andrea Dunbar

You'd hope that by the time Andrea Dunbar burst onto the scene in the eighties, as another astonishingly young female working-class writer from a Northern city with a deeply precocious and gritty play, that things would have moved on. But she was also criticised by her home city, in this case Bradford, for portraying it in a bad light, and was not offered the mentorship she needed. In fact, her story feels like one of the most tragic in this book. Often, Northern women feel sustained and comforted by the places they come from, even if they move away. But life on the Buttershaw council estate only became harder for Andrea once her writing achieved success.

She was born in 1961 and wrote her first play – *The Arbor*, about a schoolgirl who gets pregnant – as a CSE assignment in 1977, so she was even more of a prodigy than Shelagh Delaney. She'd joined the drama course after she was set an essay titled 'Why I Don't Like Cooking' as punishment for not bringing the ingredients to her home economics lesson. She wittily argued that it was middle class to be making raspberry pavlovas – what the people on the estate needed was to cook joints of meat. Her school's head of drama asked her to join his course and her life changed forever. *The Arbor* premiered at the Royal Court, London, in 1980 when she was nineteen. It was based on her own experience of living on an estate and giving birth to a stillborn baby after an abusive relationship. A friend at the women's refuge where she was staying had entered her green-ink filled exercise-book pages into a national youth competition and the Royal Court's director Max Stafford-Clark recognized her talent. He then commissioned her next play, *Rita, Sue and Bob Too* – another autobiographical piece about two girls having an affair with the same married man – which transferred to New York after its London run and became a hit film in 1987. Its tagline was 'Thatcher's Britain With Its Knickers Down'.

Newspapers described her as the new Shelagh Delaney, and the *Daily Mail* (always to be relied on for a disparaging quote about a working-class Northern woman) described her as 'a genius straight from the slums with black teeth and a brilliant smile'. *Black Teeth and a Brilliant Smile* became the title of the unconventional biography Yorkshire-born Adelle Stripe wrote about her in 2018. It uses Andrea's voice to recount her story of becoming a feted writer, while at the same time struggling to hold her life together on the estate where she was bringing up three children from three different dads, being patronised by London-based cultural figures who wanted her to churn out more material about the life she was struggling to live, and being criticised by family members, the council and other residents for making Buttershaw look bad. At the time of the film, Bradford was launching its 'Bradford's Bouncing Back' campaign to increase business to the city. I lived there then, and remember it as one in a long line of alliterative campaigns to convince people that Bradford wasn't in terminal post-industrial decline ('Bradford's Bloomin' Boomin'!' I've made that one up, but they can have that for next time . . . ).

Andrea's mother blamed the fact that she had (a small amount of) money from the films for the fact that she was able to, effectively, drink herself to death. She actually died of a brain haemorrhage after falling off a pub stool, aged just 29, which may not necessarily have been due to her heavy drinking. Although the city of Bradford has failed to memorialise her as fully as it has done for its famous sons J. B. Priestley, Frederick Delius and David Hockney, she has been remembered more recently with a 2010 film by Clio Barnard – *The Arbor* – which innovatively entwines an exploration of her life with a version of her play filmed in front of current residents of the Buttershaw Estate. The film mainly focuses on the story of Andrea's eldest daughter, Lorraine, whose devastatingly sad story of enduring racism (her father was Pakistani, though she was brought up as white on the deeply racist estate), neglect and the death of her mother while growing up leads to a legacy of addiction and abuse. (This is not a date-night movie. I'd recommend something more uplifting for that – *Schindler's List*, say.) Even this garnered the kind of casually insulting language which posh London newspaper writers thought was okay to use. A *Guardian* review of the film referred to Andrea as a 'slumdog prodigy', which made my jaw drop when I read it. Andrea's own story and life as a writer is explored more thoroughly in Adelle Stripe's book and in the adaptation of that into a touring play by Leeds playwright Lisa Holdsworth. In it, she imagines the advice that Andrea would give to somebody from Bradford wanting to be a writer today.

> Get a proper f***king job. Seriously. Learn to be a bricklayer, work in a shop . . . you'll be happier, healthier and you'll probably be better off. Writing is the hardest thing I've done. You see me up here, and you think I've made it. But it's not all it's cracked up to be. You make

money, but then you spend it. Come up with a good idea and they'll only want you to come up with another and another and another. And then when you haven't got another decent thought in your head . . . that's when they'll send you back where you came from. Because you'll always be an outsider to them. A novelty. You see, they think they want to hear the true voice of the north. But they don't. Because the truth hurts.

## Kay Mellor

If Andrea Dunbar's story was a soap opera, then it was a particularly dark arc in *EastEnders*, while Kay Mellor's is *Coronation Street* – still tough but with a tinge of warmth and humour, which is appropriate since she always wanted to write for that show, and eventually did. Born in 1951 in Leeds, her mum divorced her dad after being a victim of domestic violence, and raised Kay as a single parent. Kay said they didn't have much and lived in a council house but their mum let her and her two brothers dream and encouraged creativity. When Kay was 16, she became pregnant to her boyfriend Anthony Mellor and they married when Kay was seventeen. She said in an interview with the *Jewish Chronicle* that she thought it was the end of her life but they're still together and live in Leeds. She says she wouldn't know her and husband now: 'We were just a little lad and lass off the estate.' Her mum had made her promise that if she had the baby she would finish her education later, which she did when her two children were of school age, progressing to finish a drama degree at Bretton Hall College in Leeds in 1983. When she got an acting role in the soap *Albion Market*, she realised she wanted to write for it and submitted a sample script. By the late eighties she had written an episode of *Coronation Street* and storylined ten more, written seven episodes of *Brookside*, and co-created the children's drama *Children's Ward* with her fellow *Brookside* writer Paul Abbott. She said working there with fellow Northern writers Jimmy McGovern and Frank Cottrell Boyce was exciting because they were all encouraged to be passionate about their writing and, if they had a big episode coming up, to lock themselves away and write until they cried. She said they were all writing from their own lives and hadn't heard many voices like theirs on telly while they were growing up – there was nothing wrong with middle-class writers writing about their lives, she said, as long as they were passionate about it.

I first knew of her work when the 1995 drama about Bradford sex workers *Band of Gold* was broadcast on ITV. It's kind of weird to think that at the time that was filmed, I'd been living in a very grotty bedsit a few miles up the hill from Bradford city centre, above a massage parlour called Pearls where one of the other tenants informed me 'the landlord is just going for a jump' on his way to see us. It was also the time in *The Arbor* when Andrea Dunbar's daughter was struggling her way into adulthood while working in a massage parlour in Huddersfield. This gritty screen fodder was real life. Kay's blend of humour and Northern reality proved popular with drama commissioners and audiences, and she has gone on to become the queen of drama about ordinary Northern lives.

She says she usually writes about women because they seem to be much more talkative and multi-layered than men – growing up she remembered sitting in Littlewoods and her mum and three aunties all talking over each other. She formed her own production company, Rollem, in 2000 to allow her more control over her productions in a London-centric industry, and the decision has paid off. Its hits, garnering millions of viewers, include *The Chase*, *In the Club* and *The Syndicate*. She was awarded an OBE in 2009, was made a fellow of the Royal Television Society in 2016, and given a Special Recognition from industry magazine *Broadcast* in 2020.

Mindful of how difficult it is to break into the world of television from outside the industry, she has set up an award for new writers in conjunction with Leeds Playhouse and has called for television to expand outside the 'circle of trust' of the usual people in order to give more voices like hers a chance. One of those voices she supported and mentored has gone on to become a giant of TV drama: Sally Wainwright.

## Sally Wainwright

Sally Wainwright, whose hits include *Happy Valley* and *Last Tango in Halifax*, writes series that are full of social realism and brilliantly acerbic Northern women and wit. She had wanted to write for *Coronation Street* from the age of nine, and eventually did from 1994 to 1999. She says Kay Mellor took her under her wing and encouraged her to branch out from soaps and create her own original content.

Her journey was one of a determined writer who always knew that's what she wanted to do. Born in 1963 in Huddersfield, she went to school in Sowerby Bridge, studied English literature at the University of York and got a writing agent after taking a play to the Edinburgh Festival. She then worked as a bus driver while developing scripts (they do say everything ends up in your writing – she wrote a drama series called *Jane Hall* in 2006 about a female bus driver in

London) and went on to work on *The Archers* and *Coronation Street?*. After being encouraged by Kay Mellor she wrote a selection of hit TV shows.

However, she really tapped a popular seam with *Last Tango in Halifax*, which was based initially on her mother's story of sudden late-life love after meeting an old school friend on Friends Reunited. This story of increasingly entwined Yorkshire families won her a BAFTA for best writer in 2012 and a BAFTA for best series. As well as it being a cracking family drama with warm, believable characters, her signature snappy dialogue and a beautiful filming location in the Calder Valley, it really depicts something about the North that I had never seen before: multiple classes and ages all interacting in the same place but all reflecting facets of Yorkshire-ness. It was also described as quietly subversive for having three strong female leads over the age of forty.

Sally has often spoken proudly of Yorkshire and its beauty – she says she's irrationally proud to be from Yorkshire and to be a woman, so to be recognized as a Yorkshirewoman is especially satisfying. She says writing about Yorkshire isn't necessarily a conscious choice but that in order to write authentically, she needs to write in her own vernacular. We see this in the smash-hit crime drama *Happy Valley* (so-called because that's what the police call the area due to its drug use), or in her wonderful drama of 2016 *To Walk Invisible*, which told the story of the Brontë sisters in a more real way than I'd ever seen them portrayed on screen before. I felt as though they could have been young women I'd grown up with, as though I knew them.

When asked in an interview why she had only attained such a powerful position in television recently, despite having written for years, Sally had to overcome her Yorkshire modesty to say that given inequalities over pay and opportunities in the media (only 14 per cent of primetime television is written by women), she'd asked her agent whether she thought she was getting paid the same as all the other people who've won three BAFTAs for writing, 'which was a bit of a dig because I'm pretty sure I'm the only person who's won three BAFTAs for writing'. She had been profiled on the arts show *The South Bank Show* in 2017, though said she thought, given how prolific and consistent she is, they probably should have profiled her fifteen years earlier. It was clearly hard for her to say that out loud to somebody else, for reasons I identify with. It can feel like a risk to point out these inequalities: 'That's the trouble with being a woman. If you do say something like that, you sound like you've got a chip on your shoulder and you're being angry. Rather than just saying it like it is ... but I think I have got a chip on my shoulder about being fat and northern. A fat northern chip. Sounds good, doesn't it?'

## *Corrie's* Women

Nothing has done more to contribute to the aesthetic of the North than *Coronation Street*'s women. Ever since Tony Warren had the idea for a soap called 'Florizel Street' in 1959, and it was commissioned for an initial thirteen episodes in 1960, working-class Northern women have been visible in all their funny, tragic, powerful glory. As Amanda Barrie, who played Alma Baldwin, said in the documentary *Queens of Coronation Street*: 'You didn't have a voice before. If you were Northern, you played someone who was sweeping the steps in someone else's rather grand drama.'

And what a grand drama *Coronation Street* has been over the past sixty years, the longest running soap in the world and still regularly number one in the television ratings. Tony, an openly gay man (at a time when homosexual acts were illegal) from a working-class community in Pendlebury, Lancashire, created women who were real, strong and Northern in a way that had never been seen on screen. They were the women he grew up with as he was hiding under the table hearing his aunties gossiping with his mother and his gran, and they were the women celebrated in the folk culture around him. He was a child actor on BBC Radio's *Children's Hour* and has said he first got the idea when fellow actor Violet Carson (who would go on to play the legendary 'battleaxe' Ena Sharples in the soap) played the children a dialect song called 'Bowton's Yard' that described the occupants of a street of terraced houses, each in turn, up to Number 12.

I was an avid watcher from the mid-eighties until 2013. The reason I eventually stopped was because I knew there was a storyline looming in which the trans character Hayley Cropper (the first permanent trans character in a long-running serial when she appeared in 1998), played by the sublime Julie Hesmondhalgh, was going to die (in a powerful 'right to die' storyline in which she killed herself while suffering terminal pancreatic cancer). Having been deeply invested in her love story with geeky Roy, the street's acceptance of her transformation, and her eventual marriage (once it was legal by 2010, possibly partly because of the impact of this groundbreaking screen relationship), I didn't think I could cope with her death, after Hesmondhalgh's departure from the street was announced in January 2013. It seemed a good time to bow out, so I was done by the episode in which she took a cocktail of drugs and lay down on their bed with Roy's arms around her while he played Vaughan Williams's 'Lark Ascending' (I didn't know that's what the death scene was until researching this. I definitely couldn't have coped).

Actually, perhaps that corroborates a critique of the soap in recent years. As it has competed more with the ratings juggernaut that is BBC One's *EastEnders*, it has become more and more about gritty realism and has lost some of the humour that has always been so key to its success. On the other hand, some of that humour may be what has allowed Northerners to be taken less seriously. That feels like a big statement, so let me qualify it a bit. *Coronation Street*'s characters have often been larger than life, a bit cartoonish. You could use the word 'grotesque'. Usually that's used to mean repulsive, or ugly. But another meaning of 'grotesque' is caricatured, larger than life, so exaggerated as to be outside the norm and become weird. There's a whole strain of 'Northern Grotesque' imagery – seaside postcards with their women with huge boobs and bottoms, pantomime dames, the mother-in-laws Cissie and Ada played by comedians Les Dawson and Roy Barraclough. In these caricatures, Northern women (or performances of them by men) become hyper-women. Their feminine characteristics are made bigger – they are, as the young people say, 'extra'. The thing is, lots of non-Northerners have a tendency to see even ordinary Northernness as exaggerated in some way. It is outside of their normal and can seem a bit put-on or camp. A few times when I've appeared on telly I've been described as 'like a Victoria Wood character' (thank you, anonymous Twitter people). It's as if being audibly Northern can in itself feel 'a bit much' and unreal to someone who is used to the norm of a woman who doesn't have much of a noticeable regional accent.

Many of *Coronation Street*'s legendary female characters are perceived as unreal and grotesque (which is both fascinating and a bit scary to some people). But paradoxically, they're based on how lots of Northern – particularly working-class – women do exaggerate their feminine characteristics, how they vamp and camp it up, while at the same time laughing at themselves and the ridiculousness of the world. The most common terms *Corrie* stars themselves use to describe the soap's female characters are 'strong women' and 'real women'. Bet Lynch and Elsie Tanner and Karen McDonald and Carla Connor are gloriously full-bodied, big-haired, large-gobbed characters who took up space and shone and purred and fur-coated their way down those famous cobbles and exposed their necks in deep full-throated laughs or to roar at the small, inadequate men who were the limp white mice to their big, predatory, unapologetic leopard (prints). They are the ultimate resilient copers, though their glamorous exteriors hide a lot of inner pain. When I said I was researching *Corrie*, several strong Northern women I know independently mentioned Bet Lynch's line, delivered as she sits in immaculate make-up, a silver blouse and large, swaying hoop earrings: 'You see this smile, Betty? It's not really a smile, it's the lid on a scream,' which must have struck a lasting chord for many women just getting on with things.

There again, in *Coronation Street*, the sanctimonious, grey women who disapproved of the bold, brassy women were also larger than life in their own way. My own favourite is Deirdre Barlow's mother Blanche Hunt, played by Maggie Jones. Her one-liners were the best. She's an unusual choice for some-one's favourite character, though (I always was perverse).

Back to the battleaxe versus the bombshell. That dynamic was set up in the very earliest episodes of the show, as Ena Sharples (hairnet, hatchet face, handbag) faced off against Pat Phoenix's Elsie Tanner (dyed hair, full make-up, shinier handbag) who railed against her penchant for gossip in a shouting match across the cobbles: 'We don't need sewers round 'ere, we've got Ena Sharples!' This was a matriarchal society where the women were very much in charge. It's hard to remember now how revolutionary it was at the time to hear real Northern working-class accents on the telly. The news was still read by extremely posh women wearing ball-gowns (only the ballgowns have changed really).

And it's not just the characters that are tough – the actors themselves have to be strong, especially as more and more episodes are broadcast in a week, with scenes filmed out of order and requiring emotionally demanding acting. Interestingly, the actors themselves are given an initial char-acter outline but very little other direction about how to play the character. So, really, the characters are a creation both of the scriptwriters and of the women who embody them.

Longevity is another key feature of many of the street's best-loved stars. They provide continuity at a time where more of us move around and away, the continuity that used to come from people staying on one terraced street for their whole lives. Over the years I've probably spent more time with, say, corner shop owner Rita Fairclough (played by Barbara Knox) than I have with most of my own relatives.

The soap has also been a training ground and launchpad for some of our greatest contemporary Northern female actors, including Julie Hesmondhalgh, Suranne Jones, Sarah Lancashire and Katherine Kelly. It turns out there are so many more *Corrie* women I could be paying tribute to.

As I have come to understand while writing this, if you're a regular viewer, it becomes sort of hardwired in you, like the siren song of that cornet theme tune. It entwines with your own perceptions of the North so that they are part shaped by *Coronation Street*, and your viewing of it is shaped by them in turn. Much as I thought my comic writing has been influenced by Victoria Wood, I now realise that *Coronation Street*'s language must have been a significant influence as well.

The humour and the trope of the 'strong woman' perhaps mask the fact that many of these women were suffering significant trauma in a socio-economic context that had exploited them and reduced their choices for years. Or maybe it makes that trauma and suffering palatable.

I am surprised, though, that *Coronation Street* still hasn't got enough significant ethnic minority characters. In 2020, they were advertising again for BAME scriptwriters and acknowledged they're still not representing the diverse ethnic makeup of the North. Remembering my time leading writing sessions with the hilarious young women of all-Muslim girls school, Feversham School in Bradford, I think it's a no-brainer that *Corrie* could introduce at least a couple of larger than life Asian families who would simultaneously hark back to the strong matriarchies and tight-knit interwoven families of its early years, with plenty of conflict, humour and a closer reflection of today's North.

## Screen Visionaries

I have focused so much on *Coronation Street* because its depictions of Northern women are the most iconic and the most enduring. There have also, of course, been key moments and characters in the other Northern soaps. Channel 4's soap *Brookside*, set on a close in Liverpool, featured the first pre-watershed lesbian kiss on British television in 1994. *Hollyoaks*, the more youth-focused soap, featured the first trans actor playing a trans character. It has also been the first soap to feature disabled actors playing disabled roles, such as autistic actor Tylan Grant, who responded to a national call-out for autistic actors and has been playing the role of Brooke Hathaway since 2018 (they might eventually get to the point where an autistic person on telly is allowed to have autistic friends, but we may be a way off that yet). They have also spoken out about the stigma they face as a black and a non-binary actor. Or we could go back earlier to *Byker Grove* and its pioneering work in children's drama with its gay kiss in 1994.

However, in recent years the biggest impact on the representation of Northern women on screen has come from the success of Nicola Schindler's Red Productions, founded in 1998 from the front room of her home in Manchester after she decided to produce her own work, having been a script editor for Manchester's Granada Television. The work she has collaborated on with writer Sally Wainwright, such as *Happy Valley*, *Last Tango in Halifax* and *Scott & Bailey* (as well as Russell T Davies's groundbreaking drama *Queer as Folk*), is some of the country's most successful drama. Schindler was born in Rochdale in 1968 to a schoolteacher mum and solicitor dad, and went to the University of Cambridge where, she said, it was the first time that being from Rochdale made her seem exotic. Like Sally Wainwright, she downplays the intentional representation of the North in the productions her multi-million-pound company creates, but says she is drawn to shows that feel true and authentic to her. She still lives and works in Manchester (significant when so much of the media industry is still focused on London. That is shifting, and will even more now Channel 4 is going to be based in Leeds).

Now, imagine a room full of television's most powerful people. Mostly men. Sat with their colleagues, waiters and waitresses discreetly leaning across their shoulders to fill up the wine glasses, new business cards being fingered in pockets. A diminutive, brown-haired, middle-aged woman takes to the stage and smiles. 'Thank you for the great honour of being the first old lady to deliver the annual MacTaggart lecture', she begins, then starts delivering the zingers, still smiling as she hits them. She muses on her predecessors delivering the lecture ('Kevin Spacey . . . he proved to be a good choice . . . And by an extraordinary coincidence, three people with the same surname – Murdoch. What are the chances of that, eh?').

The woman delivering this keynote address at the Edinburgh International Television Festival in 2019? Dorothy Byrne. She was born in Paisley in 1953, educated in Blackpool and Manchester, then at Sheffield University, and moved to Manchester to produce *World in Action* for Granada before becoming head of news and current affairs at Channel 4 in 1998. She said in her lecture that she couldn't believe how posh everybody was when she first went to work there. They'd all been to Westminster School. She urged the Channel 4 workers in the new Leeds headquarters to 'really move out of London. Not pretend to move out of London to your holiday home' (this may have been a reference to the difficulty involved in getting BBC workers to move from London to Salford when the Media City complex opened there in 2011 with the aim of decentralising BBC production). She went on to call on the big ideas that used to characterise television broadcasting to come back, instead of television leaving the field to books and podcasts and Ted talks. Though she pointed out that in order for those big ideas to reflect all of society, they needed to be made by a greater range of people than they are now, at a time when only 2.2 per cent of directors come from ethnic minority backgrounds and only 25 per cent of them are women. She also recounted how her former boss once sent her home because she looked flushed and unwell (he had no idea what the menopause was), called strongly for more fact-checking in news and better working conditions for female freelancers, and called Boris Johnson and Jeremy Corbyn cowards for refusing to be interviewed. She is basically as much of a Northern queen as Cartimandua, in my book.

## Ngozi Onwurah

I am conscious throughout this book of the women who slip between the gaps in the narrative. Who are forgotten or who are never noticed in the first place. The ones who succeed against tremendous odds. The ones who are doing the right thing in the wrong place or at the wrong time. Most of them are not in this book at all, of course – I don't know about them.

Ngozi Onwurah was the first British black woman to make a full-length feature film when she directed and wrote the dystopian science fiction fantasy *Welcome II the Terrordome* in 1995. It took another decade before Amma Asante made *A Way of Life*. Dorothy Byrne's statistic about how more than twenty-five years on, only 2.2 per cent of directors are from ethnic minorities puts that even further into context. *Terrordome* was panned by mainly male critics, who saw its violent representation of black people killing black people in ghettos, and being killed by white police officers, as negative and detrimental to race relations. It was not the film a black woman was supposed to be making.

Ngozi Onwurah was a girl who once scrubbed herself with Vim in the bath because she wanted to be white, like her mother. She twirled round and round in a white dress like Wonder Woman, thinking the transformation might happen if she wished hard enough. She felt guilty that boys smeared the front door of their Newcastle flat in dog poo. That didn't happen to the mothers with nice white children. Why did Auntie Eileen give her and her sister black dolls for Christmas instead of a Tiny Tears? She hated that doll, but not as much as she hated her own reflection. She said all this on film in her powerful, devastating 1988 short, *Coffee Coloured Children*, which laid bare the casual racism of 1970s Newcastle, and which she made after attending a film school in London for three years, with a grant from Channel 4.

She and her sister and brother were born to a white mother who married a Nigerian medical student and moved to Nigeria with him, until he sent her back to Newcastle during the civil war. It was supposed to be temporary as she was pregnant, but after that they never lived together as a family again. Ngozi's sister Chi Onwurah is now the MP for Newcastle Central. She originally trained as an electrical engineer (which she says was an even more sexist profession than the House of Commons) and is now an advocate for girls taking STEM subjects, as well as having been Labour's shadow minister for business and then for culture. I once performed at a Newcastle gig where she was the guest of honour, and when one of the stage lights starting flickering, she unfussily got on a chair and fixed it for us. That's the sort of multitasking you want in your MP . . .

Their mother, Madge Onwurah, is another remarkable Northern woman. She features in a 1991 short by her daughter, playing herself. She was diagnosed with breast cancer while pregnant with her son, then had a mastectomy two days after she gave birth to him. After that, she came to feel ashamed of her body and felt it would never be appreciated again. The film, *The Body Beautiful,* depicts her fantasising about having sex with a young black man 'who I loved for his ordinariness'. The scene is juxtaposed with shots of a version of the younger Ngozi as a model, being photographed and appreciated, and perhaps objectified. It is an unusual, beautiful, sensual depiction of a mother and daughter accepting their bodies, their sexuality and each other. You watch it (you can, in fact – it's free on the BFI player) and think that here's a voice to watch out for. Same with the *Terrordome* film, which starts out with a depiction of the Igbo Landing, in which a group of slaves drowned themselves rather than work as slaves. The same characters are then shown in a city where they are stuck, haunted by violence, anger and trauma, sound-tracked by songs including the Public Enemy one that gave the film its name. It came out in the same year as *Four Weddings and a Funeral.* Hugh Grant genially swearing as he gets into a morning suit for yet another wedding, it is not. Ngozi calls it her 'angry film'. The mid-Nineties, though, were a time when we were supposed to feel that inequalities of gender, ethnicity and class were over. We were all multicultural New Labour supporters now. Somehow this film burst in with a shriek when people were only prepared to hear whispers.

In the last couple of years, Ngozi's achievement in film-making has begun to be recognized by academics, film historians and audiences. Yes, it's technically rough round the edges, financed on a micro-budget as it was, with money scraped together, including some from Channel 4. But the multiple perspectives, sensory detail and direct anger wrapped up in layered storytelling which recognizes a historical perspective are all there. It only took five grand at the box office at the time. Now a world which has given birth to Black Lives Matter can recognize its brave mixture of brutality and redemption. People can watch it online for themselves, and, hopefully, cultural organisations will be able to give opportunities to determined filmmakers like Ngozi to continue to experiment and have the benefit of bigger budgets and more support.

# 9

# Sound and Vision

*Barbara Hepworth*
I am standing in a white room full of shadows and smooth
sculptures. One of them is white and curved with a hole in
it (do not think about Polos, this is an art moment). There
are brown strings across the hole, as if it is an instrument.
The piece stands on a grey plinth and is positioned so you
have a view through the hole, to the rectangular window and
then to the green space outside. Further beyond that is a
busy road, but in here there is no noise. There are smooth
lines and curves, there is peace. The sculptures are peaceful.
I think I do not understand sculptures, but, nonetheless,
they don't seem to mind. It doesn't feel like they want to be
understood, not with my busy mind anyway. Maybe they
just want me to stand still for this moment, in this room, in
this concrete building filled with art, named after a Northern
woman (as so few other buildings are).

She is in her studio, holding a hammer and a chisel. She
bangs the hammer onto the chisel, making white edges over
the black paint she had marked previously. It feels like the
stone is humming. She feels the chipping as if it is inside
her, somewhere on the upper part of her stomach. The wind

might do this work, or the sea, but it would take them years and years. She knows other people will touch this too. Pat it. She hopes they will. She wants them to feel themselves in it too. It is not a thing to be separate from. It is not separate from her.

It is 1972. A television interviewer asks Barbara Hepworth, 'Isn't the father the most important one?' referring to her nine-piece series of sculptures 'Family of Man'. 'Why isn't he the biggest?' 'He doesn't have to be the biggest to be the most important,' replies Barbara in her languorous received pronunciation. Fur cape draped over her shoulders, large, bronze geometric ring, bracelet and necklace visible. She is used to questions. Used to being asked if it isn't hard to work with such big pieces of stone and bronze and wood. Aren't they heavy? Ever since she and Henry Moore were at the Royal College of Art in the 1920s, shifting sculpture's focus and fashioning abstract objects that created their own spaces. They liked to say she was his disciple, but they were peers who learnt from each other, and the other artists and writers and thinkers in their group. In the first place she had been encouraged by a teacher (there is always a teacher) – Miss McRoben, the head at Wakefield High School for girls – to apply for a scholarship to Leeds School of Art after she had so loved the Egyptian sculptures they had looked at in art lessons and at the museum – their scale, their shapes.

By the sixties she was one of the biggest figures in modern British art. She represented Britain at the Venice Biennale in 1950 and won the Sao Paolo Biennale in 1959. Now she is an international figure. Her works travel. This is a different life now. More space, more money for materials. Commissions like the one for the winged figure outside the Oxford Street John Lewis in London, which 200 million people a year have seen since 1963. In her huge studio at St Ives, in the garden with its intense sun and shadows, she chips and hammers and marks out. Not like the years with her husband, fellow sculptor Ben Nicolson, and their triplets. Not like growing up in Yorkshire, her surveyor father driving over the hills, their form defined by the roads that sculpted them, lines and curves – though those things are all still in her. 'I know that all I felt during the early years of my life in Yorkshire is dynamic and constant in my life today,' she is quoted as saying, on the Hepworth Gallery webpage. She was an innovator, in her move away from figures to abstraction, in her direct carving into stone rather than making a maquette for a master worker to build, in her experimentation with materials, and in her wish that people would experience her work with their bodies. Now they can (except we're not allowed to touch them) in the Hepworth Gallery in her home town of Wakefield. St Ives claims her too, rightly, but she was formed in and by the landscape of Yorkshire and we can touch (with our eyes only!) the pieces she made there, and in the wide-open spaces of the Yorkshire Sculpture Park, a few miles away. 'I am constantly plagued by this little-woman attitude,' she had said in 1966, but she kept on, producing over six hundred pieces in her lifetime, recognized and loved for their relationship to nature and to bodies. Chipping away, carving out a space for herself that went far, far beyond the narrow containers and cluttered rooms mothers of triplets were supposed to fit into.

---

Of course, there have been other female artists from the North. Though not that many it seems, and none yet regarded as significant as Barbara Hepworth. There again,

*The Guardian* art critic Jonathan Jones was happy to point out: 'She is not in the same class [as] Brâncuşi, Kandinsky, Mondrian, Pollock, Rothko or Richard Serra.' Okay, Jonathan, these things are subjective. She was put in her place in her life often enough. Since I have kept my eyes open, I have begun to see traces and hints of female artists around the North, though it often feels like they are sneaking in, jostling at the edge of the page.

### Sheila Fell

When I first saw a photograph of Sheila, with her intense, kohl-rimmed eyes nearly covered by her long fringe but looking straight at the camera, with her high cheekbones and her plain black jumper, I got a shock. It looked like she was alive now and issuing a challenge. In my head I think I'd imagined a nice lady painter. It doesn't look like she was that at all. There's also a clip of her being interviewed on Border TV for a Cumbrian exhibition in 1960. She has the careful speech of someone who hasn't had elocution lessons but is trying to talk posh (a 'phone voice') and speaks quietly and diffidently. When the confident-voiced, bow-tied male interviewer asks her if she enjoyed painting at school she comes to life and laughs and shakes her head vehemently. 'Ohhh, not really, no. No, I didn't.' She said she didn't really decide to be a painter but just drifted into it, but couldn't think what else she might do. In another interview five years later she talks more confidently, sports a brilliantly sixties white cap with black polka dots, and says that since she'd began to sell better she was able to buy more expensive paints with brighter colours and got excited and carried away by colour. Similar to how Barbara Hepworth was able to experiment more once she could afford bigger materials. It doesn't quite fit with the image of artists in garrets following their every creative whim, but of course it makes sense that being able to afford better stuff can sometimes lead to better art.

The critics said Sheila painted Cumbria in a way it had never been painted before, and you can sometimes still see her works on display at the Tate and in her native Cumbria, though it feels like (usual story) she would have been even more highly recognized as the innovator she was if she'd been a man. Still, she was one of a very few highly regarded female painters in the 1950s and 60s and one of the youngest ever to be elected a Royal Academician in 1974. A miner's daughter, she lived most of her life in London after moving there to go to art school, but continued to paint the Cumberland landscapes where she'd grown up for the rest of her life. In fact, after she won a travelling scholarship to Europe in 1959 she discovered it was hard to paint anywhere else. She just wanted to capture and recapture the Cumberland hills and lakes in brooding oil tones reminiscent of Cézanne and Van Gogh.

She was born in 1931 in Aspatria, Cumbria, and an art teacher (see, I said there's always a teacher) encouraged her to go to Carlisle School of Art when she was sixteen. She said the experience was a disaster and they told her she should be a textile artist, not a painter, but she ignored them, enrolled at the Saint Martin's School of Art in London, then showed them even more comprehensively by holding a London exhibition at the ridiculously young age of 24, which sold out completely.

L. S. Lowry bought two of her paintings and went on to buy eighteen more of her works, sending her a weekly allowance; he became a friend to her for the rest of his life. He said she was one of the country's finest landscape painters.

*Tatler* magazine said in a profile of her in the 1950s that success hadn't changed her, that she still 'smoked Woodbines, is still as likely to eat in a working man's café and spends less on clothes than the average typist'. Given that Sheila died in 1979 at the age of 48 of alcohol poisoning (says one account, while another said she fell down a steep staircase), just as a *Sunday Times* profile of her came out in which she said she intended to live to the age of 104, it feels like there's a story there we've not heard enough of.

### Leonora Carrington

Another maverick lady painter was the leading surrealist artist and writer Leonora Carrington, though initially I wasn't sure it was right to claim her for the North, since although she was born in Lancashire – the debutante daughter of a Lancashire textile mill owner – she left as soon as she could (possibly propelled by her father putting her in a mental institution in her twenties. She never saw him again after she moved to Mexico in 1942 and said she was more afraid of him than Hitler) and spent most of her life in Mexico. Instead of her biography featuring mill workers at the gates, she invented her own origin story in which she said that on one cold and miserable day, her mother had fed herself with chocolate truffles, oyster puree and pheasant, lain down on top of a machine designed to extract semen from all sorts of animals, from pigs to bats to stallions, and it had turned her bored, listless being upside down, via a spectacular orgasm, and Leonora was born, a combination of human, animal and machine, on 6 April, 1917, as England shook. I think I might try answering similarly next time someone asks me where I was born (maybe in the census). Anyway, this combination of surreality and earthy humour characterised her writings and her art, which were inspired by falling in with the Surrealists when she went to study art in London. (Many of them fell in love with her pale-skinned, dark-haired beauty, including Max Ernst who called her his 'bride of the wind'. She was also friends with Picasso, Miró, and André Breton.)

After Ernst was detained when France was invaded by the Germans during the Second World War, she had a breakdown and was incarcerated in an institution in Spain for a while where she says she became 'an androgyne, the Moon, the Holy Ghost, a gypsy, an acrobat, Leonora Carrington and a woman'. (Again, definitely one for the census entry under 'How would you describe yourself?' Or perhaps a Tinder profile.) Her 1974 novel *The Hearing Trumpet* has been described as one of the finest comic novels of the twentieth century and 'the occult twin to Lewis Carroll's *Alice in Wonderland*', and since it contains paragraphs like this, I would suggest she and her work are worth more investigation:

'It is impossible to understand how millions and millions of people all obey a sickly collection of gentlemen that call themselves 'Government'! The word, I expect, frightens people. It is a form of planetary hypnosis, and very unhealthy.'

'It has been going on for years,' I said. 'And it only occurred to relatively few to disobey and make what they call revolutions. If they won their revolutions, which they occasionally did, they made more governments, sometimes more cruel and stupid than the last.'

'Men are very difficult to understand,' said Carmella. 'Let's hope they all freeze to death.'

In her introduction to the 2005 Penguin edition of the book, novelist Ali Smith laments that Leonora's life is more remembered than her work, but when she recounts the stories about her, it's easy to see why: apparently she scandalised a Parisian art party by coming wearing only a sheet, then dropping it in front of everybody; served cold tapioca she'd dyed with squid ink to guests as caviar; went off for a shower fully clothed then came back dripping; cooked an omelette for visitors to her house which she filled with their own hair she had cut while they slept; and had sentences in her author biographies on the back of her books like: 'Subjected to horrifying treatment in a Madrid asylum, she was rescued by her Nanny who arrived in a submarine'. I think I love her.

---

### Lubaina Himid

You can manage to be an international artist from the North, as proved by Preston-based Lubaina Himid, who became the oldest person to win the Turner Prize in 2017, at the age of sixty-three (the prize had just been opened up to artists over 50, which partly accounts for the fact that so many headlines were about her age. It was a bittersweet thing for her, she said, as 'I think to myself what I could have done if I'd won it at 40 . . . twenty years in front of you aren't the same as 63 years behind you'. She was also the first black woman to win the prize, and says she also considers herself to be a 'cultural activist'.

Her work is bold, colourful, satirical and deeply concerned with representations of black people (one installation shows how pages from *The Guardian* frequently have photographs of black people next to negative headlines. Another is based on Hogarth cartoons and includes cardboard cut-outs of Ronald Reagan and Margaret Thatcher kissing). She was born in Zanzibar and after her father died of malaria, her mother, a textile designer from Lancashire, brought them back to London. She moved to Preston when she was 36, saying she had to get out of London because she was broke and 'art schools were not employing black women in 1990'. She is still at the University of Central Lancashire, now as a professor of contemporary art, and says that many of her contemporaries are women like her, whose work was passed over when they were in their thirties and forties because it didn't fit what was fashionable and is now being picked up on as curators realise they missed out on diverse artists because they didn't recognize the value of what they were doing at the time.

## At the Gallery Entrance

I have seen a couple of the beautiful, intricate wood prints Viva Talbot did of steelworks, at an exhibition on the art of steel at the Middlesbrough Institute of Modern Art (people unfamiliar with Middlesbrough may now be digesting the fact that Middlesbrough has an institute of modern art. It does, and a very good one too). Born in 1900, Viva's dad was a steel company boss in South Durham, so she had unique access and was able to depict the inner workings of the factories at a time when no women were allowed in. Academic Joan Heggie came across them by accident in 2006 and then tried to find out anything she could about this woman who wasn't in any reference books (and mostly still isn't).

Some other women doing things differently in the art world include the Singh Twins from Liverpool, whose beautiful mash-ups of Indian traditional art, illuminated medieval manuscripts and pop art have not quite made it into mainstream acceptance by art galleries, but it feels like it's only a matter of time; and acclaimed Black British Artist, the flamboyant Chila Burman, born in 1957, who describes herself as a 'Punjabi Liverpudlian' and 'South Asian pop artist' and whose giant glittery ice cream titled 'Eat Me Now' was inspired by her ice cream-van owning dad. Another set of twins from Newcastle – Jane and Louise, the Wilson twins – were shortlisted for the Turner Prize in 1999. They create big video installations and, like me, seem to be fascinated by big, ugly, brutalist, modernist structures (their work has included pieces depicting a former Stasi headquarters in East Germany and a rocket launch at the giant Baikonur Cosmodrome in Kazakhstan). Then there are the visionaries who look more closely, or from a different angle. I love the photographs of Sirkka-Liisa Konttinen (who emigrated to Byker in Newcastle from Finland in the 1960s) and is still documenting the ordinary people in all their extraordinariness. Then there's Tish Murtha who also photographed the marginalised boys and girls of late seventies and early eighties Newcastle. As a working-class woman her position as documentary photographer was, as she said, 'from the inside', having grown up as one of ten children in a council house in Elswick. Tish died at the age of just 56 in 2013 of a sudden brain aneurysm but her work is being collated by her daughter in books such as *Youth Unemployment* and there are efforts to keep remembering her work, given how easy it is for talented women to slip out of the frame.

It has been exciting therefore to read, as this book is being finished, of a film by rare Northern female filmmaker Carol Morley (born in Stockport in 1966) whose 2011 drama-documentary film *Dreams of a Life* about 38-year-old Joyce Vincent, whose body lay undiscovered in her bedsit for three years, shows her acute sympathy for lives lived under the radar. Carol became fascinated by the archive of Sunderland-born artist Audrey Amiss whose headmistress at Bede Grammar wrote to her 'I think you will become one of the greatest painters of the age', but who had a breakdown after starting at the prestigious Royal Academy and spent the rest of her life working for the civil service, being admitted to psychiatric wards and making unusual art hardly anybody got to see. Audrey Amiss had summarised her own lack of recognition, saying 'I was once in the tradition of social realism…but I am now avant-garde and misunderstood.' Carol brings her back to life in a film whose title comes from Audrey's description of herself in her passport; *Typist, Artist, Pirate, King* (which alone tells me this is a woman whose work I want to see more of) and recognises her as an important and original artist.

### *Sound Visionaries*
### Olive Shapley

She is holding a microphone as a crowd of curious children gather round in the terraced street. They have started shushing each other now, fingers on lips, not even making the shushing sound any more after she told them it was for radio. Imagine, the voices of people from round here on the radio! At least these miners' wives are less likely to swear than the miners. She'd had to hold a placard up for the live show to remind them 'Do not say bloody or bugger!' She nods her head carefully, encouraging her interviewee but without saying 'mmm' out loud because that will get on the recording. And this isn't about her voice. It's about the voices of ordinary people. She knew not everybody at the BBC understood this; it went against everything Lord Reith thought should happen. People should speak properly. Sound educated. But her boss understood. They were a tight-knit crew in Manchester in the 1930s. Far enough away from the top brass to do what they wanted. Yes, there was trouble sometimes, and management made it perfectly clear they didn't like these sort of programmes, but they didn't stop them.

The seven-tonne mobile recording unit safe in the street behind them was what made all this possible. Getting out and about among real people. Olive knew how to get them to talk, not feel intimidated by her posh Southern accent. Her open face, her smiling eyes. Anyway, she was one of them now. No airs and graces. There was a moment, which she later recalled in an interview for the BBC oral history collection, when she'd decided she was a Northerner, while recording the radio show *LSD* (no, it wasn't about hallucinogenic drugs – that meant pounds, shillings and pence then). In that wedding shop, the woman trying on hats. Hat after hat and the assistant saying, 'Eeee, you look terrible!' after each one, all of them laughing and laughing. That was when she decided.

Olive Shapley lived in Manchester for more than forty years and pioneered the (what now seems obvious) idea of getting ordinary people talking on the radio. But this just hadn't been done, ever since the early days of the BBC in the 1920s when you had to speak in received pronunciation to be let anywhere near a microphone. Perhaps the people in London only understood one word in six of these people who Olive zipped round the North interviewing, but she didn't care. She knew there was nothing more truthful than real people talking. They'd trust you if you'd been in their neighbourhood for a few days, or come back more than once, drunk with them in their pub, sat in their lorry.

She was born in Peckham in 1910 and went to the University of Cambridge, where she became great friends with Barbara Betts, who we know as Barbara Castle, the great Labour politician. They would both have been 'in-between' people at Cambridge, not quite fitting in with the posh people, but able to camouflage themselves well enough. To connect with ordinary people, and to convince the truly middle-class ones they knew what they were talking about. Handy qualities for a BBC producer and for a politician. Olive organised *Children's Hour* from Manchester from 1934 but then became the first producer to get out and about among real people with that giant recording truck. She produced timeless radio, which is held up as an exemplar of the medium, like 1939's *The Classic Soil*, written by Joan Littlewood, which took Friedrich Engels's writing about Manchester and offered listeners a 'microphone impression' of Manchester today and a hundred years earlier, again using interviews with Mancunians on their own territory.

After she married her boss, John Salt (great-grandson of Saltaire mill boss Titus Salt, mill fact fans), she had to leave the BBC for a while because married couples weren't allowed to work together (fairly sure it's not the married couples that cause the problems . . . ) and they moved to New York where she made documentaries about Harlem's black neighbourhoods and produced a fortnightly newsletter for *Children's Hour* in which children spoke about their experiences. After the war, she started producing *Woman's Hour* and for twenty years innovated frank discussions about things like the menopause, women's pay and periods. It feels like telling the truest story possible in people's own words was her greatest motivation.

She was much loved in her community in Manchester, and in the sixties she used the space in her large house in Didsbury to start a refuge for unsupported single mothers (she refused to use the then derogatory phrase 'unmarried mothers'), then in the seventies took in displaced Vietnamese Boat People. Not only was she quite clearly a good egg and a deserved honorary Northerner, but she was an important radio pioneer whose legacy lives on in many broadcasting techniques still in use today and, most crucially, in the attitude that ordinary people's voices should be heard.

## Ethel Leginska, Cosey Fanni Tutti, Hannah Peel and Northern Futurism

She was supposed to wear evening gowns, but instead she had her hair bobbed and wore something closer to a tuxedo, a black velvet jacket, a slim skirt and a white shirt. The audience in their evening gowns and dinner jackets sat up straighter in their seats as she walked confidently across the stage and sat down at the piano. They had heard about this English woman who commanded the stage, who could run through an entire Chopin programme without a break and who was so much more expressive than other pianists. She thought stiffness was the worst quality a concert pianist could have. How could you feel the music if you weren't relaxed from your shoulders down to your fingertips? She was more relaxed on stage than in real life. There, under the spotlight, in the quiet, apart from the coughs and the rustles of the programmes, there was just her, the piano and the music. The custody battle with her husband over little Cedric went away. But it wasn't just the big things. It was the little things. The journeys to the recitals. The loudness of the city, trying to juggle the dates when she would be performing and seeing her son. These things she couldn't control. Music she could. Which is why she wanted to learn and learn and keep on learning. Why should there be any barriers in music? It was for everyone. She could compose and conduct and build her own orchestras who could play pieces exactly the way she knew they should be played. No need for everybody to be so rigid about this. Music sounded better when it flowed from people who felt free, and the piano especially could reflect every mood, every feeling, all there is in life, all that one has lived. She could speak through the piano more easily than she could with her own voice.

Ethel Leginska was born Ethel Liggins in Hull. Ethel Liggins does not sound like the name of an acclaimed concert pianist who wrote operas and symphonies, was the only woman to conduct major orchestras – including the Berlin Philharmonic and the New York Symphony Orchestra – and founded both the Boston Philharmonic Orchestra and the Women's Symphony Orchestra of Boston. Ethel Liggins sounds like the name of a girl born in Hull in 1886. One who seemed to fuse with the piano as if it was part of her own body and who was giving public piano recitals at the age of six. A wealthy Hull shipping family paid for her to study at top conservatoires in Europe and by the time she was 16 she was giving public performances in London (where somebody suggested that the more Slavic 'Leginska' would sound just that bit more impressive).

Not that Ethel was any slouch at publicity. When she injured her finger in a door in 1916, she sent the X-ray photograph to a music magazine for them to publish. Stress was a constant feature of her life, though. She had several 'nervous breakdowns' and once went missing for four days before a performance at New York's Carnegie Hall, being found 190 miles away in Boston. She continued to teach, albeit with fewer opportunities to lead orchestras. Her second opera debuted in Los Angeles in 1957 where she had settled, with her leading the orchestra. She'd first done that over thirty years earlier, but even then women were only just beginning to break through into the world of classical music. What a pioneer, and one who could so easily, without the patronage of a wealthy family, have stayed in Hull and never had her astonishing musical talent heard beyond her own front room.

———————

Another Hull-based musical and artistic pioneer couldn't have been any more different on the surface. In contrast to Ethel's tuxedo suits, she was most famously photographed in basques and stockings. She lived in a squat, and one of her most well-known pieces involved her sitting on a swing on stage while weeing in a perfect arc. Rather than operas and symphonies, she produced industrial music which throbbed and pulsed with metallic shrieks and was aimed at producing extreme pleasure or pain. Cosey Fanni Tutti (born Christine Newby in 1951) believed absolutely that 'art is life and life is art' and makes me think of a review of Ethel Leginska's opera *Gale* from 1935 which said she waved a baton 'as if she believed it possessed some superhuman power'. Ethel and Cosey were both all in with their work – body and soul. As part of the collective art movement COUM Transmissions, Cosey represented Britain at the Ninth Paris Biennale and she worked for two years on an exhibition called 'Prostitution', which showed at the ICA in

London in 1976. This had involved her taking part in shoots for porn magazines and films and questioned the relationship between sex work and money, and art and money. In contrast to many of the artists she worked with, she hadn't been to art school (though had wanted to – her domineering dad insisted she get a job straight after she left school) but was swept up into the hippy and beat scenes that came to Hull in the late sixties, and came to strongly believe that anyone could be an artist and that art should be accessible. Her autobiography *Art Sex Music* is a brilliant depiction of that time, and also makes it clear that her relationship with art guru Genesis P-Orridge was one of coercive control by them. But it opened up a world of freedom to her. She was open to collaborations with other artists, musicians and creatives and to questioning all existing norms and values. Working in the absurdist DADA tradition, she took part in actions, events and happenings everywhere from the streets of Hull, to London warehouses and international arts venues. The life she was expected to have of marrying a man, having his tea on the table every night and bringing up a family was not for her. For the people living that life, they probably couldn't get their heads round one in which you took your cat for a walk and it pooped out one of the used tampons you'd been using in your art installation because it liked eating them. Cosey is still making music and art today and is another female artist whose work was remembered and re-evaluated in the late 2010s and during the time of Hull's City of Culture festival.

---

Hannah Peel grew up in Barnsley from the age of eight (she was born in Northern Ireland in 1985) and it feels like a long way from there to being nominated for an Emmy for her music for a *Game of Thrones* documentary in 2019. Her electronic music beeps and pulses and swirls and swishes. She has opened for Paul Weller and Alison Moyet, wears very cool shiny clothes and interestingly-shaped glasses on stage, and is acknowledged as one of the most exciting electronic composers working in Britain today. In 2016 she recorded an album inspired by her grandmother's response to music during her battle with dementia, called *Awake But Always Dreaming*. With her band The Magnetic North she has also made a concept album about the Lancashire new town Skelmersdale and how it became the home of Transcendental Meditation (honestly that is not something who has been to Skelmersdale would expect to happen. Either the concept album or the meditation. And it's an album of gorgeous songs).

---

Also inspired by thinking about dementia, Hannah created her alter ego Mary Casio – an elderly pioneering electronic stargazer who has long dreamt of leaving her terraced house in Barnsley and is able to travel, in her mind, to Cassiopeia. In 2016 she premiered Mary Casio in Manchester with a piece combining analogue electronics and a thirty-three-piece colliery band, then released an album of the piece recorded at Barnsley Civic Theatre, which was awarded number one electronic album of the year by *Electronic Sound* magazine. One of the tracks features a recording of her grandad singing in Manchester Cathedral in 1927, one of the first recordings made of a choirboy. When I heard these pieces, titled things like 'Sunrise Through the Dusty Nebula' and 'Andromeda M31', with their aforementioned pulses and bleeps, plus gorgeous brass band horns that sound like the lamenting horns played by the Black Dyke Mills Band at my dad's funeral, but in space, I thought, hang on – this is the sound of Northern Futurism.

Then I thought, what's Northern futurism? And I realised it's this. It's the sound of the past, that stirs the Northern nostalgic soul, but it's also a questing spirit driving us into the future. Into the stars, beyond where we've ever dreamt we could go. To where we were always told we could never go. In Hannah's work it keens, but it joyously opens its shiny brass throat and laughs and reaches and joins with other instruments and voices to imagine a better future. I don't think Hannah is the only Northern Futurist. Cosey Fanni Tutti is one too, though her sound is the clanging metal of the North's industrial past meeting the joyous pulses and sirens of an unimagined future soundspace. Now I think of it, I met another Northern Futurist in a very cold warehouse in Manchester. For some of the time, I was lying down on the floor in a room full of cushions, my head on a pillow. Then there was another room full of clanging music that hurt my ears and I had to leave. Then I was taking part in a discussion about neurodiversity (the idea that people having different types of brain, including autism, ADHD, dyslexia and OCD, is actually a human strength). That was why I'd been invited, but it gave me the chance to discover the work of Nwando Ebizie and her multimedia installation 'Constellations'. She is also partial to a shiny stage outfit, and is multiple things – singer, poet, performance artist, musician. I knew she'd created an alter ego called Lady Vendredi, a time-travelling blaxploitation pop star, but it turns out that, according to her online biography, that alter ego has now created her own alter ego called 'The Baron', 'a transvestite, transracial, tap-dancing Northern comedian'. That fusion of the North's past with the multiple identities of the diverse future are also pure Northern Futurism (I know I've lost some of you here. You're thinking, can't we go back to finding out about some sports stars and suffragettes everybody had forgotten about, then have a nice cup of tea?). Nonetheless, this feels like the perfect point to meet our final group of women – the Northern women of the air – as they take us into the future with a healthy dose of recognition that we will always carry the past with us.

# 10

# Explorers of Earth and Air

## *Queen of the Desert: Gertrude Bell*

Perhaps Gertrude Bell's life is the most extraordinary in this whole book. She seemed to live not one life, but twelve. Any one of the things she did might have merited inclusion. She was the first woman to win a first-class degree in modern history, for example, from St Margaret's College, Oxford, in 1868. As the daughter of a prosperous North East iron family from Washington, her destiny was to be a debutante and a society lady doing good works. It definitely wasn't to set off on two round-the-world journeys, making her one of the greatest female explorers of her age. Or to famously cling to a rope for fifty-three hours – FIFTY-THREE HOURS! – on an unclimbed part of the Alps, when her expedition was caught in a blizzard in 1902.

That was before she taught herself Arabic, travelled to remote tribal villages, learnt the politics of the Middle East, spent the war as a sort of female Indiana Jones as a spy in Cairo and, by 1917, had gone to Baghdad and got herself a job in charge of liaising with the Arabic population. Oh, and she'd taught herself archaeology at this point too, founding the Baghdad Museum of Archaeology, which survives to this day. She led in persuading the British to grant the Arabs their independence and rule Iraq (then Mesopotamia) themselves. She underestimated the strength of the Shia majority, though, who didn't really want to be ruled by the Sunni-supporting king she helped install and who rose up in revolt in 1920, leading to the deaths of hundreds of British soldiers and 8,000 Iraqi troops. However, the Iraq she helped create with her policies lasted thirty-seven years until Saddam Hussein's Ba'ath party seized power in 1968.

She revelled in her role as a lone woman in diplomatic circles in the Arabic world, and as mediator between the British and the Iraqis, and she predicted she would be remembered there, as she apparently is, even if she isn't in Britain. She was given the nickname 'Khatun' in Iraq, which means 'fine lady'. In one of her letters home she said, 'As we rode back through the gardens of the Karradah suburb where all the people know me and salute me as I pass, Nuri said, "One of the reasons you stand out so is because you're a woman. There's only one Khatun . . . For a hundred years they'll talk of the Khatun riding by." I think they very likely will.' Her letters home became increasingly depressed and in 1926 she took an overdose (possibly accidental) of sleeping pills and died, far too young (I have written that so many times in this book), at the age of fifty-eight.

It feels like she deserves more memorialising than the 2015 *Queen of the Desert* film by Werner Herzog in which she was played by Nicole Kidman, and which focused more on her personal life (a series of passionate attachments that didn't go anywhere) than her diplomatic achievements, and currently has an 18 per cent critic score on Rotten Tomatoes.

## Queens of the Air: Amy Johnson and Helen Sharman

Flowers. That's what you get given when you come back down to earth (if you're a woman). Flowers that smell fresh and sweet, not of engine oil or rocket fuel. You carry them in your hands and don't have anywhere to put them. Often you have to hold them in one hand because everybody wants to shake the other one. Some people actually just want to touch you. Pat your shoulder, your suit that has been above the earth with you. They think you're magic in a way, that your flight might transfer something to them. An ability to leave things behind maybe.

Everybody wants to know what it was like being up there. What you saw. What you ate. Whether you were lonely. You tell them about the vivid, vivid blue of the sea, the bright white of the sun. You have had a view that most of them will never have. A lot of the time your body was confined, squashed and held in. You ached, you ached all over. But sometimes there were moments of sheer exuberant joy and you leapt up and stretched out and felt like you could stay awake forever and that the next flight could be powered just by your own happiness and sense of freedom.

You know that you are now an ambassador of the air, that you can inspire other women to do what you have done. It is a responsibility and a passion. Your own journey had seemed unlikely, but you knew you could do it, knew you had the skills and the training, even though you believed yourself to be completely ordinary. You knew what you had done was extraordinary and that you must tell the world about it, tell the girls who think that this isn't for them, that it is, it can be, if they believe. So you must keep a brave face on, only occasionally let out that there were moments when you were lonely, moments when you were exhausted, moments when you thought it was all going wrong. You are a pioneer and people are excited to be in the same room as you, to touch the clothes you wore, the machine you flew in. You will tell them about all the people who helped you, who joined in fixing problems, who laughed with you and ate with you, the loved ones who sent you on your way with such encouraging messages. But it is you alone they are interested in, the idea of a woman on her own in the vastness of the inky black sky as billions of sparkling stars look on.

———————

Amy Johnson only had a hundred hours of flying experience when she set off from England to Australia in her brilliantly named tiger moth plane, *Jason*, on 5 May 1930. She had set a course on a map using a ruler and flew without any radio equipment or knowledge of what the weather would be. She had a compass, a parachute, a sheath knife, a revolver, plus a Thermos flask of tea and some sandwiches. To be honest, all expeditions can be made okay if you set off with a flask of tea – though personally I would be keen to skip the several crash landings, the fuel leak she had to repair in mid-air, the sandstorm, and everybody wanting to take her out to dinner at night when she'd just spent another twelve hours in a cockpit trying to work out whether that white thing was a cloud or some ocean waves. Nineteen days later she made it to Darwin in Australia to what would become a familiar sight for her: excited crowds applauding, waving their hankies and throwing their hats in the air; dignitaries ushering her to platforms to make speeches, leading rounds of 'hip hip hooray' and giving her more bunches of flowers. So many bunches of flowers.

It was the time of the Depression and Amy's astonishing achievement as the first woman to fly solo from England to Australia was headline news all over the world. Of course she beat herself up about how she hadn't snatched the record for the fastest flight ever after her various mechanical and landing problems meant she couldn't top Bert Hinkler's record time of sixteen days, but she would go on to set other records, such as the fastest flights from London to Moscow and to South Africa, India and Japan. (Can I confess at this point that I had always thought those long pioneering flights were continuous? I didn't realise that it was actually a journey of seventeen planned stops in places from Vienna to Baghdad to Singapore to refuel, sleep, repair *Jason* and fill up that Thermos flask. Plus, in one instance, to have a group of tribespeople run towards her with knives and machetes, though luckily it turned out they were friendly, if a bit baffled that this woman talking in a jolly way about how 'tip top' the British Empire was had just fallen out of the sky into a clearing on the edge of their jungle.)

It seemed that once she'd had her first taste of flying, she couldn't stop. This young middle-class woman from Hull had been born in 1903 and studied economics at the University of Sheffield, among mostly men. She then went to work as a legal secretary in London but got hooked on flying after taking a short flight and went for lessons. Most of the (few) other women flying at the time were much posher and had significant access to money. Amy's instructors told her 'you're not a flier' but she ignored that, and also qualified as the first female ground engineer for good measure, later becoming president of the Women's Engineering Society. (Actually, I find it inspiring to know she wasn't a particularly naturally gifted pilot – just an extraordinarily determined one.) She had a turbulent private life and after her sister's suicide and the difficult break-up of a relationship, she decided she was going to make the fastest flight to Australia (I would just have sat with a bar of Dairy Milk). Her ever-supportive father, who ran a fish import and export business, and a peer called Lord Wakefield each put up half the money for a £600 biplane, which she christened *Jason*, and without much fuss or fanfare she set off from Croydon Airfield, little knowing that she was going to become a global sensation, on the front page of every newspaper and celebrated as one of the world's most pioneering women.

During the Second World War she joined the Women's Air Transport Auxiliary, which ferried planes between RAF airfields (one of 128 women who did this), but tragically her plane crashed off Herne Bay one night in 1941. She bailed out into the freezing sea but her body was never found (there are many conspiracy theories, such as that she could have been a spy, or shot down by friendly fire, but it's most likely that it was simply an accident). She was only 37 and seemed set to have many more years ahead of flying adventures and record attempts and encouraging other young women into engineering and flying. Actually, she still has encouraged many other women into these fields, as the memory of her achievements lived on. There are twin statues of her in Hull and Herne Bay, with words she said in a speech in 1936 etched on her flying cap: 'Believe Nothing to be Impossible'.

---

Helen Sharman echoed those words after she became the first British person and the first European woman to blast off into space almost exactly sixty-one years after Amy's epic flight. She urged: 'We should push forward, not only our individual boundaries, but also the boundaries of what humans believe is possible.' However, she described herself as 'ordinary' (as Amy did too), and said nothing unusual had ever happened in her life growing up in a nuclear family in Sheffield (she means a two-parent kind of family, not radioactive people) and then going to the local comp. She studied chemistry at university and then went to work for Mars Confectionary, making better ice cream and chocolate. For some people this would be enough – to know you'd made an excellent contribution to the world – but then she heard an advert on the radio saying 'astronauts wanted' and that anybody could apply. Well, not quite anybody – you had to be fit and hold a science degree. She thought at first, why would it be me? But then realised it definitely wouldn't be her if she didn't apply. Out of 13,000 people, it *was* her, and after eighteen months of rigorous training with the Russians (who were backing the trip in the interests of international cooperation), she was shot into space in May 1991 for an intense week of carrying out plant experiments, exercising for two hours a day and experiencing fun stuff like pushing little bits of bread through the air and seeing them land in her fellow astronauts' mouths. Plus seeing one of them, Sergai, dressing for dinner in a tie, which stuck up in the air the whole time. She was only 27 when she went up, currently still the sixth youngest out of the over 500 people who've travelled into space.

In her autobiography, *Seize the Moment*, she said she loved the weightlessness and just randomly being able to do somersaults during breakfast, and lots of the footage that exists of her on the space station consists of her smiling. She said she could see the curve of the earth and its bright blues, contrasted with the deep black of space outside the Mir space station. She felt safe, apart from one scary moment when there was an electrical failure and some lights went out, which would have been worse if the fans had also stopped because they circulated air, which is quite important when you're in space where there isn't any. I get the impression she's fairly fed up of being asked how she went to the toilet in space, but in an interview with the British astronaut Tim Peake they both agreed that it's very human for people to be fascinated by all the visceral stuff even in the midst of the engineering and scientific miracle that is space flight.

Talking of Tim Peake, when the former army commander set off into space in 2015, he was routinely described as 'the first British astronaut'. For people like me who could vividly remember the astronaut advert and how Helen Sharman, a fellow Yorkshirewoman, had been picked, it was strange to see her being erased from history before our eyes. She has at least been made a CMG in recognition of her ongoing contribution to space and technology educational outreach, has a star on the Sheffield walk of fame, has several honorary doctorates, and numerous school houses and buildings have been named after her. But perhaps the greatest legacy she has is in the exploring minds and hearts of all those people who have looked up into the night sky and now know that it is possible to travel to places we had only been able to dream of before.

### *The Possibilities of War: Lilian Bader, Hilda Lyon and Rachel Parsons*

So many women got opportunities to do things they had never done before during the First and Second World Wars, though it shouldn't have taken global carnage for that to happen. Some of the windows clamped shut again straight afterwards, and some have stayed open – a chink, at least. Here are three women who have flown pretty much under history's radar but have not quite been forgotten due to the efforts of people who recognize how easily this can happen.

Black History Month has highlighted the story of Lilian Bader who was born in Toxteth in 1918 to a merchant seaman from Barbados, who served in the First World War, and a British-born mother of Irish origin. She fought back against rejection and prejudice to become one of the first (possibly actually the first) black women to serve in the armed forces, though shockingly her first attempt to do so ended when she was asked to leave her job as a canteen assistant at Catterick Camp in North Yorkshire after seven weeks, when her father's Caribbean birth was discovered (this was the father who fought for Britain in the First World War). She returned to domestic service but felt ashamed when some soldiers asked her why she wasn't doing war work. She felt like she couldn't tell them that 'a coloured Briton was not acceptable, even in the humble NAAFI'. She had already struggled to find employment; she had been kept in the Liverpool convent where she had been placed after being orphaned at the age of nine, and where she stayed until she was 20 because, she said, 'I was half West Indian and nobody, not even the priests, dare risk ridicule by employing me.'

According to her page on the Second World War memory site Living Memorial, after hearing on the radio that black people who had been turned down by the army were being accepted into the RAF, she joined and found herself standing out 'in a sea of white faces' but someone told her she looked nice in her uniform which cheered her up. She trained as an instrument repairer, which was a trade newly opened to women, and her capability shone out. By 1941 she was a leading aircraftwoman, and was then promoted to acting corporal. She met and married a young black tank driver called Ramsay Bader and had to leave the forces in 1944 when she became pregnant. They went on to have two sons, and she studied for a degree and then trained as a teacher. Her struggle against prejudice to take up a vital war role has been recognized in recent years and in 2020 she was memorialised in the Oxford Dictionary of National Biography.

She sits with charts and diagrams strewn over her desk. Her trustiest tool is a slide rule and she is an expert in the shaping of air, but would never put it as poetically as that. She knows how air moves and how objects, especially flying objects, move through it. Sometimes she does a year of calculations for something that will never be made because a higher authority steps in and stops it – a biplane bomber which was to have bombed Berlin, for example. Hilda Lyon was an unassuming farmer's daughter from Market Weighton in East Yorkshire; she was a genius of mathematics and engineering and went on an early 'joy-ride flight' of the ill-fated R101 airship when she was working on it. She had always shone out as bright, having her hand up in class at primary school before other children even knew what the question was. She was one of the most important aeronautical engineers in her field, and shapes based on her designs are still in use in submarines today (it is still called the 'Lyon shape'). Many of her classic scientific papers are still regularly cited. Yet after I mentioned Hilda Lyon in my show when I took it to Beverley in East Yorkshire, a woman from the town told me indignantly afterwards that she had never heard of her. 'Why haven't we got a statue of her in our market place?' she fumed. 'We've got a statue of a man called Giant Bradley, but his only apparent skill was ... height.'

Born in 1896, Hilda went to Beverley High School then to the University of Cambridge, where she graduated with a degree in mathematics in 1918. Well, they didn't actually award degrees to women then, even if they'd excelled as Hilda did. They called them 'titular degrees' and the women were not on the degree list or at the graduation ceremony but were mailed certificates in the post. There was a second vote on the issue in 1921 (the first one in 1897 prompted a riot) but even though women had just been doing men's jobs during the war (or because women had been doing men's jobs during the war ... ) it was still a no. Anyway, she went on to work for aeronautical companies, carrying out research on things like friction and drag (if you want to see friction and drag, look at the men's attitude to women getting degrees at Cambridge). She said she was a 'country bumpkin' at first but excited by seeing maths theory set to real-world applications. Her biographer, Nina Baker, points out that as the aviation industry came with less baggage than other fields of engineering – because it was so new – there were more opportunities for female engineers there. Hilda was involved in the design of the R101 airship – actually she pointed out that wind tunnel tests based on small models were inaccurate and a more rounded shape at the front would be better. This was never tested in real life because the R101 exploded on its maiden commercial flight to Paris, killing forty-eight of the fifty-four people on board, ending the airship programme.

After beginning to research abroad, initially in the US (which is why she luckily wasn't on the R101's official maiden flight), she was called back to East Yorkshire from a post in Germany in 1932 because her mother was ill (it must have been a scary time to be in Germany – just as the Nazis were ascending to power and Jewish students and staff were being marched out of the university). Very unusually for the time, she was able to continue her research at home as her work was so valuable to her company and she could do some of it at local university libraries like Leeds and Hull. She carried on working through the war, but sadly died in 1946 after an operation for an ovarian cyst, with – I have written this for so many women – so much work still to do. Her loss was mourned as a sad and significant one by the aeronautical world, and a colleague recalled her painstakingly accurate work. When I first performed my show, there were very few mentions of Hilda Lyon, but I can see there is now much more online and a short biography, as well as a blue plaque in Market Weighton. Perhaps that statue won't be too far behind.

Beams of light search the sky looking for Zeppelin and aircraft. Women make this searchlight equipment at the Parsons factory in Heaton, Newcastle. They're overseen by Rachel Parsons, daughter of the inventor of the steam turbine and and a passionate scientist herself. She is one of the first three women to study Mechanical Sciences at Cambridge in 1910, though as we know from Hilda Lyon, she's not allowed a degree.

Rachel directs the family company while her brother is fighting in the war. When women are prevented from keeping the jobs they had taken on during the war, in favour of returning men, Rachel and her former suffragette mother, Katherine, set up an all-women engineering company Atalanta, to mobilise the extraordinary talents of the women they have overseen working in factories - and found the Women's Engineering Society. They are passionate about women mobilising together to try and open the doors to work that are being slammed in their faces. At one point Rachel stands for parliament.

Tragically, she was brutally battered to death by her stable-worker in 1956 in a dispute over his pay. Her passing was reported as the tragic death of a lonely, eccentric heiress, who the judge called "quarrelsome and uncontrollable", a piece of victim-blaming which seems to have contributed to her murderer getting only a ten year sentence for manslaughter. One of the most pioneering and determined women in early engineering was reduced to being portrayed as a "difficult woman" rather than the forgotten feminist hero she was.

### Voyagers in Space and Time:
### Professor Monica Grady and Doctor Who

We see a conference room full of people watching two screens, then applause starts, and cheering. A lot of people stand up. There is a 'Yay, yay, yay!' and the camera pans across to capture the source: a middle-aged woman wearing a blue and white striped top and cardigan and a bright yellow lanyard round her neck – a woman who describes herself on her Twitter profile as 'short, round, busy, bespectacled and bossy'. She is pumping her arms up and down in the air, as if she's celebrating the best goal ever, laughing joyously and saying 'fantastic!', her face on full ecstatic beam. Her happiness overspills to a man stood next to her, who she envelops in a hug, still laughing. He is a reporter it turns out, and asks her 'What did you make of it?' as if that wasn't the most obvious thing in the world. Still clenching her fists and laughing she says, 'Sorry, David, I didn't mean to hug you like that but I'm so excited! It's landed, it's landed!', her voice distorting the microphone. 'You've waited years for this,' he says and her laughter becomes mixed with happy crying. 'I've waited years,' she agrees, alternating between laughing and crying as she says again, 'It's fantastic, it's fantastic, it's really, really wonderful, I'm going to cry!' You feel like this is how some women might react to the emotion of giving birth if only they hadn't just pushed a human being out of themselves after several hours of knackering effort. Pure oxytocin joy. She tries to pull herself back: 'Sorry, sorry, sorry, I'll try to be a professional scientist, it's an amazing moment for European space agency history.' David says, 'The emotion just came over you.' And, it all whooshes up in her again like a rocket launching a lander to Mars (which is what she is celebrating): 'It's unbelievable, we've waited so long and now it's happening!'

On *Desert Island Discs* several months later, she said she felt she looked a fool. But of course, Kirsty Young said, the reason the clip went viral was because such unselfconscious joy was heart-warming. It made science look like rock and roll. Monica Grady had been celebrating ten years of her own personal work on the project coming to fruition – and thirty years of planning in total. The Philae lander landed on Mars in 2014 to take photographs and samples and, just before her interview with Kirsty, after a nerve-wracking seven-month silence, it had woken up and said, 'Hello Earth. Can you hear me?'

Born in 1958, the oldest of eight children, raised by teachers in Leeds, Monica said she noted down the time the sun went down and the street lights went on in the street outside her bedroom window every night for a year. Growing up in a close family she described as calm and loving, she remembered all of them watching Neil Armstrong landing on the moon, but had no idea of what her own future path might be until she answered an advert after graduating from Durham University to work with Colin Pillinger, studying lunar samples. She discovered that moon rocks are beautiful. Their colours are so clear — not like earth's rusty, cracked rocks — because they haven't been rained on. It got her into meteorites, which she says feel amazing to hold - having something four hundred million years old in your hand that no one else has ever touched and is a capsule containing the entire history of the universe. Monica talks with such passion and clarity about her work, it's no wonder she is one of our top space communicators.

Her work now involves using meteorite data to investigate where life on earth came from and to look for intelligent carbon-based life forms on other planets (I sometimes think we don't have that many intelligent carbon-based life forms on this one . . . ). This proud Yorkshirewoman, who has Yorkshire's white rose tattooed on her arm and chose Meat Loaf's 'Bat Out of Hell' as her first *Desert Island Discs* track, is sharing her infectious enthusiasm and expertise in a way which shows us that scientists can be very down to earth as well as, indeed, rock and roll . . .

---

Finally, does it seem strange to end this chapter and this book with a fictional character? We have already seen that the ways in which culture and the media represent Northern women can have a massive impact on how we are perceived. I knew that one thing I wanted to do in this book was challenge some of the ingrained stereotypes and prejudices about Northern women. To show that we are multiple and complicated and interesting – and that perhaps the only thing we have in common are the social and cultural and economic factors that hold us back because the centres of power are so strongly located in London and the South East in this country.

I have long said that I wished there would be more depictions of Northern women as associated with the future – because so much Northern imagery is concentrated on nostalgia and the past (and, yes, I am aware of the irony of saying this in a book with a big historical component and which is very, very enthusiastic about, for example, the enduring legacy of *Coronation Street*'s women). As we have seen with so many creative women, the imagination truly has the power to change things. It is where the seeds of the future are sown, it is where we can plan virtually for potential realities. For a long time, these virtual futures were ones in which women had equal rights to men. Thanks to the efforts of the suffragists and suffragettes, these dreams of the future have now come true, even though there is still a long way to go until all equal rights are realised in reality.

When the actor Jodie Whittaker was growing up in Skelmanthorpe in Huddersfield, knowing that being an actor was the only life for her, she wanted to play roles that nobody had ever imagined a young girl from Huddersfield could play. She had an idea of what the roles couldn't be

– she even told an interviewer that there could never be a female James Bond or Doctor Who, for example. So she was as surprised as anybody else when she *did* get cast as the thirteenth Doctor, in 2018, to a chorus of both joy and criticism (one male fan on a forum said 'It's called a Time Lord not a Time Lady'). Jodie said at a BBC press screening in Sheffield of her first episode: 'It feels completely overwhelming, as an actor, as a feminist, as a human, as someone who wants to continually push themselves and challenge themselves and not be boxed in by what you're told you can and can't be. It feels incredible!'

She says she doesn't see the Doctor as a Yorkshire character – she was just doing her own accent from the beginning of the long audition process, as the producers had told her to use her own voice. For me, I think it is actually significant that this iconic space and time traveller, who was first introduced by the BBC in 1963 as an educational way to explore different histories and cultures, and who has generally been a man with an RP accent (except Christopher Ecclestone's Ninth Doctor in 2005, who famously replied, 'Lots of planets have a North' when his companion Rose Tyler asked him how come he had a Northern accent if he was an alien), was finally a Northern woman.

The show was previously filmed in Cardiff, but Jodie's series have been filmed in Sheffield. As Jodie's Doctor crashed through the roof of a tram headed to Grindleford, passengers were sceptical to hear they were being invaded. One of them said, 'We don't get aliens in Sheffield.' to which the Doctor could only respond, as so many women have to being told that their existence is wrong or impossible, with the unarguable fact of her being there: 'Well, I'm an alien, and I'm in Sheffield.' As her future companion PC Yasmin Khan investigates the evening's strange goings on and asks if anything out of the ordinary has happened, her superior replies, 'It's the night shift in Sheffield, everything's out of the ordinary.'

Towards the end of the episode, as the Doctor prepares to save the day, she dons goggles, leather gloves, a brown leather work apron and a welding mask, then fires up a blowtorch in order to fashion a new version of the Doctor's multi-purpose tool – the sonic screwdriver (so a woman is seen doing engineering on the telly – how often does that happen?). It also poignantly links to a nearly-forgotten aspect of the city's history.

Sheffield is known for its steel industry, and a statue of two women in work gear (including goggles and an apron exactly like the one Jodie's Doctor is wearing) was erected in 2016 to commemorate the previously unsung women who worked in the city's foundries during the First and Second World Wars to produce vital things for the country's war effort, such as artillery shells, crankshafts for aeroplanes, and tank treads. The hundreds, possibly thousands, who shifted away from their domestic lives to do this were told to keep it quiet, and worked twelve-hour shifts amid the dangerous molten metal, six days a week for much less pay than the men, until the men came back and they were informed with a note in their pay packets that they would no longer be needed. No official thanks, no appreciation, until a group of former Women of Steel went round giving talks in the steel-works and in public about what they'd done during the war to anyone who would listen and a local newspaper started a campaign for a statue to commemorate them. It is thanks to former steelworkers like Kathleen Roberts, Kit Sollitt, Ruby Gascoigne and Dorothy Slingsby, who spoke out when they were in their eighties and nineties, that these women will have a permanent legacy in the city and long overdue recognition of their crucial role.

———————

Imagine that hammer was first wielded by the women of Cartimandua's tribe at a time when they could not even have imagined that women could ever be told they were not capable enough to shape their own weapons, necklaces and destinies, just as they imagined the goddess Brighid did, she who they sculpted and painted and evoked in their stories, and who was a smith, a prophet and a poet.

———————

They do not say, 'If you can see it, you can be it,' but perhaps it is to that rhythm that the hammer slams down. It clangs through history, liquid iron hot in the cauldrons the Pendle witches peered into, to see the future when it felt like they had little power at all beyond whatever they could muster in their imaginations.

———————

It echoed as the suffragettes broke windows with hammers inscribed 'Better broken windows than broken promises', furious that male politicians were refusing to allow them their rights as citizens, no longer believing that words could change things. It smoothed the metal on which 'Deeds Not Words' would be carved into the statues that would finally be cast and poured from furnaces when a wave of centenary celebrations led to recognition that women's power had stayed as resolute as steel all this time.

---

It bore down in the hands of women who mended their aircraft and voyaged in blue skies where men and women had believed for thousands of years that only birds could fly, and in the hands of a sculptor who reshaped how we saw and felt the rolling moors of the North.

---

We saw it again, not in the endless depictions of Northern women as victims of a killer on the streets, but in new generations of women forging their own futures in what could become their own Northern Powerhouse, in a television time traveller who was just a little way ahead of where women are moving, and in the hands of thousands of little girls who haven't yet been told that those toys are not for them.

---

This book is for all of them.

# Acknowledgements

This book started as a show which was one of several shows I imagined making during my PhD in Northernness and comedy. One of them would have involved me being sterilised live on stage. I imagine the world and my womb are better off for my decision to do one about Northern women instead. I particularly want to thank the wonderful actor Joanna Holden who said she'd always wanted to play Hylda Baker, which made me realise a show haunted by that redoubtable music hall star could be possible (because Northernness is haunted - but that's another type of book). Joey, and the show's director, the brilliant Annie Rigby, one of the country's finest female directing talents (but she's based in the North East, so not enough people know that) helped me so much in working out how to tell the stories of the many women I began to discover.

I also want to thank my Facebook friends and audiences who crowd-sourced so many of the initial women I researched and, the many projects across the country from 2017 and 2018 which began to highlight forgotten women with articles, books, events, plaques and statues. Not least

Carol Bell and the team at the Great Exhibition of the North which commissioned the show. Also the team of wonderful Northern women who worked to bring it to life and to people- including Laura Brewis, Carole Wears, Josie Brookes, Danielle Giddens and Natasha Haws.

I knew there should be a book but didn't think I had time or capacity to write it and am so grateful to Genevieve Pegg of Harper North for asking me at just the right time, as a winter lockdown loomed, and for providing a publishing experience that, although conducted via Zoom at the strangest time ever, has felt full of Northern care and warmth. The team at Harper North who have worked on this are women who have the most extraordinary attention to detail and sharpness, which is what it feels the women whose stories we're bringing to life deserve. I'm grateful also to Jenny Heller, my literary agent, for her acute contractual eye and I know, if times were different, for what would have been more exciting days out in - gasp- non-Northern cities.

A splendid Northern man, Colin Potsig, spent a lot of time in that lockdown insisting I put myself and my voice into this book, and being my first and most exacting reader- so very big thanks to him for performing the opposite of an erasure.

Finally, a huge and humble thank you to all the women mentioned in the book, whose stories are inspiring and galvanising and uplifting (and to all those who wrote or made or disseminated the sources I was able to use to find out about them). I kept trying to get away from the cliche of Northern Grit, but couldn't in the end. Though again and again, something else kept coming up- something about solidarity and care and community and love- here's to that.

# Author's Note/Sources

The research for this book began with the research for my show *Where There's Muck There's Bras*, commissioned by the Great Exhibition of the North in 2018. (Well, actually it began with my research on Northernness and women in comedy, at which point I discovered there's a lot, lot less written on Northernness and Northern women than I think there should be. This means I'm even going to reference my own PhD here. If one of you then reads it, that's probably doubled its readership).

I also include here a non-definitive list of book sources and suggested reading which will be useful for anyone interested in more information on the women mentioned within and also of the online sources I've drawn on directly.

## 1 The Forgotten Queens of the North

Dave Russell's seminal book on how the Northern identity is constructed in culture *Looking North: Northern England and the National Imagination* (Manchester University Press, 2004) has been very helpful to my thinking on the region in all sorts of ways and he points out that "the North has generally been coded as masculine…and set against a more effeminate South" though paradoxically "The North has certainly been the key site for England's 'strong women'…both real and fictional". He gives the examples of the politicians Bessie Braddock and Barbara Castle, the Bronte sisters and cyclist Beryl Burton, all of whom are featured in this volume.

I even got a pun into the title of my PhD…*Stand Up and Be (En) Countered: Resistance in solo stand-up performance by Northern English women marginalised on the basis of gender, class and regional identity.* (2018): Available online: https://etheses. whiterose.ac.uk/20722/

*Cartimandua: Queen of the Brigantes.* Nicki Howarth (The History Press, 2008)


## 2 The Hildas

*Hilda of Whitby, a spirituality for now.* Ray Simpson (BRF Books, 2014)

https://www.english-heritage.org.uk/visit/places/whitby-abbey /history-and-stories/st-hild/

https://www.pilgrimageandcathedrals.ac.uk/blog/st-cuthbert's -ducks-1446120484

*She Knows You Know: The Hylda Baker Story,* Jean Ferguson (Breedon Books Publishing Co Ltd, 1997)

https://www.comedy.co.uk/features/comedy_chronicles/strained -relationships-hylda-baker-and-jimmy-jewel/

*Lost Olympics: The Hilda James Story,* Ian McAllister (emp3 Books, 2013)

https://www.ishof.org/hilda-james.html

A definitive Coronation Street fan site: https://coronationstreet.fandom.com/wiki/Hilda_Ogden


## 3 Sibyls, Suffragettes and (re)Sisters

*The Lure of the Lancashire Witches,* Jennie Lee Cobban (Palatine Books, 2011)

Mother Shipton:
https://www.bbc.co.uk/legacies/myths_legends/england/north
_yorkshire/article_1.shtml
https://www.bbc.co.uk/news/uk-england-york-north-yorkshire
-41470751

Women chartists:
https://sheffieldtimewalk.wordpress.com/2018/01/13/sheffield-the
-road-to-womens-rights/
https://richardjohnbr.blogspot.com/2007/10/aspects-of-chartism
-women-chartists.html

Suffragettes:
*First in the Fight: 20 Women Who Made Manchester*, Helen
Antrobus and Andrew Simcock. (iNostalgia Ltd, 2019)
*Rebel Girls: How Votes for Women Changed Edwardian Lives*, Jill
Lidington. (Little Brown, 2006)

Lilian Bilocca:
*Headscarf Revolutionaries: Lilian Bilocca and the Hull Triple-
Trawler Disaster*, Brian Lavery (Barbican Press, 2015)

Women Against Pit Closures:
https://www.royalexchange.co.uk/in-conversation-with-the
-women-against-pit-closures
https://www.ncm.org.uk/whats-on/women-in-the-miners-strike

Fracking Nanas:
https://www.independent.co.uk/news/uk/home-news/fracking
-protest-lancashire-shale-gas-drilling-uk-cuadrilla-latest
-a8602771.html
https://www.theguardian.com/environment/2019/oct/13/dont
-frack-with-us-the-victorious-nanas-of-lancashire-activism

4 Politicians

https://www.suffrage-pioneers.net/the-list/margaret
-wintringham/
*Red Ellen: The Life of Ellen Wilkinson*, Laura Beers. (Harvard
University Press, 2016)

https://www.parliament.uk/about/living-heritage/transforming
society/electionsvoting/case-study-radical-politicians-in-the
-north-east/introduction/about-the-case-study/

https://mmwonderwomen.wordpress.com/2018/03/05/ellen
-wilkinson/

https://www.plutobooks.com/blog/ellen-wilkinson-and-the
-jarrow-crusade-october-1936/

*Politics and Power: Barbara Castle*, Lisa Martineau. (Andre
Deutsch, 2011)

https://spartacus-educational.com/PRcastleB.htm

https://www.theguardian.com/politics/2002/may/03/obituaries
.anneperkins

https://www.yorkshirepost.co.uk/news/politics/betty-boothroyd
-speaks-her-mind-politics-yorkshire-and-making-history
-1778432

http://www.bbc.co.uk/legacies/myths_legends/england/liverpool
/article_1.sht

https://www.bbc.co.uk/news/uk-politics-11149803

https://www.politicshome.com/thehouse/article/betty-boothroyd
-i-am-a-bit-timid-but-im-dealing-with-the-giants

http://kenningtonnews.blogspot.com/2010/01/magic-mo
-mowlam-our-mischievous.html

https://www.jocoxfoundation.org/aboutjocox

https://www.theguardian.com/education/2020/oct/19/students
-from-northern-england-facing-toxic-attitude-at-durham
-university

https://www.theguardian.com/politics/the-northerner/2013/may
/03/emma-lewell-buck-labour-south-shields

https://www.theguardian.com/politics/2016/dec/18/naz-shah-mp
-bradford-british-muslim

https://www.yorkshirepost.co.uk/news/politics/am-i-british-or
-muslim-first-im-yorkshire-both-says-baroness-sayeeda
-warsi-dewsbury-303371

https://www.independent.co.uk/news/uk/politics/jeremy-corbyn
-s-top-woman-angela-eagle-journey-through-labour
-a6731846.html

https://www.manchestereveningnews.co.uk/news/greater
-manchester-news/mp-angela-rayner-hits-back-13309268

https://twitter.com/angelarayner/status/1307273752133144576
?lang=en

https://www.blackpoolgazette.co.uk/news/politics/mpeas-pod
    -labour-politicians-mixed-bbc-parliament-broadcast-1373987
https://www.telegraph.co.uk/politics/2020/04/03/lisa-nandy-profile/
https://www.theguardian.com/culture/2021/feb/24/leftie-comic
    -tory-baroness-standup-sayeeda-warsi-nick-helm-channel
    -4-cancer

## 5 Sportswomen

https://www.bbc.co.uk/news/uk-england-leicestershire-41737483
https://www.theguardian.com/sport/blog/2019/aug/26/beryl
    -burton-liquorice-allsorts-shake-up-cycling
https://www.barnsleychronicle.com/article/17205/dorothy
    -delighted-after-asher-smith-ends-59-year-wait-for-medal
https://www.fifa.com/news/lily-parr-the-pioneering-star-2593969
https://www.yorkshirepost.co.uk/news/people/inspirational
    -woman-dewsbury-highlighted-duke-and-duchess
    -cambridge-2441127?amp
https://www.yorkshirepost.co.uk/sport/other-sport/special
    -anniversary-looms-swimmings-1960-olympic-games
    -heroine-anita-lonsbrough-2950595
https://www.examinerlive.co.uk/lifestyle/nostalgia/nostalgia-how
    -fly-helped-anita-4944406
https://athletemedia.co.uk/article/from-super-saturday-to-the
    -scotland-500-kat-copeland-mbe/
https://www.olympic.org/nicola-adams
https://www.theguardian.com/sport/2012/aug/06/beth-tweddle
    -london-2012-olympics
https://www.yorkshirepost.co.uk/sport/big-interview-jessica
    -ennis-1877938
https://www.theguardian.com/society/2012/feb/24/tanni-grey
    -thompson-talking-about-disability-transcript
https://www.theguardian.com/sport/2012/aug/31/hannah
    -cockroft-paralympics
https://www.uefa.com/womenschampionsleague/news/0254
    -0e17867f833a-ed9c11599285-1000--meet-the-nominees
    -lucy-bronze/
https://www.skysports.com/football/news/11095/12147078/steph
    -houghton-man-city-england-captain-lifts-lid-on-career-in
    -sky-sports-driving-force-docuseries

https://www.stephhoughton.com/about-steph-houghton/
https://www.ukhillwalking.com/articles/features/12_female_uk
    _hill_runners_who_have_set_the_pace-9928
https://www.theguardian.com/lifeandstyle/2019/jan/18
    /ultrarunner-jasmin-paris-montane-spine-race-winner
    -mens-record-express-milk

6 Writers

*The Blazing World and other writings*, Margaret Cavendish.
    (Penguin Classics, 1994)
https://plato.stanford.edu/entries/margaret-cavendish/
*The Brontes: A Life in Letters*, Judith Barker. (Abacus, 2010)
*The Life of Charlotte Bronte*, Elizabeth Gaskell. (Penguin
    Classics, 2018)
*Charlotte Bronte: A Life*, Claire Harman. (Viking, 2015)
*In Search of Anne Bronte*, Nick Holland. (The History Press, 2016)
https://www.peterrabbit.com/about-beatrix-potter/
https://www.newyorker.com/books/page-turner/the-unjustly
    -overlooked-victorian-novelist-elizabeth-gaskell
https://gaskellsociety.co.uk/elizabeth-gaskell/
https://www.historyextra.com/period/victorian/bronte-sisters
    -anne-charlotte-emily-who-were-they-house-famous
    -write-books/
https://www.encyclopedia.com/women/encyclopedias-almanacs
    -transcripts-and-maps/banks-isabella-1821-1887
http://www.annebronte.org/2019/05/19/gentleman-jack-anne
    -lister-and-the-brontes/
https://www.annelister.co.uk
https://historicengland.org.uk/research/inclusive-heritage/lgbtq
    -heritage-project/love-and-intimacy/
    anne-lister-and-shibden-hall/
http://www.jeanettewinterson.com/journalism/about-anne
    -lister/
https://readingbug2016.wordpress.com/2017/03/01/the-secret
    -garden-by-frances-hodgson-burnett-1911/
https://www.bbc.co.uk/news/resources/idt-sh/the_life_and_loves
    _of_anne_lister
*Gentleman Jack: A Biography of Anne Lister*, Angela Steidele.
    (Serpent's Tail, 2019)

*Journey from the North,* Storm Jameson. (Bloomsbury, 2013)

https://www.theguardian.com/film/2012/mar/20/novelists-plead
-poverty-after-hollywood

https://slate.com/culture/2013/08/literary-grudge-match-a-s
-byatt-margaret-drabble-their-mother-and-their-feud.html

https://archive.nytimes.com/www.nytimes.com/books/99/06/13
/specials/byatt-possessed.html

https://www.encyclopedia.com/women/encyclopedias-almanacs
-transcripts-and-maps/jameson-storm-1891-1986

https://www.theguardian.com/books/2017/jan/14/winifred-holtby
-author-south-riding-feminist-campaigner

https://www.telegraph.co.uk/culture/books/9145903/The-story-of
-the-friendship-between-Winifred-Holtby-and-Vera
-Brittain.html

http://www.halifaxpeople.com/Phylis-Bentley.html?fbclid=IwAR
1wGMAInVxRRFrDa2QHAJPGKehgfE1hmGT-LflLi45
mfwxhIBGtdy6j89E

*Why Be Happy when You Could be Normal,* Jeanette Winterson.
(Vintage, 2012)

https://www.theguardian.com/books/2012/may/12/jeanette
-winterson-professor-manchester-university

https://www.theguardian.com/books/2019/jan/04/pat-barker
-women-carry-the-can-long-term

https://www.theguardian.com/books/2010/jul/02/beryl
-bainbridge-obituary-author

https://www.theguardian.com/culture/2011/jan/17/linda-grant
-interview-life-writing

7 Women with Microphones

https://www.theguardian.com/media/mediamonkeyblog/2014
/nov/25/viewer-offered-bbcs-steph-mcgovern-20-to-correct
-her-northern-accent

*Let's Do It: The authorised biography of Victoria Wood,* Jasper Rees.
(Orion, 2020)

*How to Be Champion,* Sarah Millican. (Trapeze, 2017)

*A Coward's Chronicles,* Marti Caine. (Arrow, 1991)

https://e-space.mmu.ac.uk/607213/1/Northernness%2C%20
Gender%20and%20Manchester%27s%20Creative%20
Industries%20Milestone.pdf

290 — KATE FOX

https://web.archive.org/web/20120910042334/http://freespace
.virgin.net/scott.wills/kenickie/art006.htm
http://pennyblackmusic.co.uk/magsitepages/article/9683/Pauline
-Murray-Interview
https://thirdway.hymnsam.co.uk/editions/september-2014/high
-profile/being-herself.aspx
*Memoirs of a Not So Dutiful Daughter,* Jenni Murray. (Black Swan,
2018)
*Till The Cows Come Home,* Sara Cox. (Coronet Books, 2019)


8 Stage and Screen

https://www.theguardian.com/books/2010/sep/18/jeanette
-winterson-my-hero-shelagh-delaney
https://www.theguardian.com/books/2019/oct/05/tastes-of
-honey-selina-todd-review-shelagh-delaney
*Black Teeth and a Brilliant Smile,* Adelle Stripe. (Fleet, 2017)
https://www.independent.co.uk/arts-entertainment/theatre-dance
/features/andrea-dunbar-life-arbor-rita-sue-bob-black-teeth
-brilliant-smile-a8945401.html
https://www.bbc.co.uk/news/entertainment-arts-48348751
https://www.artangel.org.uk/the-arbor/born-to-write-and-die/
https://www.thejc.com/culture/features/kay-mellor-a-passionate
-writer-1.436451
https://rts.org.uk/article/dorothy-byrne-wickedness-s-been-going
-decades-still-wickedness-and-we-should-expose-it
https://autisticnick.com/2019/03/04/disability-and-soap-operas/
https://en.wikipedia.org/wiki/Ngozi_Onwurah
https://www.theguardian.com/film/2020/jul/23/has-terrordomes
-time-come-how-a-black-british-film-found-its-moment
https://pdfs.semanticscholar.org/e5f6/68fe96d1d1d535c2ef68456ffa
97c8b934cd.pdf


9 Sound and Vision

*Barbara Hepworth: Art and Life,* Eleanor Clayton. (Thames and
Hudson, 2021)
https://www.theguardian.com/artanddesign/jonathanjonesblog
/2015/jan/21/barbara-hepworth-henry-moore-tate-britain
-modernism

https://thelowryblog.com/2020/06/01/sheila-fell/
https://www.newyorker.com/magazine/2020/12/28/how-leonora
 -carrington-feminized-surrealism
*The Hearing Trumpet*, Leonora Carrington. (Penguin Modern
 Classics, 2005)
https://biography.yourdictionary.com/ethel-leginska
*Art Sex Music*, Cosey Fanni Tutti. (Faber and Faber, 2017)


10 Explorers of Earth and Air

*Queen of the Desert: The Extraordinary Life of Gertrude Bell*,
 Georgina Howell. (Pan, 2015)
*Seize the Moment: The autobiography of Britain's first Astronaut*,
 Helen Sharman and Christopher Priest. (Victor Gollancz,
 1993)
*Amy Johnson*, Constance Babington Smith. (Daredevil, 2021)
https://www.blackhistorymonth.org.uk/article/section/bhm
 -heroes/black-history-month-firsts-lilian-bader/
https://livingmemorial.org.uk/portfolio_page/lilian-bader/
https://www.theengineer.co.uk/late-great-engineers-hilda-lyon/
https://womenengineerssite.wordpress.com/2018/10/09/hilda
 -lyon-airships-windtunnels-and-submarines/
*Adventures in Aeronautical Design: The Life of Hilda M Lyon*, Nina
 Baker (independently published, 2020)
https://womenyoushouldknow.net/dr-nina-baker-engineering
 -legacy-hilda-lyon/
https://www.irishnews.com/magazine/entertainment/2018/09/26
 /news/jodie-whittaker-i-was-lucky-i-could-keep-my-own
 -accent-as-doctor-who-1443632/
https://www.yorkshirepost.co.uk/news/people/moving-story
 -sheffields-remarkable-women-steel-2882899